I0813217

PHILIP ROTH

Philip Roth

Stung by Life

STEVEN J. ZIPPERSTEIN

Yale
UNIVERSITY
PRESS

New Haven and London

Yale University Press books may be purchased in quantity for educational, business, or promotional use. For information, please e-mail sales.press@yale.edu (U.S. office) or sales@yaleup.co.uk (U.K. office).

Frontispiece: Photo taken December 1, 1968, just before the appearance of *Portnoy's Complaint* (Bob Peterson/Getty Images)

Set in Janson type by Integrated Publishing Solutions.
Printed in the United States of America.

Library of Congress Control Number: 2025932269
ISBN 978-0-300-25155-5 (hardcover)
A catalogue record for this book is available from the British Library.

Authorized Representative in the EU: Easy Access System Europe, Mustamäe tee 50, 10621 Tallinn, Estonia, gpsr.requests@easproject.com

10 9 8 7 6 5 4 3 2 1

ALSO BY STEVEN J. ZIPPERSTEIN

Books

The Jews of Odessa: A Cultural History, 1794–1881

Elusive Prophet: Ahad Ha'am and the Origins of Zionism

Imagining Russian Jewry: Memory, History, Identity

Rosenfeld's Lives: Fame, Oblivion, and the Furies of Writing

Pogrom: Kishinev and the Tilt of History

Edited Books

Jewish History: Essays in Honour of Chimen Abramsky (with Ada Rapoport-Albert)

Assimilation and Community: The Jews in Nineteenth-Century Europe (with Jonathan Frankel)

Zionism, Liberalism, and the Future of the Jewish State (with Ernest S. Frerichs)

The Worlds of S. An-sky: A Russian Jewish Intellectual at the Turn of the Century (with Gabriella Safran)

To Susan, who has inspired nearly every line while teaching me there are more important things than these lines

What did I prize most in him? What do I miss most
about him? His titanic scrutinizing engrossment
with every last vicissitude of existence, his raptness
and his rapture, his lucidity, his being perpetually
wide awake as if he were being stung by life . . .
—Philip Roth, "In Memory of Richard Stern"

CONTENTS

Introduction, 1

1. Father, Mother, Family, 15

2. Genesis, 24

3. Indignation, 47

4. Goodbye, 57

5. Apprenticeship, 74

6. Marjorie Morningsickness, 85

7. *Hocker*, 96

8. Portnoy, 104

9. Grand Old Man of Letters, 119

10. "Thinness of Culture," 133

11. Lonoff, 146

12. "Fuck the Middle Ground," 164

13. Facts, 181

14. "He Understood . . . Only What He Understood," 192

15. Maletta, 205

16. America, 218

17. "Old Age Is a Massacre," 236

18. Horror at Home, 249

19. Everyman, 264

20. Ghost Writer, 275

Conclusion, 285

Notes, 297

Acknowledgments, 327

Index, 331

PHILIP ROTH

Introduction

The appearance of the most famous of his books—*Portnoy's Complaint* in 1969—was likened in *Life* magazine to the Second Coming. Philip Roth dated Jackie Kennedy (once), slept with Ava Gardner, dined with Alger Hiss (Roth circled the dinner table repeating the words "pumpkin" and "typewriter"). Single-handedly, *Portnoy's Complaint* upended censorship laws in Australia. The 1969 film version of his novella "Goodbye, Columbus" did much the same for the American movie industry. At a gathering he attended in the early 1960s of Israeli and American Jewish writers in Tel Aviv—with Roth having merely one recently published novel and a collection of short stories to his credit—it was generally agreed that the American Jewish reading public now defined itself by whether they liked him or loathed him. Roth had just turned thirty.[1]

From the start, and with no sign of abatement after his death in 2018, Roth's work as well as his person have elicited vastly different reactions—praise, often lavish, or denigration, often vociferous. In some quarters an emphatic disdain, or so it seems, by those who have scarcely, if ever, read him. When Lisa Halliday's novel *Asymmetry* was published in 2018—clearly based in part on a love affair with Roth when she was in her twenties (he was then in his late sixties)—Ayten Tartici in the *Yale Review* compared Halliday's expansive, broad novelistic vision (Halliday, the author of this one book) to the feeble narrowness of Roth. How could the writer of fiction as "sweeping" (the reviewer's term) as Halliday's take seriously someone as restrictive as Roth, who "after all wrote nine novels about his own literary alter-ego Nathan Zuckerman," this being a prime example of "outsized attention to the male ego at the expense of all else."[2]

In stark contrast, novelist Joseph O'Neill once listed, with no intent to be comprehensive, the range of issues preoccupying Roth over the span of his thirty-one books: "Jews in America (and Israel and Europe); the social history of Newark; sex, marriage, illness and aging; the prostate gland; pain, persecution and disgrace; the political landscape of post-war America; masturbation; death; life; Nixon; racial and sexual politics; childhood; the dealings of men and women; and baseball."[3]

There is good reason to believe that Roth—despite rubbing shoulders with the Kennedys, a spate of famous and infamous romances (never, rumors to the contrary, with Barbra Streisand), furious spats (he wrote a full-length novel in reply to a bad review, a stingingly bad one)—viewed himself as something of an isolate, living much like an "unchaste monk."[4]

Then and later, Roth scrutinized meticulously the twists and turns of his reputation while taking incredible risks with books that critics sometimes deemed readily disposable: These included the dense baseball saga *The Great American Novel* and the extravagantly jokey, anti-Nixonian *Our Gang* (here Nixon ends up in Hell, still campaigning for high office against the

Devil). To be sure, Roth meticulously annotated the arrival of nearly every one of these books with well-placed interviews or essays explicating their meanings, all this performed with donnish patience and rhetorical skill. As a young man he considered a legal career—imagining the ideal life where he was employed by the Anti-Defamation League protecting Jews from harm—and he knew well how to argue his own case effectively, while also integrating into his fiction lengthy essay-like interludes where characters disagreeing with him were, time and again, allotted the best lines.

In his early twenties, then the author of no more than a small cluster of short stories, nearly all in college publications, he cautioned his girlfriend Maxine Groffsky—later the model for Brenda Patimkin in his widely praised novella "Goodbye, Columbus"—to save his letters, advising her that there might well be interest in them in the future. When famous, he cultivated a spate of biographers even while insisting, as he put it in the late-life novel *Exit Ghost*, that literary biography was "the lowest of literary rackets," at best, "a lightweight approach to human character."[5] Particularly once actress Claire Bloom's bleak, acidic portrayal of their marriage was published in 1996, with most reviewers taking its accuracy for granted, Roth feared biography's lethal staying power, its capacity to outlast a writer's best books, convinced that Bloom's book sabotaged his chances of winning the Nobel Prize.

And biography would come to bite him badly though the 2021 authorized biography of Roth by Blake Bailey ended up having an immeasurably more harmful impact on its author. In a Fitzgerald-like saga of rise and fall, Bailey was, in the span of little more than a week, acclaimed on the front page of the *New York Times Book Review*, then almost immediately eviscerated. His 898-page book was soon pulped by his publisher Norton in reaction to claims that Bailey, when a teacher at a private school years before, had groomed underage girls for sex once they turned seventeen or eighteen. There was also a separate accusation of rape. The blowback meant that, for some, Roth would be conflated with his disgraced biographer.

Hence the need for a new biographical study, all the more so since few contemporary writers have shown themselves to be quite as self-referential as Roth, and few self-referential writers have managed, for so very long, to be quite so cagey, so slippery. Of course, there is no reason why writers or others should be expected to ease the work of biographers. What do we know or, for that matter, care about the private lives of E. L. Doctorow (how many know his first name?), Ian McEwan, or Alison Lurie—all accomplished novelist-friends of Roth's? But Roth feels different. He cultivated, despite endless complaints, the tantalizingly intimate comparisons between his own résumé and those of his protagonists—Zuckerman, or Tarnopol, or Kepesh, sometimes also Philip Roth. He described life with the use of protagonists who, as often as not, looked, spoke, dressed, and acted strikingly, often identically, like himself.

As his friend the writer David Plante has noted, Roth showed himself to be lavishly candid, freely acknowledging matters most others worked hard to hide. (The most famous of his books is built around masturbation, one of very few sexual acts still a source of embarrassment in the 1960s.) Yet he was enamored by secrecy, by the masks used in situations intimate or otherwise. I overheard several conversations at his funeral—a rather small affair of some seventy or eighty, for which Roth himself had drawn up the list of invitees—between people who knew one another well but who only that day discovered a shared friendship with Roth. He conducted an affair, known by nearly no one except for the two of them, with a woman living half a mile away from his Connecticut home, sequestering this relationship for nearly twenty years before eventually depicting it in copious detail in his 1995 novel *Sabbath's Theater*. This, he said, was the favorite of his books—perhaps because he felt no need to hide away anything of himself, his fantasies, nightmares, or appetite. Nowhere in this book, unlike in so many of the others, do we find the angst, the shame of a good Jewish boy or the buttoned-down man that he was and, at the same time, was not.

"Making fake biography, false history, concocting a half-imaginary existence out of the actual drama of my life *is* my life," he put it in his *Paris Review* interview. "There has to be some pleasure in this job, and that's it. To go around in disguise. . . . To pass oneself off as what one is not. To *pretend*."[6] The protagonist of his novel *The Human Stain*—who resigns from a long and distinguished academic career after being savaged as an anti-Black racist, having lived his life as a Jew when actually a light-skinned African American—declares that the essential "trick to living in the rush of the world . . . is to get as many people as possible to string along with your delusions."[7]

He saw making fake biography as essential to the making of his fiction. "Searching into the life and character of the real Philip Roth," wrote the novelist J. M. Coetzee, "[is] a questionable enterprise under any circumstances." A close friend of Roth's, Bernard Avishai, in his incisive analysis of *Portnoy's Complaint*, says much the same: "My book is not a biography of Roth, I hasten to add. If anything, it aims to leave readers doubting that there could be a problem for which a biography is the solution."[8] Roth treated most efforts to collapse the relationship between his life and art as the byproduct of indolence, the inability to understand the basic workings of fiction. Is it true that it is preordained for Roth's biographers to meet a dismal fate?

Roth himself would do much to provide a reply to such skepticism. In the many memos to his biographers—he explored the prospect of several before settling eventually on Bailey—he acknowledged the ways in which his books drew on his own experiences and on those close to him. Certainly, this doesn't mean that his fiction is transparently autobiographical. Rarely does

Roth simply replicate his experiences, though at times he does just that. Mostly he captures their emotional valence, the imprint left behind. And while he frequently insisted on masking the details, he drew directly from the life around him. For instance, Roth insisted vociferously that the voluble, brilliantly theatrical Palestinian Ziad of *Operation Shylock* bore no resemblance to Edward Said, lambasting the *New Yorker*'s vaunted proofreaders for misspelling the name in their review of the book as "Zaid." Yet, in an outline he prepared for the book, one finds a Roth note: "George Ziad (Edward Said)."[9]

Often, he declared he trusted the actual, palpable events of life far more than the fiction he read so assiduously and that he so thoroughly integrated into the fabric of his writing. Arguably, he drew on books for the writing of his novels more so than any other widely read English-language novelist of his time, while remaining distrustful of books as a source for inspiration. "Philip Roth is a writer's writer," says literary scholar Aimee L. Pozorski. "He cherishes the books of others as much as we do his." This reliance on books is apparent throughout: "Goodbye, Columbus" provides a gloss on David Riesman's then-influential *The Lonely Crowd.* His first novel, *Letting Go,* is meant as an extended conversation with Henry James. Flaubert's shadow rests heavily on the next novel, *When She Was Good.* Fierce, unresolved combat between Freud and Nietzsche is foregrounded in *Portnoy's Complaint.* And then there's evidence of Lionel Trilling, Conrad, Edna O'Brien, Genet, Thomas Mann, Céline, Shakespeare, Melville, Kierkegaard, Arthur Schlesinger, Camus, Joyce, always Kafka. Eventually, as literary biographer Michael Gorra observes, Beckett too, "but better—better because it's set in the entirely recognizable social landscape of old age."[10]

Yet Roth took to heart the chasm between "the written and unwritten world"—a term popularized by the social thinker/guru Paul Goodman—distrusting the capacity of books to turn life into abstractions or ideology. These demons would have to be extracted if credible fiction was to happen. So earnest, so unflinching was his commitment to a life of writing. "Of all contemporary novelists," wrote critic James Wood on hearing of Roth's decision, at the age of eighty, to retire from writing, "he is the one who has made writing seem a necessary and continuous act, inextricable from the continuities and struggle of being alive."[11] And so astonishingly funny. A good example—this cited by Wood as his own favorite—is how Zuckerman decides in *The Ghost Writer* that the lovely young woman he spots at the home of writer Emanuel Lonoff is the real Anne Frank, whom he would manage to woo and marry, thus persuading his father that he isn't the self-hating Jew his detractors have accused him of being: "I kept seeing myself coming back to New Jersey and saying to my family, 'I met a marvelous young woman while I was up in New England. I love her and she loves me. We are going to be married.' 'Married? But so fast? Nathan, is she Jewish?' 'Yes, she is.' 'But who is she?' 'Anne Frank.' "[12]

And while suspicious of the intrusiveness of biography, *The Ghost Writer* astutely sums up the essential impulses behind the writing of such work—namely the interplay between literature's achievement and its author's imperfections: "When you admire a writer you become curious. You look for his secret. The clues to his puzzle." This is what the young, eager writer Nathan Zuckerman says to Lonoff. James Joyce's biographer Richard Ellmann characterizes this same tension as the chasm separating the "erratic and provisional" surface of a writer's life and the "splendid extravagance" of the author's prose.[13] The unruliness of *shmutz*, as Roth refers to it, and civilization's demands is just where Roth constructs so many of his thirty-one books.

Despite acknowledging that such matters are at the heart of his fictional imagination—these explored with a fluency rivaling that of Mario Puzo (Roth's *Portnoy's Complaint* bested Puzo's *The Godfather* on the *New York Times* bestseller list)—Roth made it hard to speak credibly about his own secrets. "Getting people right is not what living is all about anyway," he writes in his novel *American Pastoral.* "It's getting them wrong that is living, getting them wrong and wrong and wrong and then, on careful reconsideration, getting them wrong again. That's how we know we're alive: we're wrong."[14]

Ever since the writing of the first short stories in the mid-1950s, he sought to expose the fissures in the lives of his characters. "Epstein," one of his first stories to appear in a major magazine, told of a middle-aged Jewish man stumbling into adultery. What interested Roth here, as he put it, is "how—and why and when—a man acts contrary to what he considers his 'best self.' "[15] Neil Klugman, the aimless hero of his prize-winning 1959 novella "Goodbye, Columbus," discovers that while quite nearly everything about his new love interest Brenda is distasteful—except, of course, her sinewy body—he sees himself likely slipping into the role of a prospective Jewish groom. Forty years later in *The Human Stain*, Roth has Coleman Silk marry a woman he cares little for just because her wild semitic hair might well shield him once children are born, protecting him from revealing his deepest secret: that he is Black "passing" as a white Jew. No one in Roth's novels—except the explosively compulsive, failed puppeteer Mickey Sabbath of *Sabbath's Theater*—lives forthrightly with their deepest, ugliest inclinations.

There was nothing that intrigued Roth more than what it felt like before such fissures surfaced. Although known for his astringency, no preoccupation of his was keener than the innocence, the tenderness, even the freedom of one's earliest years. Roth remained certain—much like Jean Genet, whom he admired greatly—that "to create is always to speak of childhood" with the moments just on the cusp of adolescence the closest to bliss. "Bring it all back," beseeches Nathan Zuckerman's brother, stricken with impotence because of a heart condition in his 1986 novel *The Counterlife:* "bring back those summers at the Jersey Shore, the fresh rolls perfuming the grocery basement in the

Lorraine Hotel, the beach where they sold the bluefish off the morning boats . . . the most innocent months of his most innocent years."[16]

In writing his life, among the questions that immediately surface are these: From where the inspiration for the "most unforgettable character I've met ever," as Roth puts it in *Portnoy's Complaint:* the portrayal of the alluringly possessive Sophie Portnoy. Not a description of his own mother Bess, and yet the use of the knife as a weapon with which to bludgeon her boys to eat was, it seems, a part of his mother's repertoire. Her obsessive cleanliness was legendary: Roth and his brother were known not to use the toilets in their friends' houses because none was as clean as their own. As an adult, Roth would be described by those who knew him as a wild man with Purell in his pocket.

And the source of his ferocious ambition? His punishing routine was set in motion in his mid-twenties and maintained with few interruptions until his last published word. ("There's the most beautiful park in the world just down the street from me"—he lived in New York on 79th Street near Columbus Avenue, and said this to me in his early eighties—"and yet I can't allow myself to spend time there.")

Why devote so many pages to Jews? His knowledge of the Jewish religion was, as he readily admitted, sparse; his interest in Judaism was passing at best. Yet he would probe nearly every aspect of contemporary Jewish life: the passions of Jewish childhood, the pleasures and anguish of postwar Jewish suburbia, Israel, diaspora, the Holocaust, circumcision, the interplay between the nice Jewish boy and the turbulent one deep inside. Among the most urgent of such interests was what it meant for a Jew to go "wild in public," as he wrote a few years after *Portnoy's Complaint.* It "is the last thing in the world that a good Jew is expected to do—by himself, his family, his fellow Jews, and by the larger community of Christians whose tolerance for him may be tenuous to begin with. . . . He is not expected to make a spectacle of himself, either by shooting off his mouth or by shooting off his semen, and certainly not by shooting off his mouth about shooting off his semen."[17]

At the same time, his insistence on seeing himself as an American writer is never in conflict with his Jewishness. Writing a friend from Italy in late 1959 soon after the appearance of his first book, *Goodbye, Columbus and Five Short Stories*, he admitted, "I miss, these past few days, the hot aggravation of American summers, the vulgar, loud, sweaty charm of the beach, and the traffic. . . . I've felt my Americanness so very much." Why it took such effort to understand all this, as he explained to another friend decades later, was that "To be an American involves trying to find out what it means to be an American . . . from his childhood a foreigner in America wondering what an American was, and then he realized that this very condition *made* him an American."[18]

His was a fervent, if skeptical patriotism, a kinship forged amid the Second World War, in a milieu smitten by President Roosevelt and perhaps still more resolutely by his wife, Eleanor. Eventually it included a heightened awareness of the absurdly constrained lives of the writers he would come to champion in Prague and elsewhere in Soviet-dominated Eastern Europe. He loathed Nixon and Johnson, George W. Bush and, of course, Trump because he remained convinced that they all contravened the very core of what America ought to be—a belief forged in the 1940s and '50s and that never abated. His was an America where there is no contradiction between love of country and allegiance to one's Jewish family, and no credible reason for Jewish self-hatred. American Jewry, as he puts it in *The Counterlife*, is "seething with self-love . . . seething with confidence and success. And maybe that's a world-historical event on a par with . . . Israel."[19]

Eventually he was preoccupied with Israel and Palestine too: Few if any American novels have more intelligently investigated Israel's dilemmas than Roth's *The Counterlife* in 1986 or

Operation Shylock in 1993. And from the start, long before his imagination was whetted by Israel, he had an acute interest in the Jewish catastrophe in the Second World War. Already in the 1950s before the writing of "Goodbye, Columbus," he sought to write about Anne Frank and then sold a play to *Playhouse 90* about the controversial Vilna Jewish council head Jacob Gens. Shortly afterward, he wrote a short story about a Jewish refugee that would be made into an episode of *Alfred Hitchcock Presents*. The first novel he attempted to write—never completed—was about an American Jewish businessman who planned to travel to Frankfurt to kill a German in an act of revenge.

Survivors were among his closest friends: the Romanian writer Norman Manea (Roth chose a burial site beside Manea's future plot), Israeli Aharon Appelfeld, and Czech Ivan Klima. He felt an intense kinship with Primo Levi and played a decisive role in introducing Holocaust victim Bruno Schulz's previously little-known work, now recognized as among the masterpieces of twentieth-century prose. His ever-more-rageful responses to antisemitism would culminate in the 2004 *Plot Against America*, with deep Jewish kinship expressed in its very first lines: "Fear presides over these memories, a perpetual fear. Of course no childhood is without its terrors, yet I wonder if I would have been a less frightened boy if Lindbergh hadn't been president or if I hadn't been the offspring of Jews."[20]

Reluctant earlier, but by the late 1980s Roth was prepared to acknowledge just this indebtedness. In an interview with Asher Milbauer, a friend born soon after the Holocaust in one of the rare shtetl-like spots of postwar Romania, Roth said:

> I have two audiences, a general audience and a Jewish audience. I have virtually no sense of my impact upon the general audience, nor do I really know who these people are. Counterbalancing the general audience has been a Jewish audience affording me, really, the best of both worlds. With my Jewish audience I feel intensely their expectations, disdain, delight,

> criticism, their wounded self-love, their healthy curiosity—what I imagine the writer's awareness of an audience in the capital of a small country where culture is thought to mean as much as politics, where culture is politics . . .[21]

Finally—a few words about Roth on women and men, together and apart. His treatment of women remains a matter of controversy, and I describe now only one episode regarding his life with women beyond his books.

In the mid-1970s, soon after the end of one of his longest romantic relationships—some six years—with Barbara Sproul, a young theology scholar, Roth entered an affair with another beautiful woman, a writer living upstairs, unhappily married. Encased in secrecy ("It was," writes Janet Hobhouse, "not my reputation he was trying to protect, but his own comfort"), this was one of several sexual relationships of his that was lavishly lubricated by talk. Her depiction of him—no more than a dozen or so pages in a memoirlike novel unfinished at her untimely death and published posthumously—may well be the most compelling of all Roth's biographical portraits: "I admired his fasting. I admired his stony separateness and self-sufficiency. I admired the smallness of his needs, the steadiness of his routines: his exercise weights, his evening runs, his early nights. All the symptoms of his current loneliness and depression I read as choices heroic and exemplary. I admired the way he organized his existence around the two pages a day he set himself to write."[22]

Soon enough, the affair came to its end, with Roth moving away after noticing a bottle of lithium she had been prescribed. This, as he saw it, spelled trouble. Now, "the great man tired of it all, longing for his peace and routines, bored with . . . the little bird in all her feathers and delightful youth—too much of that youth." The story ends here, but then again, it doesn't. Some years later they reconnect, meeting over lunch; he tells her that he didn't much like her book on Gertrude Stein but enjoyed her new fiction. Soon afterward she is diagnosed with cancer, and he accompanies her to chemotherapy sessions and sits with her for hours as she awaits news about whether her tumor has shrunk. Roth remains with her for the remainder of that day when the bad news she receives kicks in. And when shortly afterward she dies penniless, Roth finds and buys for her a plot near that of her mother. Visiting her grave often, he'd kneel, "imagining her young and beautiful again, looking up at him and laughing: *Now* you love me."[23]

That last line I quote is not mine but Blake Bailey's, drawn from his biography, a vigorously researched work yet one curiously tone-deaf to the writing at the epicenter of Roth's life. It is a huge volume overflowing with much useful information, alongside a summation that is suffused with envy for the longevity, the variety, the stupendous stamina of Roth's sexual activities. And while reviewing some of the same documents as did Bailey, I came to see how Bailey's all-too-fixed interest in Roth's sexual life not infrequently obscured Roth's far keener preoccupation with literature.

A telling example is found in Bailey's treatment of Roth's once-close friendship with novelist Alan Lelchuk. Although he admired Lelchuk for his daring on and off the page and his late-night sexual escapades, Roth limited even his restaurant meals—typically no more than two weekly, as Hobhouse had observed—ever fearful that they would interfere with his strict writing routine. Bailey cites accurately a letter to Lelchuk of the late 1960s among Roth's papers in the Library of Congress. The woman mentioned, Alice Denham, stands out in the history of *Playboy* magazine as the only woman to have published a short story in the same issue where she was featured as a nude. (Later she would publish the book *Sleeping with Bad Boys*, detailing her sexual encounters with many of the leading writers of her day, including Roth.) In the letter, Roth writes Lelchuk:

"I wouldn't put my dick in Alice Denham if I were you. You might want to apply for a Guggenheim someday, and I understand Henry Allen Moe [the foundation's seventy-five-year-old president] is hot for her."[24]

It is typed and one and a half pages, and it is what Bailey chooses *not* to quote or mention that illustrates a fundamental difference between our books. Here, in a letter written nearly a decade before *The Ghost Writer* (widely considered among Roth's finest books), there is a foretaste of its eventual plot and even a glimpse of the makings of *American Pastoral*, which would appear nearly thirty years later but started around this time and was put aside. And while Roth's interest in his friend Lelchuk's sexual experiences arguably deserves some mention in his biography, there was nothing of greater importance to Roth than his books, his true loves, and the only reason that justifies spending years of one's own life writing and rewriting a book about him.

1

Father, Mother, Family

"At times it seems that Roth has written one immensely long and surging roman-fleuve," writes Claudia Roth Pierpont in her study of Roth's work.[1] If so, at its heart is father, mother, family—roughly in that order.

In the 1959 novella "Goodbye, Columbus," Philip Roth made certain to move Neil Klugman's parents away from New Jersey, consigning both to Arizona so that its hero might be free to enjoy an aimlessness unlikely if they were close by. Elsewhere in his writing, the father hovers close at hand, ever ready to pounce with a barrage of emphatic, endlessly repetitive lessons regarding work and family, an edgy bundle of good will, rage, and manhood. A cousin has vivid memories of an argument between Roth and his father about Philip's late-night hours spent with girlfriends, an argument so fierce that Philip, then in his first year in college, jumped out of the front window to escape the fray. Roth would deny this ever occurred, but, then again, he is one of our greatest masters of fiction.[2]

Roth dressed up his father, Herman, as a charming curmudgeon in his brilliant evocation of second-generation American Jewish life: his memoir *Patrimony*. Elsewhere in his fiction, Roth had him die, years before his actual death, with the word "bastard" on his lips—likely in retaliation for Roth's uncomfortably revealing family portrayals in his character Nathan Zuckerman's early writings. By far the most unadorned and straightforward of all his descriptions of Herman may well be found in an essay Roth wrote for *Harper's* in the immediate wake of the success of *Goodbye, Columbus and Five Short Stories*, published in 1959. Now that he had experienced the first taste of fame, he was perhaps more willing to speak with little artifice about the tension at its center: his hunger for independence and its cost with his father.

He starts it off—the reminiscence is entitled "Beyond the Last Rope"—with a very brief but also lavishly enthusiastic description of his mother, depicted as a woman of unrivaled competence, cheerfully setting aside all household norms every summer when the family fled Newark's heat for Bradley Beach. Here, without complaint and in ramshackle "kibbutz-like" pandemonium, she would share cramped iceboxes and soapy bathrooms in multifamily bungalows.[3]

Soon Roth leaves his mother aside, now recalling the freedoms he would experience on the beach—especially the "examination of someone else's body." He remains convinced that he kissed more during those summers than he would for the remainder of his life and with girls from magical-sounding spots like Bogota, New Jersey. Also on the beach are Syrian Jewish girls, nothing like the Jews he knew back home, "whose cocoa-colored skin was that color all year round," their faint mustaches, indifferent air, and brown bellies making his stomach churn. At the ocean's edge, he learns not only to swim and drive

Philip Roth with his mother and older brother Sandy at Bradley Beach, where the Roths spent most summers during Philip's childhood and much of his adolescence. (Courtesy of the Philip Roth Personal Library, Newark Public Library)

but, more importantly, how "to flirt, to drink, to pose, to swindle, to do everything."[4]

By the time these summers are nearing their end, on the cusp of his exit to college, he has a steady girlfriend with whom he tests boundaries, sexual and otherwise. Together they take risks—perhaps the most daring is swimming beyond the last of all ropes, no longer intimidated by fear of the deepest water and cavorting with the most self-confident summer swimmers. Yet, startlingly, the feelings he remembers at such moments are as exasperating as they are joyous: marvelous in their sense of freedom but also unsettling in what it means to have abandoned the warmth, protectiveness, and attentiveness of his parents' admonishments. Now side by side with "Serious Swimmers," Roth finds himself hankering for the restrictions of the recent past that he has, of course, loathed but now misses. These the themes that will take center stage for him for the remainder of his writing life.

The reminiscence then moves to the parent most responsible for these once-overpowering (in retrospect, also comforting) constraints. Roth tells how his father, who typically joined them only on weekends, managed sometimes to arrive midweek in the early evening after a full day's work. He would surprise the family at around 7:30 just as they were ready to sit down for dinner. Dinner would wait as Herman changed into his bathing suit, heading to the beach with his two boys by his side. And with this he would transform himself, as Roth saw it, shedding his sweaty workday clothes, stripped free to enter the blessed waters of the Atlantic: "Finally, I would watch him lower himself into the water to swim, and then to turn over and float on his back. Behind us the sun was perfect and red, and when its light broke out on the water I knew I was seeing something beautiful. My father floated so still—he worked so hard—and then he came in and was glowing, like the sea, from those last pure spikes of light."[5]

Nothing here of Herman's obstinance. Just a glimpse of unlikely transcendence: the product of nothing more than a dunk in the Atlantic before retiring to a homemade meal in a simple summer cottage beside a loving wife and adoring boys.

Much of Roth's writings over the years would be forged out of the incomparable pleasure of such moments and the impossibility—if also the undesirability—of replicating them. "I wanted to be ten despite a lifelong determinedly anti-nostalgic stance. I wanted to be ten," Roth writes many years later in *Operation Shylock*, "and when the voluptuous earthiness of women other than my momma was nothing I yet wished to gorge myself on."[6]

There is a self-sufficiency in this that he had relished—a calm happy equilibrium altogether different from what it feels like to cross into the uncharted waters of adulthood and beyond. Roth would come to write his age's most probing, uncompromising examination of freedom with *Portnoy's Complaint:* a study of a hapless neurotic, unfettered yet miserable, estranged from family, wifeless, childless, momentarily even impotent. Widely viewed as a celebration of the libertine sixties, there, at the core of his imaginative life, was the prospect—impossible to replicate if also unwelcome—of living a life much like insurance salesman Herman or that of his own boyhood, where joy was made of little more than a quick swim, dinner beside one's loving and loyal kin, and love for no woman other than his mother.

Soon after Herman's death, Roth wrote literary critic Alfred Kazin and his wife, Judith, a note thanking them for their condolences, adding that he considered sending the following ad to the *New York Review of Books:* "Unemployed son, 56 years of experience, excellent credentials, seeks new position."[7]

> I remembered—with the luxurious sense of having been blessed—the Sundays of my own childhood, the daylong round of visits, first to my two widowed grandmothers in the slum where my parents had been born, and then around Camden to the households of half a dozen aunts and uncles. During the war, when gasoline was rationed, we would have to walk to visit the grandmothers, traversing on foot five miles of city streets in all—a fair measure of our devotion to those two queenly and prideful workhorses, who lived very similarly in small apartments redolent of freshly ironed linen and stale coal gas, amid an accumulation of antimacassars, bar mitzvah photos, and potted plants, most of them taller and sturdier than I ever was. Peeling wallpaper, cracked linoleum, ancient faded curtains, this nonetheless was my Araby, and I their little sultan . . . what is more, a sickly sultan whose need was all the greater for his Sunday sweets and sauces. Oh how I was fed

> and comforted, washerwoman breasts for my pillows, deep grandmotherly laps, my throne![8]

It may well have been during such visits where Roth first heard of the talk of Tarnopol—Peter Tarnopol, the first of his writer-protagonists whose therapist describes him as at "the top of narcissists in the arts." Tarnopol was the name of the largest town in the region of his paternal grandfather's native Kozlov, a busy railway depot packed with Jewish-owned stores, taverns, and grain dealers in an overwhelmingly impoverished, craggy region hugging the Russian empire. Its tenuous linkage to Austria-Hungary—above all, Vienna, where a cluster of his mother's relations had resided for a time—would be touted by Roth's relatives: "We may have been ordinary people, but our affiliations were not without grandeur."[9]

Not only was much of the Roth family's life built around relatives, but the celebration of such ties was featured in an elaborately organized family association, with claims of being the largest group of its kind in North America. Roth's immediate family eagerly participated in this—the Flaschner Family Association—launched by relatives on his mother Bess's side who were the first to come to the United States. Herman served as president for a year in 1943, and Bess was one of its recording secretaries. The association boasted a membership of four hundred at its height and included among its services a private bank with no-interest loans, scholarships for members' children, and yearlong activities designed to enhance family ties for young and old.[10]

The group published a quarterly newspaper full of prideful gossip, sponsored a family song ("Three Cheers for Our Family / And Ever Heed Our Call"), and had its own stationery adorned with the message "Remember Your Family"; and even produced a family crest with the eagle at its center culled from the Austro-Hungarian flag. It held annual banquets in grand chandeliered halls, galas interspersed with numerous casual activities like picnics, baseball games, tugs-of-war, and Purim parties. Newark was well known at the time (according to historian Dan Oren, himself a relative) as a city made up of a multitude of such extended families often organized into comparable associations, with most of their members living close to one another.[11]

By the early 1950s, the Flaschner association announced a change in its priorities, shifting away from financial assistance, since most of its members were reasonably secure, to solidifying the allegiance of the new generation. The fact that so many of its young had served in the military in the Second World War and then in Korea provided what was deemed to be ample evidence (as announced in *Flaschner Family: Victory Edition*, issued in 1951) of the readiness of the younger members to devote themselves to kin as well as to nation: "We are extremely proud of the courage, loyalty, and full sense of patriotic duty for Country and Family."[12]

The priority of family cohesion is repeatedly trumpeted: "It is the children of the family rather than ourselves that we must think of at all times, and so the educational program will be furthered and protected so that the human urge for betterment will be one of the outstanding factors . . . "[13] All this was in rather muddled, postimmigrant English, with barely concealed anxiety regarding the waning loyalty of the young.

Nearly all such Jewish associations (hundreds existed in America by the 1920s and '30s) were first launched to help ease integration into American life, to alleviate the poverty and loneliness of life in a new, uncertain world. Such concerns had now been overshadowed by the fear that the younger generation was too comfortable in the New World and was untethered from allegiances older relatives took for granted.

The *Victory Edition*, Roth recalled, was a prized family possession. In his faux-autobiographical story "'I Always Wanted

You to Admire My Fasting'; or, Looking at Kafka," Roth has his father display the volume with pride when his son's Hebrew teacher Franz Kafka comes to their home for dinner. He presses the book onto Kafka to whet his appetite for the pleasures of family life: "A family association of over two hundred people located in seven states, including the state of Washington! Yes, relatives even in the Far West: here are the photographs. Dr. Kafka, this is a beautiful book we published entirely on our own for five dollars a copy."[14]

Curiously, the 1951 commemorative volume makes no mention of the catastrophic fate of the family left in Europe. The only oblique reference: "Herein is information of the Elders of our Family. It is strange that neither Lemel Flashner [*sic*], or any of his children or their offspring have we been able to contact. To our knowledge none have ever left Austria."[15]

Roth remembers relishing the gatherings, particularly encounters with "exotic" relatives from as far away as Boston. "In our lore," he writes in *The Facts*, "the Jewish family was an inviolate haven against every form of menace, from personal isolation to gentile hostility. . . . 'Hear, O Israel, the family is God, the family is One.' "[16]

What he took away from all this remains both straightforward and, unsurprisingly, ambiguous. Roth, despite his commitment to his Roosevelt-inspired country, admitted that he never felt altogether at ease with gentile America, in sharp contrast with someone like the *Paris Review*'s rich, self-assured George Plimpton. Its embrace he distrusted, if also desired. In contrast, there was his family's hold from which he fled, and then spent much of the remainder of his life scrutinizing for its resilience, which he understood could be altogether rejected only at one's own peril. Flaschner flags and songs, family baseball pageants and banquets—its awkward, well-meaning attempt to hold onto him and his contemporaries—offered Roth a welter of lessons in the wages of freedom, betrayal, and allegiance. Perhaps he had this in mind when he wrote so movingly in *The Human Stain* of Coleman Silk's betrayal of his mother—and the rest of his African American family—which permitted him to live free from their constraints, if also free from their overpowering, nurturing, and suffocating love. In the end Roth leaves unanswered whether Silk's flight was all for naught.

> Murdering her on behalf of his exhilarating notion of freedom! It would have been much easier without her. But only through this test can he be the man he has chosen to be, unalterably separated from what he was handed at birth, free to struggle at being free like any human being would wish to be free. To get that from life, the alternate destiny, on one's own terms, he must do what must be done. Don't most people want to walk out of the fucking lives they've been handed?[17]

2

Genesis

. . . to notice anything, really, other than
that I had miraculously made it from
my unliterary origins to here . . .

Newark—distant yet just across the water from the Republic of Letters—would distinguish itself by prodigious work. "The men worked fifty, sixty, even seventy hours a week; the women worked all the time," writes Roth in *The Anatomy Lesson*. It was these men and women who would weigh on him always: "Jewish fathers bursting with taboos," mothers painstakingly fastidious if also vaguely amorous, and their sons "boiling with temptations."[1] They provided the most volatile challenges of his adolescence and eventually a potent inspiration for his fiction.

"Work," as literary critic Ross Posnock observes, is the last word of "Goodbye, Columbus": a love letter to Newark, the city where Philip Milton Roth was born March 19, 1933. Bereft of the features that characterized America's more celebrated cities—New York, San Francisco, or New Orleans—"not even a joke like Brooklyn or Oshkosh or Peoria," as native son Leslie Fiedler put it, by the early 1940s Newark was a city of half a million people. It was still packed with jobs, most of these back-breaking labor in factories often little more than down the street from where the workers lived, the bulk of them still immigrants or children of immigrants. Here, as literary critic Mark Shechner put it, "To be a hustler was a term of high praise, as high almost as being a *mensch*."[2]

At Newark's height in 1925, it was home to 1,688 factories, with the city a leader in the manufacturing of paint, chemicals, drugs, costume jewelry, hats, leather, electric light bulbs, and beer. During Prohibition, it was one of the country's busiest hubs for the importing of bootlegged Canadian liquor. The city's white-collar employees were numerous as well, with insurance companies employing more than thirty thousand. City boosters then insisted that there was no item in America whose origin couldn't be traced to Newark.

"When my father bought this factory," says the Swede, the high school football star at the helm of his father's factory in Roth's *American Pastoral*, "there were trolley cars on Central Avenue. Further down were auto showrooms. . . . There was a factory where somebody was making something in every side street. . . . Kiler made watercolors, Fortgang made fire alarms, Lasky made corsets, Robbins made pillows, Honig made pen points."[3] A compact place, less than twenty-five square miles with much of it marshland or the airport.

Its geography benefited it while also rendering it oddly indeterminate: Built between Philadelphia and New York at the convergence of two rivers, for a century it served as a convenient industrial and commercial depot. Well into the 1940s, it boasted a robust civic culture with a wide array of theaters and restaurants, the cavernous Mosque Theater (the site of important political rallies), and Bamberger's, a flagship department store. Once an "uncouth and unthinking Industrial Frankenstein," said the head of its splendid library system John Cotton Dana, it had remade itself into "a model of cultural refinement."[4]

To be sure, such boosterism often fell flat. An oft-repeated claim was that Newark's "Four Corners" downtown intersection was "the busiest traffic center in the world." Its airport, opened in 1931, was described at its start as "the busiest in the country." The Pulaski Skyway—completed in 1932, crossing the Passaic and Hackensack Rivers and linking Newark with New York—was anointed at its opening as "the outstanding highway engineering achievement in history." Newark's boulevards themselves would be lavishly extolled: "The straight, spacious reach of Broad Street from Lincoln Park to Military Park . . . ranks among the attractive thoroughfares of the country." It was claimed that French toast was invented at one of the city's Jewish-owned restaurants.[5]

But its dreadful side, well before its eventual decline, was undeniable. The city's poorest neighborhoods included some of the most primitive housing in the country. Wooden structures filled the streets of the mostly impoverished Third Ward. Newark's Ironbound neighborhood, with a population largely from Portugal and Spain, was covered almost year-round by soot from nearby factories. On hot summer days, the city not only sweltered but stank. Many of Newark's buildings had no running water or heat, and before Prohibition the streets of the Third Ward were packed with speakeasies and taverns. (A selling point of Roth's Weequahic neighborhood was its ban on taverns.) Overall, it was a city with a multitude of small, modest houses, most with barely any space between them, the stoops providing the most accessible air. "A very ugly town" is how Rabbi Joachim Prinz first described Newark, having fled Berlin in 1939 and finding himself, much to his dismay, forced to accept a rabbinic position there.[6]

But Prinz acknowledged that it was also very interesting. While scouring its Jewish community's grandees to help renovate the thousand-seat Palladian-like Temple B'nai Abraham, he discovered Newark's impressive Jewish elite, many of whom, close friends, lived in the same ornate apartment building. Prinz himself, who later gained a national reputation as a significant voice in the civil rights movement, would always insist that Newark's Jewish grandees were the most outstanding group of its kind in the country.

At Newark's pinnacle were two vastly different figures—curiously enough good friends—both generous philanthropists whose stature among Newark's Jews was said to rival that of Bernard Baruch, Roosevelt's famed Jewish financial wizard. Louis Bamberger, owner of the city's great department store, would be the lead benefactor of Newark's Museum of Art and the founding donor of the Institute for Advanced Study at Princeton. And Abner "Longy" Zwillman—genial, philanthropic, and well read (though self-educated)—was at the helm of one of the East Coast's most profitable and deadly underworld dynasties. The FBI listed him among the most wanted in the country and one of the six leading figures of "Murder, Inc.," with enterprises including, at their height in the 1930s, illegal liquor, waterfront extortion, tax evasion, jury tampering, and obstruction of justice.[7]

Hailing from the city's slums, Longy (the affectionate name due to his lanky build) was a gangster (likely a murderer), and a fiercely devoted son whose mother shopped in furs and diamonds. He bankrolled the Minutemen, one of the most forceful and violent anti-Nazi groups in the country made up of thugs, including a sprinkling of celebrated local boxers, who in the 1930s regularly beat up the pro-German sympathizers in Irvington and other German American neighborhoods.

Under the leadership of ex-boxer Nat Arno supported financially by Zwillman, the Minutemen announced they would do battle with Nazis the very minute they learned of one of their gatherings. With Zwillman in control of local police and Newark City Hall, pro-Nazis often found themselves unprotected, with the police going so far as to inform the Minutemen of anti-Jewish activities. Stink bombs were tossed into Nazi meetings, and pro-German activists were beaten with bats and iron bars.

Describing one such incident, Arno said, "It was one of the most happy moments of my life. It was too bad we didn't kill all of them."[8] As Roth described with undisguised admiration: "Longy eventually made it big. But even at the top, when he was teamed up with Bugsy Siegel and Lansky and Lucky Luciano, his closest intimates were the friends he'd grown up with in the streets, Third Ward boys like himself, who it took little to provoke. . . . Meyer Ellenstein, another street kid from the Third Ward ghetto—when he was mayor of Newark, Ellenstein all but ran the city for Longy."[9]

His generosity extended far beyond Jews: Zwillman covered the cost—singlehandedly and anonymously—of the city's soup kitchens. He purchased an African American social club to save it from demolition. When Zwillman killed himself in 1959 during a Senate investigation, Prinz delivered the funeral oration with a throng standing outside to pay their respects. Perhaps because Newark was a city made up of newcomers, it was more tolerant of the victimless crimes such as bootlegging or illegal gambling with which Longy was most closely involved; his more violent activities were little more than rumors for the longest time.

Indeed, the presence of gangsters in the city's Jewish life was pervasive. According to literary critic Mark Shechner, who until the age of eleven lived in Roth's neighborhood, Weequahic was "a natural blending of the commercial sphere with the underworld."[10] Longy's office was upstairs from Newark's most celebrated Jewish-owned restaurant, the Tavern, whose New Year's Eve dinner menu featured turkey, chicken, steak, veal, and shrimp, but no pork. The eatery was located just behind Abraham Block's candy store, a gangster favorite where the Minutemen liked to gamble. Former bootleggers owned another Jewish favorite, the Log Cabin Grill. Prinz would come to learn that nearly all the richest Jews in his congregation were in business with Zwillman.

This is the contour of Roth's early life, and he would revel in stories of Zwillman, the Minutemen, and the gangsters huddled at the city's candy stores—his earliest tales were built around gangster glory and folly. In general, neighborhood stories would be his forte from early on, certainly as early as his first years in college and often the way he introduced himself to people he cared about. And he would also rehearse tales of less dangerous, exotic locals: gentiles. Here is one of his riffs told at Yaddo in the late sixties:

> Then there were Italians. . . . They were the Americans . . . we didn't have any Wasps. I didn't have a sense of what they were really. What you have is Italian and Colored, Negroes, Italians, Irish; Italians I knew, they were something like Jews. And the guys were tougher. And they looked a certain way. They looked like George Wallace. I liked them when I worked at Klein's [department store] and ate with the Italian guys in the cafeteria. Girls were very sleek and thin. I didn't respond to them. Guys had a sort of comedy-like appearance like Dean Martin. As Jews we knew the hysteria, the emotionality, and we knew the piety. These guys were in another wavelength.[11]

Newark's economic slippage was long in coming, with the Second World War only delaying the inevitable. Never blessed with the range of institutional fixtures that defined other cities—an orchestra, a baseball team, a major museum—and with the Pulaski Skyway now easing access to New York City, local cultural life starved. Moreover, Newark—in contrast to Chicago, Philadelphia, or Dallas—was unable to absorb its nearby regions with their crucial tax revenue, these suburbs being the destination of so many of its residents, including nearly all its Jews. With Newark now cash poor, African Americans who were encouraged in the 1920s to move to the city to fill industrial jobs, positions left empty by the stoppage of foreign immigration, found themselves jobless, thrown out of work as Newark slid into economic decrepitude.

Newark's rise and then its fall, the deterioration of cozy ethnically inflected villagelike neighborhoods, the sense that it once enjoyed a precious self-sufficiency despite its proximity to New York—these would nurture a nostalgia denser and more resilient than that of the country's other declining industrial hubs. Roth's writings would figure prominently here, despite his abhorrence of sentimentality. Still, his imagination was never more robust than when fixed on his youngest years there.

"In my childhood imagination," said Roth in an interview in the early 1990s, "Newark was always the East Coast of the American mainland. Beyond that was the Hudson River, which was not that easy to cross in the old days. New York was to us as Europe was to New York." His was a capacity to "stand both inside and outside the child's mind": this how George Orwell identified Charles Dickens's genius. Roth often admitted that he was puzzled by the resilience of childhood recollections, with their capacity to inspire: "Look," says Zuckerman in the epilogue to *The Facts*, "this place you come from does not produce artists so much as it produces dentists and accountants. I'm convinced that there is something in the romance of your childhood that you're not permitting yourself to talk about."[12]

When Roth spoke of Newark, as he did even in the very last of his novels, *Nemesis*, nearly always it was that smallish slice of it, Weequahic, at the city's southwest corner, this the neighborhood of his birth. Named for its Indigenous inhabitants and built on a subdivided farm, by the time of his birth it had emerged into a self-sufficient Jewish townlet no more than a twenty-minute bus ride from downtown Newark but distant from anything except itself. There was nowhere else in his youth (except Bradley Beach, where his family escaped the summer heat) that Roth spoke of with comparable pleasure and a fixation on the smallest, most precious details.

Weequahic was largely inaccessible to Jews until the 1920s because of exclusionary covenants (the first who managed to settle there were less recognizable German Jews), but its population was soon as much as 95 percent Jewish. Once Beth Israel Hospital, by now the city's best, announced its plan to move there in 1923, Weequahic emerged as the center of Newark's Jewish life.

Among its many pleasurable features was freedom from anti-Jewish taunts that made life in the older Jewish neighborhoods uncomfortable and sometimes unsafe. Roth recalls how his paternal grandfather, Sender, who lived in the overwhelmingly impoverished Third Ward, would yell at neighbors who called him a kike. No more than a few miles away, Weequahic had a suburban feel with its tree-lined streets and single-family homes. No factories were permitted—the closest was on the other side of the neighborhood's vast, beautiful park. "Orderly" was the depiction typically used in real estate advertisements.[13]

Weequahic—though certainly not expected to be a lifelong feature in Roth's work and never as exacting in its detail or persistence as James Joyce's excavation of Dublin—reemerged in book after book. Roth, convinced of the need to fix his fiction as close as possible to reality, drew on his old neighborhood for the backdrop of an idyllic (if also exceedingly regimented) childhood, a tumultuous adolescence, the rise and decline of the American city, and eventually the site of a fascist takeover and the terrors of an uncontainable epidemic.

Roth's Weequahic was roughly middle class, with the poorer Jews living nearer to the commercial streets and the wealthier ones (mostly doctors and lawyers) in single-family homes close to the park. The neighborhood was made of two distinct sections—Lyons Avenue up to Chancellor being the wealthier part with the largest houses, many of them boasting finished basements. These, Roth and his friends valued greatly because of their promise of at least some privacy and, once adolescence arrived, the prospect of a modicum of sexual activity. "I'm an authority on Newark," writes Roth in *The Anatomy Lesson*. "Not even on Newark. On the Weequahic section of Newark. If the truth be known, not even the whole Weequahic section. I don't even go below Bergen Street."[14]

Weequahic's grandest jewel was its three hundred–acre park, with its lake, golf course, even riding stables. The park was designed by Olmsted Brothers, the firm founded by the sons of Frederick Law Olmsted, creator of New York's Central Park. Weequahic Park sought to replicate, as local historian John Johnson wrote, the look and feel of the Anglican Northeast. And little more than eight miles away at the foot of the Watchung Mountains was Crystal Lake, with a fishing and boating lake, merry-go-round, boxing ring, and Olympic-sized swimming pool.

Impressive too was the local high school, which still, well into the 1970s, boasted the lowest dropout rate in the country and the highest number of graduates who went on to earn Ph.D.s. From its start in 1933, Weequahic High School took itself very seriously, adorning its entrance with a lavish New Deal mural (one of the most celebrated in the state) portraying an array of scholars in worshipful frames under the heading "The Enlightenment of Man," including a Jewish scholar enraptured by a book. Roth grew up, as he told Bailey, amid "a culture with a tremendous *respect* for books." The school's principal during Roth's years wrote book reviews for the *Newark Evening News*. A French teacher, the model for Murray Ringold of *I Married a Communist*, came to his job with a Ph.D. from Johns Hopkins.

"Perhaps by definition a neighborhood," writes Roth in *American Pastoral*,

> is the place to which a child spontaneously gives undivided attention; that's the unfiltered way meaning comes to children, just flowing off the surface of things. Nonetheless, fifty years later, I ask you: has the immersion ever again been so complete as it was in those streets, where every block, every backyard, every house, every *floor* of every house—the walls,

> the ceilings, doors, and windows of every last friend's family apartment—came to be so absolutely individualized?[15]

Not only idyllic in his imagination, Weequahic was cleverly engineered to meet the needs of newly Americanized Jews enjoying their first experiences away from crowded immigrant neighborhoods. Its commercial streets were planned with considerable forethought. Local activist turned entrepreneur Michael Stavitsky bought an entire block, making it into the locale of many of Weequahic's most attractive, well-patronized stores. Ads for local shops sought to make it amply clear that Jewish patrons could expect to be treated better there than downtown. Johnson shows in his dissertation on the neighborhood how such expectations continued to be nurtured well into the 1950s: A full-page advertisement in a Weequahic Jewish newspaper in 1958 urged "For Real Values—Shop Bergen St," with a listing of stores featuring cigars, shoes, men's clothing, furs, hats, jewelry, linen, handbags, fish, and sportswear—as well as a reminder from Manoff Fisheries to "order your Passover fish now."[16]

"Our lower-middle-class neighborhood of houses and shops—a few square miles of tree-lined streets at the corner of the city bordering on residential Hillside and semi-industrial Irvington," writes Roth in *The Facts*, "was as safe and peaceful a haven for me as his rural community would have been for an Indiana farm boy."[17]

Yet this would be the breeding ground for Roth's frenzied portrait of youth in *Portnoy's Complaint*, with its ravenous hunger for freedom, barely containable eruptions of sexuality, and oceanic parental devotion.

"In other words," Roth's Zuckerman says in *The Counterlife*, in response to an impromptu lecture on the origins of ancient Israel at the home of an Israeli West Bank far-right radical, "it didn't all begin up that outside flight of wooden stairs where

Grandma and Grandpa lived on Hunterdon Street. It didn't begin with Grandma on her knees washing the floors and Grandpa stinking of old cigars. Jews didn't begin in Newark, after all."[18]

Sender, his paternal grandfather, was a hatmaker—hardworking, taciturn, a distant presence. Roth described him in his nonfiction book *Patrimony*, published in 1991, as "an elongated man with an undersized head—the forebear whom my own skeleton most resembles—and about whom all I knew was that he smoked all day long, spoke only Yiddish, and wasn't much given to fondling the American grandchildren."[19] Family lore had Sender studying to be a rabbi back in Galicia, but there is no indication that he possessed any special access to Jewish texts, none that he remained pious. His son Herman's most treasured heirloom from him was a shaving cup embossed with Sender's name that rested for years at the local barbershop, where he enjoyed his Saturday razor shaves—doubly prohibited by Jewish law.

His paternal grandmother, Bertha, Roth describes as "a simple old-country woman, good-hearted, given to neither melancholy, nor complaint." Unlike the more distant grandfather and blessed with singular generosity, she frequently hosted immigrant relatives, even as she invited her granddaughter Sonny, her mother, and her diabetic brother to live with her—in addition to seven children (two died in infancy). And the household sometimes included Sonny's father, a gambler, usually penniless. Sonny recalls, with considerable fondness, sharing a bed with Bertha until her marriage. The Flaschner publications singled out Bertha as the family's greatest exemplar of kindliness.

Their bustling, overcrowded neighborhood with some of the worst housing in the city was described by Roth in *I Married a Communist* with the exactitude of a meticulous social historian:

> a tiny neighborhood swarming with kids: kids in the alleys, kids crowding the stoops, kids pouring out of the tenements and stampeding from Clifton Avenue down Broad Street. All

> day long and, during the summertime, through half the night you could hear these kids shouting to one another. . . . Everywhere you looked, bands of kids, battalions of kids—pitching pennies, playing cards, rolling dice, shooting pool, licking ices, playing ball, making bonfires, frightening girls.[20]

Roth's father was the first child in his family born in the United States. When fourteen, in eighth grade, Herman left school to join his father and three brothers at a hat factory. Once he married Bess, they settled in Weequahic, where he sold shoes, then opened his own shop, which failed in the Depression. After some odd jobs, he was hired by Metropolitan Life as an insurance agent with a clientele including Newark's poorest. Sandy was born in 1928 and Philip five years later. "His resolute dutifulness, his relentless industriousness, his unreasoning obstinacy and harsh resentments, his illusions, his innocence, his allegiances, his fears were to constitute the original mold for the American Jew, citizen, man, even for the writer, I would become."[21] Roth's memoir *Patrimony* was a book-length monument to Herman's raw, rambunctious, and generous temperament.

Perhaps the most pronounced quality of the father in *The Plot Against America* is his "breathtaking perseverance." Work is what Herman Roth excelled at, surviving bankruptcy twice while always putting food on his family's table as an insurance agent. His son would later capture Herman's experiences—as branch manager, husband, father, widower, and, finally, elderly man dying a slow, painful death.

Herman labored hard to protect his sons from sexual mishaps—much to Philip's distress—and was terrified that they would get one of their girlfriends pregnant. He could be hotheaded, capable of volcanic anger, jarringly intrusive, but he was also the chosen confidant of relatives in trouble. Little if anything of the repressed father of *Portnoy's Complaint* resembles Herman Roth, whose presence in the family—indeed, anywhere he went—was keenly felt. He broadcasted his loves (family, Newark, FDR, boxing, Israel) as loudly as his hatreds (Nixon, antisemitism, all criticism of Israel).

Late in life, Roth would greatly enjoy reciting his father's favored, often fractured sayings. When served an especially spicy dish, he would exclaim, "This is as hot as Aunt Blanche": a relative, as Herman explained, who was the madam of a New Orleans brothel and later the mistress of a senator. At a celebration at Bradley Beach for V-J Day, Herman announced while dancing with the family in a conga line: "From here on, boys, we're going atomic!"[22]

No other family member so preoccupied Roth. His first novel, *Letting Go*, begins with a plaintive letter about his father. Bucky Cantor, the Job-like protagonist of Roth's last novel, *Nemesis*, was worse off than an orphan, with his mother dead and his father—a deadbeat, a gambler—nowhere to be seen. By far, *Nemesis* is the most tender of all his books, with its full-length evocation of the fatherly love enjoyed by Bucky's girlfriend.

Herman would readily admit that his was a tendency to *hock*, to push until the other agreed to his benevolent advice—this, a quality shared by son as well as father. Roth once summed up Herman as "a cross between Captain Ahab and Willy Loman."[23]

Indeed, the most terrifying moment of his childhood, as Roth describes at the start of his autobiography *The Facts*, was the sudden hospitalization of his father when Philip was eleven, with Herman given only a 50 percent chance of recovery from an appendectomy. The prospect of fatherlessness, Roth admits, struck him at the time both "as scary and a little taboo"; at the time, he knew only two boys without fathers, and "everything either of them did or said seemed determined by his being a boy with a dead father."[24]

Roth speaks at length in his autobiography of his father. In stark contrast, the description of his mother, Bess, is dispensed

Herman Roth, argumentative, strong-willed, and a fiercely devoted, loving father. (Photograph by Barbara C. Sproul)

with in little more than a sentence—but what an extraordinarily packed run-on sentence, this portrait of a son enraptured:

> The link to my father was never so voluptuously tangible as the colossal bond to my mother's flesh, whose metamorphosed incarnation was a sleek black sealskin coat in which I, the

> younger, the privileged, the pampered papoose, blissfully wormed myself whenever my father chauffeured us home to New Jersey on a winter Sunday from our semiannual excursion to Radio City Music Hall and Manhattan's Chinatown: the unnameable animal-me bearing her dead father's name, the protoplasm-me, boy-baby, and body-burrower-in-training, joined by every nerve ending to her smile and her sealskin coat.[25]

Bess looked nothing like the combustible, bristly Sophie Portnoy. She was slim, a careful dresser, an impeccable housewife, and a scrupulously attentive mother. Philip was her favorite, something on which both sons concurred. This caused Sandy much distress when he was young, yet he acknowledged it with little rancor later.

But Sandy would also admit that he recognized in Sophie Portnoy more than a passing snapshot of his mother. When upset, she would lock the boys out of the house. When they would hide under the bed escaping her momentary fury, Bess would sweep the floor to ferret them out. She terrified Philip when a young boy with her harsh discipline, which he would later dismiss, or insist it wasn't at all unusual, or that these slips were fleeting amid all else that enveloped this happy household.

Roth acknowledged an intense desire to please her, to be an impeccably good Jewish boy while at the same time—in his friend Benjamin Taylor's judicious description—bursting with "inner anarchy." The residue left in the wake of this favored if frenetic childhood lingered, and not infrequently Roth dreamed of re-creating it somehow: He suggested, half-jokingly, to his friend Albert Goldman, with whom he was close in the early 1970s, that they collaborate on a Beckett-like play depicting a brothel for nice Jewish boys. Here, a motherly prostitute would bathe and powder you, then put you in a child's pajamas (the same, of course, that Roth wore in his childhood) and tuck you into bed, where you'd fall asleep listening to "a little radio with an orange dial." The next morning, a soft voice would call, "Wake up, dear, it's time to get up." For that, Roth said, he'd gladly pay fifty dollars.[26]

What Bess brought from her upbringing—hers was a monied family, the wealth eventually lost in the Depression, and her parents were both distant figures in Philip's life—was an indefatigable devotion to cleanliness, strict routines for meals, bedtimes, and all else. "Obsessive," as well as "fanatical" and "a control freak" is how Roth's cousin Florence described Bess. Roth fiercely disputed the depiction, though he acknowledged that no one he knew had a cleaner house.[27]

"Our household ran like a clock. What could be more comforting for a child than that?" asks Roth in a memo to Bailey. Still, how might a child like him—headstrong, as he himself would later admit, lavishly celebrated, his mother's favorite—not have felt hemmed in by such strictures? He leaves this question unasked. "He comes from a nice happy household," Roth writes in "His Mistress's Voice," a story published in 1986, "with a mother who cooked and a father who worked and stood for brushing teeth and doing homework and represented sanity and order—a calamity at his house was missing lunch."[28] Roth laughed at, and sometimes bitterly excoriated, those who took for granted that he had been reared by the likes of Sophie Portnoy, which he was not. Yet there was a resemblance. Few readers of *Portnoy's Complaint* will forget Sophie Portnoy's fixation on her son's eating, her conviction that the failure to eat properly was certain to cause damage—physical, eventually financial—and to save him, anything was justified including the use of a knife:

> So my mother sits down in a chair beside me with a long bread knife in her hand. It is made of stainless steel, and has little sawlike teeth. Which do I want to be, weak or strong, a man or a mouse?
>
> Doctor, *why*, why oh why oh why oh why does a mother pull a knife on her own son? I am six, seven years old, how do

> I know she really wouldn't use it? . . . What can she possibly be thinking *in her brain?* How crazy can she possibly be? . . . Why a *knife*, why the threat of *murder*, why is such total and annihilating victory necessary—when only the day before she set down her iron on the ironing board and *applauded* as I stormed around the kitchen rehearsing my role as Christopher Columbus in the third-grade production of *Land Ho!*[29]

This, Sandy told his wife, Doreen, is just what their mother threatened to do, with Bess holding a knife above her boys if they refused to eat. Not a sign of lack of affection, the opposite of course, but a clear indication of unwillingness to compromise on what she knew to be right. And she may well have carried this into her later life too: Barbara Sproul, Philip's lover in the late 1960s and early '70s, remembers Bess visiting Roth's Connecticut home, where she queried Barbara on her use of the dishwasher after dinner, a machine with which she appeared to be unfamiliar. Late that night, Barbara heard noise in the kitchen, where she found Bess removing the dishes from the machine, rewashing them one by one. A "domestic ingenuity . . . on par with Robinson Crusoe's" is how Roth would later capture her with, as he insisted, unfettered admiration.[30]

She was a demure, well-liked woman, an avid fan of Pearl Buck and *Ladies' Home Journal*, intently devoted to her husband and her boys and far calmer than Herman. Over the years, friends of his who met Bess often said they found her less physically attractive than Roth had led them to believe, but the real force in the family. Sandy's older son Jonathan described Bess as far more feared than Herman, quieter but more formidable.[31]

Criticism of Bess enraged Roth. No doubt, this was partly because of the fallout from *Portnoy's Complaint*. Roth would remain furious with Ross Miller for years, long after dropping him as the first of his authorized biographers, because of Miller's inclination to collapse the differences between his mother and Sophie Portnoy. "How could the author of PC [*Portnoy's Com-*

plaint] have come from a quiet, well-functioning family?" This question Miller would time and again ask him, with Roth insisting that the one and only truthful response was simply, "Well, he did—and that's the biographical enigma."[32]

By and large a woman of "cool reasonableness" is how Roth's close friend and literary critic Judith Thurman captured Bess. (Roth himself used the very same depiction in describing to his friend Ted Solotaroff his mother's disbelief when told that her son might well be a better writer than *Exodus*'s Leon Uris.) And Roth would readily acknowledge that it was an outsized response to one's parents'—imperfect, but by no means monstrous—behavior that is at the core of Alexander Portnoy's anguish.[33]

And it seems that Roth's recollection of a happy home with loving parents is by no means fanciful. Sally Priesand, the first female rabbi ordained by a rabbinical seminary, knew Roth's parents as congregants in a small synagogue in Elizabeth, New Jersey, just down the street from Bess and Herman's home. "My last memory of the two together . . . I happen to have looked out of the window and saw the two of them holding hands and walking down the street."[34]

Roth recalls in a memo to his biographers the central role played by whistling in his family life:

> Both my father and mother were expert whistlers. . . . And one of my strongest memories is of walking the one block home from school every weekday at lunchtime, heading up the driveway to the back door at 91 Summit Avenue and as I sprung up the stairs to our second floor flat hearing my mother whistling away in the kitchen having just heated up my soup and prepared my sandwich in the kitchen. . . . I knew what that whistling signified—a very happy parent.[35]

Roth was an unyielding, gorgeous boy, worshiped by his mother. "Very obstinate and very territorial" is how Roth later described himself as a child.[36] Sandy was the handsomer of the two and artistic (he had a talent for drawing much like the older brother in *The Plot Against America*), but he was certainly less assertive than his sibling, operating throughout his life at a much lower decibel level. Adored by his younger brother when growing up, Sandy was the object of great admiration when, after the army, he sought to pursue life as a painter. But when he abandoned bohemia for advertising, Philip scored Sandy as a consummate sellout.

In Roth's childhood there was nothing as consuming as his passion for baseball: "sacred heart, my inviolate homeland."[37] Usually positioned in right field (not the best of players), this was as close as he would come, likely ever, to feeling himself an integral part of America. Not quite as powerful, but close, were joyous moments like Truman's unexpected 1948 victory or the thunderbolt of FDR's death.

Still, it was baseball that most linked him to America. "Rather than growing up intimidated by the monolithic majority," he would later explain to his friend the French philosopher Alain Finkielkraut, "or in defiance or in awe of it—I grew up feeling a part of the majority composed of competing minorities, no one of which impressed me as being in a more enviable position than our own."[38] That majority was, of course, the Jewish one.

His Jewishness was from the start—later too, despite intermittent reading—constructed mostly instinctively: the closest of his lifelong friendships, his loathing for antisemitism, a blithe contempt for Christianity far transcending his overall disregard for religion. These are its building blocks far more than books. Few of the books that left the greatest imprint on him in his adolescence—except the biblically inflected novels of Howard Fast—had any Jewish content at all, although once he encountered Saul Bellow and Bernard Malamud he recognized an immediate kinship. Still, his first Jewish influences were more sensual than cerebral, distinguishing him from the likes of Norman

Podhoretz, Alfred Kazin, or Irving Howe—the figures at the center of New York's Jewish intelligentsia. Roth's relationship with these rather more ponderous and self-consciously erudite figures—long before the appearance of *Portnoy's Complaint*—was that of a rather puckish, obstreperous outsider.

All the boys he ran with were Jewish, and the girls he dated were Jewish too. "Discussions about Jewishness and being Jewish, which I was to hear so often among intellectual Jews once I was an adult in Chicago and New York, were altogether unknown," he writes. "We talked about being misunderstood by our families, about movies and radio programs and sex and sports, we even argued about politics though this was rare since our fathers were all ardent New Dealers. . . . About being Jewish there was nothing more to say than there was about having two arms and two legs." Still in his thirties, he would express amazement at the oddities of *goyishe naches* or gentile pleasures, like the apparent joy experienced by the Kennedys in rafting side by side on Snake River.[39]

Even enthusiasm for boxing took on an undeniable Jewish coloration. Herman greatly enjoyed taking his boys to the local ring, which he did often. Boxer "Slapsie Maxie" Rosenbloom, said Roth, was at the time a greater local celebrity than Princeton's Albert Einstein. In an unpublished memoir, Weequahic-born Robert Leonard Berkowitz recalled that in the summer of 1942, with dreadful rumors circulating about the fate of relatives in Poland, the fight of his second cousin and Newark native Allie Stolz at Madison Square Garden was viewed by Jews as one small but crucial way of wreaking revenge. No fewer than four thousand Jews from Weequahic and nearby Clinton Hill packed the Garden to cheer the Jewish boxer. Others came from the Bronx, Brooklyn, and Jersey City. Stolz's defeat that night for the worldwide lightweight boxing championship—widely viewed as unfair—was seen as something far more consequential than the contest for a title. "At the table, at the shul, with people, with cousins and relatives and friends," Stolz later reminisced, "I really felt I was representing Jews."[40]

At Home in America—so historian Deborah Dash Moore entitled her study of second-generation Jews—sums up with more than a whiff of irony just how those like Roth were reared. Besotted by love for a country run by Roosevelt side by side with his presidential adviser Bernard Baruch, his parents knew they were newcomers never likely to fit in altogether but saw themselves as preparing the way for their Americanized children. And while Roth insisted that he never felt poor—his parents, even in the wake of Herman's financial mishaps, never let on how worried they were about money—he came of age acutely attuned to the vagaries of wealth, the differences between the classes. Asked once by the wife of the well-known and well-born conservative intellectual William Buckley, "What is your background?" Roth answered, "I didn't have one. We were too poor."[41]

Early on, starting at Chancellor Elementary School, located adjacent to the most favored of the neighborhood's baseball fields, Roth bonded with a clutch of garrulous, bright, eager boys, all good students—nearly all eventually doctors—several with better grades than Roth. Remembered by some for his caustic humor, others described him as the most hilarious comic in his circle. High school teachers interviewed soon after the appearance of *Portnoy's Complaint* admitted they were surprised by all the hubbub since the Roth they recalled wasn't an especially remarkable student: "A quiet boy, intelligent but unimpressive," said one of them, adding he didn't think much of the new book.[42]

Most crucial were his close male friends: "Three or four of us," as he would later describe, "wandering the streets at night, shooting craps in the back of the high school with flashlights, girls, going after your date to this gathering place called Syd's on Chancellor Avenue and telling your sex stories. It was that verbal robustness, people talking, being terrifically funny, playing ball, competing, the energy flowing out. . . . Appetite. Maybe that's the word. It was the appetites that were aggressive."[43]

In taped conversations with Alan Lelchuk in 1968, on the cusp of the appearance of *Portnoy's Complaint*, Roth sought to describe his adolescence and the extent to which it was as captured in the book. He recalled that his most memorable evenings were spent in the finished basements of his wealthier friends, listening to the sugary bass-baritone voice of Billy Eckstine and his big band. Roth's favorite was "I'm in the Mood for Love"—a song that proved, time and again, the most captivating of all for the purpose of high school romance.

Eckstine, in contrast to Tony Martin, wasn't "a bar mitzvah thing," as Roth described it, but Black and smooth and sexy. Newark was then a major center for African American music, which Roth and his friends sought out with whatever money they had, purchasing records at the Savoy, the local mecca for "race records." At the time Billy Eckstine was the greatest sensation of all. Roth recalls hearing him perform at the Mosque Theater, the large downtown venue for political as well as musical events, where the crowd went crazy with admirers running up and down the aisles. At dance parties, "he was the guy who sang in your ear and your girlfriend's ear and . . . could get your girlfriend to do stuff for you." Roth recalled fondly dancing to Eckstine with the lights off in those finished basements, where you could "glide the girl against the wall." No sex—the prospect of soiling your pants at best.

Roth had no idea what the future might hold. Soon before his high school graduation, Herman urged his son to study Spanish so that he might go into the banana trade then dominated by Jews. (His father fretted far less about Philip's future than Sandy's, whose plans to work as an artist he resisted strenuously.)

Most of Roth's time outside of school was spent hanging out with his closest friends, listening to music on the radio, gambling for small stakes (sometimes taking money to pay back debts from his mother's purse), and maintaining throughout a B-minus average.[44]

According to Roth's cousin David Cohen, it was his father Irving Cohen—the inspiration for the raw, dogmatic Ira Ringold in Roth's *I Married a Communist*—who encouraged him to pursue his literary dreams. Herman thought writing was frivolous, Cohen told me.[45] "Mildly constrained still by the taboos . . . from the religious orthodoxy of my immigrant great grandparents," augmented by Herman's financial difficulties along with his limitless pride in his son, is how Roth would describe himself until the age of sixteen, when these shackles would begin to feel unbearable. His friend of the late 1960s and early '70s, the music critic Albert Goldman, suggests that Roth began at just this time to cultivate his own distinctive brand of comedy: this inspired by "the Jewish living room, the candy store or luncheonette, where after school the kids take turns driving each other over the edge of hysteria." Goldman says Roth told him he had first learned to be funny "when he was a child, probably on those daily walks from Chancellor Ave. grade school . . . to the little Hebrew school 15 minutes away. In that precious quarter of an hour, those highly regimented Jewish kids could blow off steam and subject the pyramided pieties of their world to a healthy dose of desecratory humor. For a few minutes they could afford to be bad."[46]

3

Indignation

Citizen Tom Paine was the first "serious book" Roth recalls having read. It begins with Paine bursting into Benjamin Franklin's London home—insolent, unkempt, a mid-twentieth-century pent-up adolescent in the guise of a late-eighteenth-century English farm boy. He quickly charms a bemused Franklin, much as he would the thirteen- or fourteen-year-old Roth. Paine here is belligerent: "inside him, something burning uneasily." He introduces himself as a working man, desperate to flee class-ridden rotten England for the openness, the promise, of America. Franklin helps him, setting Paine on a path whereby he would emerge as a writer—celebrated, accursed, forever indispensable. "I had just finished reading about somebody . . . who wasn't afraid to say anything" is how Roth captures his sense of the man at the start of *I Married a Communist*, "an unsavory man with a smoldering intellect and the purest social ideals."[1] It's clear why the adolescent so loved him.

"Our first real awareness of literature came from Phil," Bob Heyman, a friend of Roth's from high school, told a reporter after the appearance of *Portnoy's Complaint*.[2] Roth remembered starting to read real books at sixteen or seventeen once Sandy began to bring them home while on leave from the navy, and soon afterward from the bookstores in Greenwich Village, where he lived briefly, trying out life as an artist. The titles that moved him were diverse, yet predictable, including Thomas Wolfe's *Look Homeward, Angel*—much like *Citizen Tom Paine*, it too an overheated tale of a writer misunderstood, shunned, morally superior.

There were in the family constellation some who modeled unorthodox paths. Bess's younger brother Mickey was a bachelor artist, indifferent to bourgeois norms, who supported himself as a photographer using every opportunity to fly to Europe, where he would study the Old Masters. And there was his cousin Florence's husband Irv Cohen—a Bolshevik trucker no less fanatical about baseball than far-left politics.[3]

Despite Herman's exasperation, Sandy sought for a time to live as an artist. But the sojourn was brief, and once he met his first wife, he abandoned his artistic dreams for a successful career in advertising. A skilled dancer, a pleasant man, also something of a hypochondriac, Sandy would eventually have two adopted sons with whom he had troubled relationships. He was successful at advertising and returned to painting only after his retirement. He gave a wide berth to his far more spirited, ambitious, and gifted younger brother.[4]

Rebellion, rage in the face of injustice—these, as critic Jesse Tisch has documented, were the themes that first captured Roth's attention as a reader. "The first thing I smelled in literature was freedom" is what he later recalled.[5] Yet by the time Roth finished high school, he resembled more the directionless Neil Klugman in "Goodbye, Columbus," with little sense of what moved him except for what he disdained. Working after his high school graduation in January 1950 in the backroom of a local department store, he befriended Italian American co-workers and attended courses at the Rutgers Newark branch, housed in a former brewery, majoring—for want of an alternative—in prelaw. Often after class he gravitated to the main branch of the Newark Public Library, where Neil Klugman is employed in "Goodbye, Columbus," meandering around its open stacks, spending as much time as he could away from home.

The decision to leave the next year for Bucknell, as Roth later described it, was the byproduct of a passing conversation with an acquaintance—an unattractive, cloddish neighbor who was enrolled there and boasted of his new gentile girlfriend. Roth claimed this is why he set his sights on a middling school, deep in rural Pennsylvania with Baptist roots, known, if at all, for its engineering major. Herman agreed, perhaps because he sensed their household conflicts had grown out of hand. Whatever the reason, Roth arrived as a sophomore at Bucknell in 1951, unsure of where life might take him. He briefly joined a Jewish fraternity to satisfy his father. By the time he graduated, he would emerge as the campus's best-known intellectual rabble-rouser, now published in a campus literary magazine that he started and edited, surrounded by a loyal cadre of devotees—including Bucknell faculty—convinced he was an extraordinary talent.

Roth found the place mostly intellectually benign, mediocre even, when compared with Rutgers-Newark with its left-leaning largely Jewish faculty who had sought refuge there because McCarthyism had limited their prospects for teaching at better schools. Still, Bucknell provided him with his first encounter with lively—mostly gentile—intellectuals. And it was there that he would begin to speculate, at first vaguely, about a literary career of some sort. Never in high school, as he later told Alan Lelchuk, did he for a moment contemplate spending his life reading and writing.[6]

But right there were models for just such a course. There

was professor-poet John Wheatcroft, who later served as a judge for the Pulitzer; Mildred Martin, the college's severest of literature teachers; as well as a fetching bohemian couple, Charlotte and Bob Maurer, the husband at work on a dissertation on e. e. cummings and the wife whimsical, attractive, deftly opinionated, and one-time secretary to the fabled *New Yorker* editor William Shawn.

Also at Bucknell, much as he had hoped, he found a smart, attractive girlfriend (later a French literature professor at NYU) and two or three clever Jewish boys—all literature-besotted—who together with Roth launched the literary quarterly *Et Cetera.* Here Roth published his first short stories, all inspired by the then-ubiquitous J. D. Salinger and Truman Capote. *New Yorker*–style vignettes left their mark, as well. In Salinger, Roth discovered, as he later told Claudia Roth Pierpont, "this sense of talking, of confessing. It was indecorous." No longer did he feel the need to sequester his more overtly rebellious side, unlike at home.[7]

By far, Roth's most controversial piece in *Et Cetera*—with no hint of Salinger but a large dose of Swift—was an attack on the editor of the college newspaper the *Bucknellian.* So biting was the essay that it resulted in a formal investigation and reprimand. What Roth announced in this *Et Cetera* column was that the editor—a popular student, also a cheerleader—produced a paper whose content was so dreadful that it would even be improved if handed over to a bunch of monkeys.

There is "a theory," Roth wrote, "that if a thousand monkeys were chained to a thousand typewriters for an unspecified number of years, they would have written all the great literature that has been set down in the world by human beings." He then asks, "what [is] holding back Miss Roemer?"[8]

The school administration was livid, but his bohemian friends—the Maurers as well as his favorite literature professor

Dr. Martin—all cheered him on: "I imagine that only Bob and I, and possibly Mildred remember how long you've been a master satirist," Charlotte wrote Roth, in 1972, soon after the appearance of *The Breast.* "After Portnoy came out, and both Harry [Charlotte's son] and I read it, we agreed that it was a masterpiece, though not a Great Book. This one, I think, is both."[9]

Now Bucknell's most tough-minded and uncompromising writer, Roth relished the role and his new literary camaraderie. Bucknell's poet Wheatcroft was someone for whom "literature was not one's field of interest but one's calling . . . and that faithfully scrutinizing a revered literary text was a secular act of worship that could make the spirit soar," as Roth would later write. Mildred Martin, an expert on T. S. Eliot, assigned in her seminar (students were admitted only after careful selection) two hefty books weekly, these spanning the canon of Western literature. "There are no 'guys,' Mr. Zuckerman, in *Pride and Prejudice,*" as Roth recalls in a lightly fictionalized version of these moments in *My Life as a Man.*[10]

Most compelling were the Maurers—both young and bright, indifferent to bourgeois enticements—with a snug rented brick house filled with throwaway furniture and soon Roth's home away from home. Here he ate and drank regularly, babysat the Maurers' children together with his girlfriend, and listened to radio coverage of the McCarthy hearings.[11]

He regaled the Maurers and his other friends at Bucknell with stories of the oddballs, small-time hoods, the exotica of Jewish Newark. This was his first audience beyond the clutch of Jewish pals back home with whom he shared the local lore he knew best and that would soon come to dominate his fiction. Bob possessed a particularly capacious imagination—one, as it turned out, incapable of tethering to an academic career. Later, having finished his dissertation and divorced from Charlotte, he left a secure position teaching at Antioch to join the Peace

Corps, where among his tasks was tutoring Chilean boys in baseball. Charlotte, who would try her hand at writing without success, spent much of her life raising horses for harness racing. She was a tough critic if also a great admirer of Roth. He remained close to both Maurers, as well as to their two children. Charlotte wrote him years later, soon after a party they attended together, where she boasted about how—fleetingly—intimate they were once. She was now able to chastise herself for her critical excesses: "Do you remember sitting in the living [room] at 50 Brown Street and me asking you, in my second-hand New Yorker way, 'But what does this sentence *mean?*' "[12]

Here's a glimpse of restless, bookish Bob Maurer, whose charismatic and engaging imprint on Roth was considerable at the time. Writing in 1966, just about to leave Málaga, where Bob had brought the family to an "old house on the beach":

> There through July and August. Then probably a drive north, perhaps as far as Holland, and maybe a look at Paris, which [Charlotte] hasn't seen and I saw only from a GI's lowdown view just after the war. Across to England to see friends, maybe Scotland or Ireland. Frankly we have soul-deep doubts about this part. Just the thought of Britain still chills us; even the sound of their voices here in Madrid brings back the odor of brussels sprouts and B and B bedrooms.[13]

Into most of the stories Roth published in *Et Cetera*, he blended a Capote-like "charm and softness and mild alienation," as he later ruefully admitted. From Capote he drew "an adolescent arrogance with hints of sex, even prostitutes, a sort of wildness even madness," as Roth later recalled. The link to Salinger—ever-more tenuous as time passed—retained some pertinence too: Random House's Jason Epstein later described *Portnoy's Complaint*, much to Roth's distress, as "the Holden Caulfield of the sixties."[14]

By far, the most impressive story he published at that time

was "The Final Delivery of Mr. Thorn." It appeared in *Et Cetera*'s spring 1954 edition and is largely unrecognizable against the backdrop of the stories Roth would begin to write a year or two after his graduation, with several included in *Goodbye, Columbus and Five Short Stories.* "Gently and without sound dawn dipped morning . . . " is how it starts. Nonetheless, foregrounded here were concerns that would continue to weigh heavily: the limits of one's obligations to others; rage as something essential but also devastating; how to embrace, as a writer, the demands of realism alongside life's implausible, irrational side. Here in "The Final Delivery of Mr. Thorn," as in his much-celebrated short story "Eli, the Fanatic" written four years later and included in his collection, was an exploration of the inadequacy of rational explanations for life's twists and turns.[15]

Thorn, a mailman who recently lost his wife, is slated to retire the next day. He is devout with simple tastes (he tends to satisfy his hunger with American cheese) and lives mostly inside of his head. He has no friends, not even acquaintances, with his radio providing his only companionship—especially an early morning talk show whose inane hosts, a husband-and-wife team, dominate his imagination. Yet what he can't stop thinking about is a letter that he cannot bring himself to deliver, which he is certain will inform an elderly couple of their soldier-son's death.

At first ruminative and depressive and then increasingly fantastic once Thorn's radio dies, the story follows him as he goes off to buy a new one. Returning, he finds that his home has shrunk in size and is now no more than one single room, where he finds a man waiting who identifies himself as employed by the United States government. The undelivered letter sits right in front of them on a table next to Thorn's bed, with Thorn convinced that he is to be arrested: "The FBI man is sitting so close he could reach out and grab it, and he'd have all the evidence he'd need." The government official will eventually reintroduce himself as a post office authority there to fill out a form regarding Thorn's retirement. When he leaves, Thorn faints: "He felt as though he was an idiot or a slave or, what's worse (he thought) a child. Why, he was even on the floor, he noticed, like an infant, for goodness sake. He had not been angry for a long time (and especially angry like this: that is not *at* somebody)."

It's a windy night. As he ponders what to do, he puts the letter on the windowsill; "half in the room, half outside and then he went to bed. . . . Something had told him that the letter wouldn't be there in the morning."[16]

He awakens the next morning, as usual at 6:25, and nothing remains of the letter. Suddenly at peace, he finds himself able to sleep until 9 a.m.—all the pains once afflicting him have disappeared. And no longer does he feel the need to listen to the radio with its aimless banter.

Roth was reading Aldous Huxley's *Brave New World* when Harold Itzkowitz first met him in the summer of 1953. Both were employed as counselors at a YMHA camp Forest Lodge. While their first conversation was about the book, subsequent talks were mostly about other people at the camp, politics, and popular musicals. A favorite pastime of Roth's was dirty word scrabble, where the winner came up with the filthiest. Itzkowitz recalls that Roth's antics over the summer would become legendary. Particularly memorable was Roth's announcement to the campers on parents' visiting day that something terrible had happened: The director's wife, Marian (whom he despised), had lost her chastity belt. Roth now set in motion a camp-wide hunt, the hoax in full view of the visiting families.[17]

Roth now stood just over six feet: he was trim and lightly muscled: photographs taken of him at the time show him playfully showing these off. His look then and later was rather more rugged than classically handsome like Sandy's. But sexual energy both exuded. Roth tended to fall in love quickly—sometimes just minutes after a first encounter—this a lifelong trait.

Unsurprisingly, he was very popular with the girls—even Marian, according to Itzkowitz, was known to have been attracted to him. (When Harold returned a decade or so later as camp doctor, one of the first questions Marian asked was about Roth's whereabouts.)[18] Roth spent his first camp summer courting a tall, pretty girl from Pittsburgh, with whom he was having sex by the session's end. When she returned the next year, she took for granted that they would continue their romance, but Roth had found someone new. He had just been approached by Maxine Groffsky at the pool. With a thin, beautiful body and reddish hair, she was, for Roth, irresistible. She was seventeen, Roth was twenty-one. His friend Betty Lehman—soon married to one of Roth's closest Weequahic buddies—remembers him watching Maxine as she walked on the beach, blurting out in amazement, "She walks like a gazelle."[19]

Groffsky told me that she spotted Roth first, found him handsome, and as she was about to embark with two other swimmers on a skit about the discovery of the biblical Moses floating in the water, she walked over to him and—like Brenda Patimkin in "Goodbye, Columbus"—asked him to hold her glasses.[20] Roth captures this moment in the first beautifully crafted paragraph of "Goodbye, Columbus": "I watched her move off. Her hands suddenly appeared behind her. She caught the bottom of her suit between thumb and index finger and flicked what flesh had been showing back where it belonged. My blood jumped."[21]

They would date for the next two and a half years, with Groffsky having just graduated from high school. The relationship ended abruptly, as did so many of Roth's, with Groffsky saying to me that among the many famous men she knew over the course of an exceptionally eventful life—she would serve as an editor of the *Paris Review* and later emerged as a leading literary agent—Roth's impact on her was negligible. Perhaps so. But the influence of Roth's fictional treatment of Groffsky would not only serve to propel him, with astonishing suddenness, into literary importance but would also make her (particularly once the film version of the novella starring Ali MacGraw appeared a decade later) into one of the age's most significant cultural emblems.

4

Goodbye

Yes, love is slavery.

Roth graduated from Bucknell in 1954 and began studying English at the University of Chicago. The choice to study English was inspired by his teacher Mildred Martin, his friendship with the Maurers, and the success of *Et Cetera.* By his junior year at Bucknell, he was already contemplating the prospect of a literary life, probably as an academic.

The first impression he left on those he met in Chicago—this is how his new classmate Ted Solotaroff, soon a close friend, first saw him—was as someone gravely buttoned-down: "He looked like he had strayed into class from the business school." It was now that Roth took on the collegiate look, replete with Brooks Brothers shirts and the like, that would become his lifelong trademark. Beneath it all, as Solotaroff and others soon discovered, was one of the funniest, wildest wits around, in a place packed with sardonic, hilarious, street-smart Jews. Together they would dissect as well as imitate Henry James, Joyce, and Bellow, and trade childhood stories, and talk sex—all of which Roth would soon turn into literature.

Already in fall 1954, Roth placed a story in the *Chicago Re-*

view, a small magazine with considerable cachet. Terser than his previous stories, "The Day It Snowed" was an exploration of the inconceivability of death against the backdrop of a child's vulnerability. Soon afterward Roth published another story, "The Contest for Aaron Gold"—which first appeared in a Cornell literary journal and was included in Martha Foley's *Best American Short Stories* and then made into a segment on television's *Alfred Hitchcock Presents.* It was the success of these stories that persuaded Roth to abandon academia for fiction. And he did so without the studiously acquired scholarly cultivation that would underpin the writings of other literary luminaries of the age, like John Updike, Robert Lowell, or Norman Mailer.

"The Contest for Aaron Gold" is less ornate yet more persuasive than any of his previous stories. Here a new pottery teacher, a refugee from Europe, is hired to work in a summer camp and is soon bullied by the camp's swimming instructor. Here, too, is a vulnerable boy Aaron Gold—a camper with few skills except a stunning capacity for art. The ceramics teacher takes the boy under his wing only to confront the limits of what can be done to help someone in distress. Ultimately, he loses the boy's trust and his summer job, all because his efforts at altruism are thwarted at every turn.

At the same time, Roth also expected to see a play of his about the Holocaust made into a Broadway production. Feeling the weight of his obligations, early in 1955 he admitted in a letter to his high school friend Stuart Lehman that he despaired of the rigors of academic study:

> School, of course, is still pretty hateful. My course in American lit from 1919–1929 is the one bright spot (although Chaucer is gradually becoming more and more enjoyable). . . . By the way, if you get a chance, and happen to be shopping around for a pretty damn good book, get hold of Cummings' novel THE ENORMOUS ROOM; I'd say that next to FAREWELL TO ARMS it's the best war novel of any war. It's a beauty—the

> man has a masterful sense of humor, and the kind of honesty which I'd like to have myself—the kind I've been talking about for the past few years.[1]

Roth was still with Groffsky, spending some two weeks of the summer of 1955 at her South Orange, New Jersey, home, where the two alternated between playing a chaste dutiful couple in the presence of parents and cavorting in private. Roth's portrait of the summer in his novel *My Life as a Man*, published some twenty years later, he acknowledged bore a close resemblance to that summer bacchanal. "At the suggestion of the adults, they would go off to the kitchen late at night and there like good little children eat oversized syrup-covered portions of ice cream out of soup bowls. Out on the terrace the adults would laugh about the appetite on those two kids—yes, those were his father's very words—while beneath the table where they sat, Zuckerman would be bringing Sharon to orgasm with his big toe."[2]

His M.A. degree now completed, he enlisted in the army, the draft still in effect. Basic training at Fort Dix in New Jersey was no less dreadful than he had imagined. Writing Bob Heyman in October 1955, he described "miserable living conditions—we're housed in the old stockade: you can imagine; our mess hall is a mile from the barracks; the CO is a lying, self-concerned bastard. . . . In short, war is hell." Groffsky, he tells Heyman, is now transferring to Barnard to be closer to him, and he admits, "In my bluest moods I'm tempted to call her and say let's get married, but since I don't have time to get to a phone, I'm still single." He sorely missed Groffsky but ends the same letter to Heyman declaring a hunger for freedom, for experiences far beyond those she or any one woman could provide: "All I know is that life is very short, and freedom very precious, and that when I get out I'm going to live right up to the hilt, and make these brief years extravagant as hell. I'm going to go where I

[w]ant and do what I want to do—if I ever figure out what that is—and BE, thoroughly, BE."[3]

He exchanged numerous love letters with Groffsky—his numbering no fewer than two hundred—these likely no less vivid than the ones captured years later in Roth's story "Novotny's Pain": "She had written down, for his very eyes to see, all those things she dreamed about when she dreamed about his body. He saw, suddenly, scenes of passion that he and she were yet to enact, imagined moments even more thrilling than those they had already known."[4]

In basic training, in the bunk just beside him, was Martin Garbus, Bronx born and Jewish, later a well-known First Amendment attorney who would become a lifelong friend. Garbus's first impression of Roth, much like Solotaroff's, was of his perfectly made bed—by far the best of the barracks. Soon enough Garbus also encountered Roth's masterful gift for comedy, thus witnessing from the start both sides of him: the well-reared Jewish boy (Garbus's upbringing in the Bronx was slipshod and loosely parented) and the barracks' filthiest, most sought-after comedian. "Funny every single day," Garbus recalls. With some two hundred men in a barracks packed with "rednecks"—no more than one or two who had gone to college—Roth provided an ample daily dose of obscene entertainment.[5]

All the while, Roth was collecting bits and pieces of data, impressions that would be absorbed into the short stories he now began to write. It was here that he encountered a Jewish soldier who managed with considerable ingenuity to avoid the more onerous chores, inspiring the most controversial of Roth's early writings: "Defender of the Faith." And here too, as he would often do in his fiction, Roth introduced unsettling aspects of himself, since he also sought to shirk responsibilities, claiming that he wasn't permitted to clean the barracks on Friday evenings because of an obligation to attend religious services.[6]

A mishap—a kettle that he yanked while peeling potatoes

to stop it from hitting the foot of another soldier—brought on a back injury, which became a recurring and excruciating problem for Roth throughout his life. Reassigned to writing press releases at Walter Reed Medical Center in Washington, DC, he had far more time for his short stories. The back pain proved so debilitating that he was exempted from military service a year early. Offered an instructorship at the University of Chicago, he returned in fall 1957 to teach and finish his doctorate but soon abandoned this plan, now concentrating exclusively on his writing.

He had remained friends with Ted Solotaroff, still at Chicago, who would become one of his most devoted and loyal advocates. A New Jersey boy—rougher and less polished than Roth—Solotaroff was a failed novelist who excelled at criticism, and he championed Roth from the start. Later as editor of the influential *New American Review*, he gave so much space to Roth's work that he found it necessary to justify the decision in a fulsome statement in the magazine, extolling Roth's singular virtues ("extraordinary wit, candor, and power . . . steady ability to touch bottom, the point in which ethnic singularities take on the universal implications of human life"): This praise was for the soon-to-be-published *Portnoy's Complaint*, huge chunks of which were previewed in his magazine with a readership of 100,000.[7]

Their friendship was complicated, weathering twists and turns, and at times seemed destined to fail. There was fierce classroom competition, and a recognition by Solotaroff soon after they met that he would never match Roth's writing ability. Then there was the meticulously grim portrayal of a character modeled closely on Solotaroff in Roth's first novel, *Letting Go*, published in 1962, which offers an exceedingly detailed description (many criticized the book for excessive length) of Ted's grim Hyde Park apartment, broken-down car, threadbare jacket, and even his awful marriage. Roth acknowledged to Solotaroff that he had "borrowed from your life (your apartment, size and layout . . .)" but insisted—by no means convincingly—that beyond these passing details there was no similarity between the novel's characters and Solotaroff or his wife.[8]

The resolutely admiring Solotaroff remained loyal, even as he took a ribbing from Chicago friends when, soon after the appearance of "Goodbye, Columbus" in 1959, he ranked it in an essay in *Chicago Review* as being as impressive as the now-canonized work of Saul Bellow and Bernard Malamud. Solotaroff describes in a memoir how his reading a draft of Roth's "The Contest for Aaron Gold" contributed to reshaping the trajectory of his life:

> Early on, Roth and I exchanged short stories. Mine was the last one I'd written, three years ago, a dialogue between an old Spanish waiter . . . and a young Puerto Rican one. . . . Phil's was about a refugee artist working as a pottery teacher in a summer camp who befriends a gifted misfit. He dismissed my story with a sentence or two as "exhausted Hemingway stuff"; I wished that I could have done the same with his, but I couldn't. . . . It was indisputably striking in its deftness and authority. After I'd had to say so, I asked him: "How did you know so much about being a potter?" "I don't," he said. "I read something about it and made the rest up."
>
> This unexceptional piece of information hit me like the Last Judgement. I, who had spent years in restaurants, could make only a derivative story out of them: Phil, who knew hardly anything about his subject's work, could make it not just credible but the significant center of the story. The difference wasn't a matter of mode or taste: it seemed simply, starkly, that of ability.[9]

By the time Houghton Mifflin contacted Roth, early in 1958, hoping to sign him as one of its authors, he had decided to take the plunge. An award from his new publisher, then a Guggenheim as well as an award from the American Academy of Arts and Sciences, provided support for a move to Rome, then Paris, where he set about finishing his first book. Once he returned to the United States, now settling in the East Village, he had already begun to emerge as something of a local literary legend. It was his ability to sit at his desk ceaselessly—coupled with the appearance of his fiction and essays in the *Paris Review*, *Commentary*, and the *New Republic*—that set him apart. Poet Robert Kelly recalled that, when in his twenties and dreaming of becoming an author himself, a writer friend who lived near St. Marks Place in Greenwich Village pointed out:

> In the tall house atop which his garret was wedged against the sky . . . a second-story apartment, elegant and writerly as it seemed to us, [where] a Real Writer could be seen, in the forced intimacy of a city summer, at all hours of the day and night working hard at his typewriter. A professional writer, and we walked in awe past his window. A few years later, that real writer was to make his mark on America with "Goodbye, Columbus."[10]

The first of the stories included in *Goodbye, Columbus and Five Short Stories* were written mostly at night while Roth was stationed at Walter Reed. And in nearly every instance, these drew on his own experiences or on tales told to him by those close to him: "I need something solid under my feet to kick off my imagination" he would tell biographer Hermione Lee years later in his *Paris Review* interview. It was his University of Chicago friend Arthur Geffen who told him a story he had heard of a Hebrew school student (the actual event, Geffen admitted to me, turned out to be altogether different from what he had first been told) who challenged his Hebrew teacher, as he stood on the roof of the synagogue, that he would jump unless the teacher admitted that all-powerful God could set in motion a virgin birth. Roth promised not to use it if Geffen, then also hoping to write fiction, did so first. But, unable to restrain himself, Roth immediately built the tale into "The Conversion of the Jews," publishing it in the *Paris Review*.[11]

And it was his brother Sandy who related to Roth the kernel of "Expect the Vandals," which appeared in *Esquire:* a tale of two American soldiers stuck on an island who continue to do battle without knowledge that the Korean War has ended. Roth's father helped inspire the writing of "Epstein," also published in the *Paris Review*, a tale of adultery in Weequahic, where the owner of Syd's hot dog eatery (later featured prominently in *Portnoy's Complaint*) was found by his wife in bed with a neighbor and Herman was called in to mediate. (In the story, Epstein discovers a rash that he fears is evidence of gonorrhea, which Roth was unable to describe without help from the magazine's editor George Plimpton.) Roth was also at work on a full-length novel (he never finished more than a few dozen pages) about a Jewish businessman who plans to go to Frankfurt to kill a German, any German, the story prompted by Herman's ferocious anti-German rants.

Though Roth would later claim he didn't then see himself writing about Jews, this is what—with the rarest of exceptions—he was doing. Rather more credibly, he would express surprise that "*any* truly literate audience could seriously be interested in his store of tribal secrets, in what he knew, as a child of his neighborhood, about the rites and taboos of his clan—about their aversions, their aspirations, their fears of deviance and defection, their underlying embarrassments and their ideas of success."[12]

The prospect that this might be the stuff of true literature, which he and those close to him at the University of Chicago saw exemplified by the likes of Henry James or Conrad, at first felt unlikely. Indeed, their embrace of Western literature was itself prompted in no small measure by a hunger to escape the parochialism of second-generation Jewish life, whose obsessions and postimmigrant malaprops seemed anything but the backdrop to serious writing. As Solotaroff later reminisced:

> Wasn't the truth rather that I didn't want to write about it, that what I wanted from writing was another self than the one that was implicated in such lives. Weren't the qualities of style I aspired to precisely those that enabled me to avoid the vulgar and painful immediacy of my character, my work, my days, my thoughts, my hang-ups? In return, the impassive prose, the fiddling with form, provided an illusionary sense of mastery—control without confrontation, refinement of surfaces, mere gestures of good taste.[13]

Suddenly in the 1950s, universities were packed with eager, intellectually obsessed Jews and with talk of the Jewish horrors of the last world war, the rise of the state of Israel, the persistence of domestic antisemitism—these now topics of widespread currency. Sartre's ruminations on antisemitism in *Réflexions sur la question juive*, translated as *Anti-Semite and Jew*, lent discussion of Jews a heightened gravitas: "Everything Sartre did in those years was an event, so the book was talked about," wrote Louis Menand. There was the acclaim of *The Diary of Anne Frank*, with the Broadway play premiering in 1955. Herman Wouk and Leon Uris and John Hersey released their blockbusters about Jews. And then came Bernard Malamud's, which, "along with Bellow's, meant the world," as Roth later recalled. Critic David Boroff, a great fan of Roth's from the start, put it this way in 1963: "The Jewish condition; the Jew in exile has spoken to the exile of all people."[14]

Yet many of these same writers also assumed that there was something hopelessly parochial, closed-off, and dull about the inner workings of Jewish life. There was more than mild defensiveness in Saul Bellow's declaration at the start of his breakthrough novel *The Adventures of Augie March*: "I am an American, Chicago born." Published in 1953, this jaunty, episodic, Yiddish-inflected masterpiece was held in place by a recognizably Jewish preoccupation with family. Its insistence on Augie's Americanism was itself meant as a way of trumpeting the book's Jewishness, if only in its elision. What Bellow sought to make clear was that his terrain—whether in Chicago or elsewhere—was no less dense or textured or promising than that of William Faulkner, a great favorite of his, as well as of so many other American Jewish writers including Roth. Irving Howe sums up this sense of kinship: "Here, though we might not have yet known it, we were closer to the Southern than to the New England writers. For where, if you come to think of it, is family in Emerson, or Thoreau, or Whitman? . . . And where is the family in Hemingway or Fitzgerald? With Faulkner . . . we might feel at home because the clamp of family which chafed his characters was like the clamp that chafed us."[15]

By early 1958 while still at the University of Chicago, Roth was writing movie reviews for the *New Republic*. (Once he stepped down—he hated nearly everything he saw—his replacement would be Stanley Kauffmann, who continued to review films there with comparable disdain for decades to come.) Leaving the university, his confidence that he could support himself as a writer was bolstered by the invitation in February 1958 from George Starbuck, a poet Roth had met at Chicago who was now an editor at Houghton Mifflin, requesting that he submit work for possible publication. Roth mentioned to Starbuck the manuscript set in Germany but pressed him to consider first a volume of his collected short stories. Negotiations quickly began, swift by any standard, with *Goodbye, Columbus* appearing a little more than a year later in May 1959. This nonetheless felt agonizingly slow to Roth: "I shall be twenty-five next year and stouter, and I feel a tiny knife in my side as I race to be a boy wonder," he wrote Starbuck during a brief snag—the tone jocular, the intent remorselessly earnest.[16]

The speed with which the book moved forward was all the more impressive since it was the Frankfurt manuscript—far from completed—that Houghton Mifflin was really interested in publishing. Yet Roth sensed while working on it that he didn't know enough about postwar Germany to bring it to life: "I have a great deal of stuff in it about the kinds of compensation given to Jews by the German government. Unfortunately, I don't know a great deal about the intricacies of the set-up," he admitted in early 1958 to an editor friend at *Commentary*.[17]

It was while Roth worked on this manuscript that a new Chicago friend, writer Richard Stern, suggested he take a stab at the story of his stay at the Groffskys', a tale Roth had just related over lunch. By now, he had broken with Maxine—he did so soon after his return to Chicago from the army—and was enamored with another woman who was somewhat older, gentile, and, perhaps most important, distant from Newark and its suburbs. Eventually, she would be his first wife: Margaret Martinson Williams, or Maggie. Groffsky was heartbroken: They had dated since the summer of 1954. She had transferred from Cornell to Barnard to be closer to Roth while he was enlisted, and the relationship, contrary to the description in "Goodbye, Columbus," persisted for two and a half years. She admits that she would have done anything for him.

"Maxine Groffsky is an enigma," one of Roth's friends told me. To the girlfriends of Roth's Newark pals, she seemed standoffish, a self-contained beauty. ("I wasn't beautiful then," Groffsky told me, "only later.") What they saw as snobbery may well have been shyness, an insecurity that others assumed inconceivable for someone so attractive and intelligent. She was the youngest of this group, just out of high school, and recalls feeling intimidated by the older crowd. Deeply in love with Roth,

Groffsky felt utterly inadequate in her command of literature: "By the time I met him, I had read nothing but *A Tale of Two Cities* in school." He sent her reading lists (among the writers he then recommended was Martin Buber) and a long poem devoted lovingly to her nose job.[18]

Some years later, thinking about her glamorous career, Roth would bemusedly recall that, contrary to his prediction that she would remain stuck in New Jersey, Groffsky soon became the Paris-based editor of *Paris Review* described as "the most desirable woman of any nationality between the Berlin Wall and the English Channel." She recounts—with much the same description as I heard from other women with whom Roth was once romantically engaged—how severe he was in his judgments about those close to him, and how tough he was on himself. Groffsky remembers being frightened of slipping, worried about disappointing him. And while miserable in the wake of the breakup, she recalls also feeling relief at having escaped his scrutiny.[19]

Reasons for the breakup with Maxine would elude Roth. It may well have had to do with the tapering of sexual hunger for her boyish, athletic body in contrast to Maggie's rounder shape, her novelty, and perhaps also her more prodigious sexual experience. A "smiling, robust, fresh-looking woman of twenty-seven with friendly, square-faced Nordic good looks" is how Roth, in one of his lighter moments, described her at the time they met. His slackened attraction for Maxine Groffsky contrasts sharply, of course, with the explosively erotic summer to which Roth now turned his fictional attention. He would later recall that the writing of "Goodbye, Columbus" was for him all but effortless, the novella finished in little more than six weeks in spurts of a thousand words a day. All this, as he later put it to Lelchuk, part of a concerted effort "to kick the past."[20]

Here, as so often in his fiction, Roth borrowed promiscuously from his own life and the lives of those close to him, with many of the details in the novella drawn directly from his romance with Groffsky. The interplay, however, between what transpired between the two of them and how Roth described it was far from straightforward. Groffsky says that in stark contrast to what is portrayed in the novella—by far the longest piece in Roth's first book—her parents were not wealthy: "No cashmeres, no Cadillac," as she put it. Others who knew the family have confirmed this as well. Her mother, she insists, wasn't the scold depicted but a much-admired, thoughtful woman. Still more striking is the contrast between Groffsky herself and the self-possessed, controlling Brenda Patimkin of "Goodbye, Columbus": Maxine's was a relationship with an older, better-educated man, and she was at Roth's beck and call. She obediently devoured the books he urged her to read, with little evidence of her having been the dominant force in their relationship—this starkly different from Roth's portrayal of Neil Klugman's strong-willed lover.[21]

What Roth likely meant by his reference to the story's value in "kicking the past" was how it captured his ridding himself not only of Maxine but of the powerful pull of Newark itself—with its promise of a tight family's embrace, pervasive Jewishness, even intellectual mediocrity. Never in truth subservient to Maxine—as Neil Klugman would be in his relationship with Brenda Patimkin—it was the prospect of being submerged by these familiar, enticing comforts that inspired Roth's fierce urgency for escape. "Goodbye, Columbus" would come to be his backward glance at the reasons for flight.

What he managed to weave into his tale of young love were echoes of *The Great Gatsby*, with its exploration of wealth's allure and underbelly. Just as prevalent are the insights of sociologist David Riesman's *The Lonely Crowd*, with the book's warnings of the rise of a consumerist "outer-directed" postwar generation; Brenda Patimkin is shaped into a vacuous poster child of the ailment. Her shortcomings are made apparent already in the novella's first sentences: "The first time I saw Brenda she asked me to hold her glasses. Then she stepped out to the edge of the diving board and looked foggily into the pool; it could have been drained, myopic Brenda would never have known it."[22]

Blind to what is right in front of her, this failing of Patimkin's includes her inability to recognize Neil Klugman's love. What unfolds in the story with cinematic visuality is his eventual perception that Brenda's myopia is a moral, not merely a physical, defect. Still, her sexual allure outweighs all else.

Never does the relationship move beyond this moment. Starting already with their first telephone conversation, he finds her shallow. "What do you look like?" is all she asks about him, with her own looks and clothes—particularly the quality of her clothing (Bergdorf's, never Ohrbach's)—an unceasing preoccupation. He finds her infuriatingly status-conscious: "'I go to school in Boston.' I disliked her for the answer": this is how Brenda informs him that she is a student at Radcliffe. (Reviewers questioned how someone so vacuous could manage to get into the school.) Her comments about her own family he finds distasteful. Even her looks, which so mesmerize him, Neil has reason to fault. In explaining the reason for her nose job, she says: "I was pretty. Now I'm prettier." And her breasts leave him unsatisfied: "tiny wings no bigger than her breasts."[23]

Above all, Neil fears her capacity for control will bear down on him, and yet he continues to toy with the idea of their eventual marriage. Then no longer would he be poor—he works as a librarian in the main branch of the Newark library—yet he remains certain that if he succumbs his fate would undoubtedly resemble that of Brenda's mother: "still more beautiful than the daughter," she looks like a "captive beauty, some wild princess, who has been tamed and made the servant to the king's daughter—who was Brenda."[24]

"*I'm* not her slave," says his cousin Doris when Neil asks whether she too will hold Brenda's glasses. It is taken for granted that Neil will babysit Brenda's younger sister, and at a moment's notice. He acknowledges that he feels in their house much like the maid Carlota, though, "not even as comfortable as that." He runs errands for the mother, and, when Brenda orders him to make love on an old sofa in the attic, he admits "I obeyed her."[25]

Two weeks pass before she asks her first real question about him, but only to test whether he plans to do something better in the future than work at the library. It's in the immediate wake of such questioning that suddenly he is drained of all attraction: "I held her . . . though at that moment I was without desire." He dreads the summer's end when Brenda returns to school, but he seems to care far more about sequestering at the library a volume of Gauguin's reproductions for the sake of an African American boy who visits the library book daily, sensing that the child's fantasy of Tahiti much resembles his own. "What was it inside me that had turned pursuit and clutching into love, and then turned it inside out again? What was it that had turned winning into losing, and losing—who knows—into winning?"[26]

In the end, Brenda herself manages to blow things up, leaving a diaphragm at home that is soon discovered by her mother, thus ensuring the end of the relationship. He learns this when visiting Brenda in Cambridge. Leaving her, he walks over to the Harvard campus, where he contemplates tossing a rock through the window of Lamont Library, whose sinks were supplied by Brenda's father's company. Rage, he acknowledges, won't now satisfy him, and he leaves for Newark "just as the sun was rising on the first day of the Jewish New Year. I was back in plenty of time for work." Literary scholar Ross Posnock speculates that "Neil's work . . . will eventually move beyond service at the information desk to include writing the novella we have just concluded."[27]

On one level, an ethnography of Jewish suburbia—its realism reminiscent of the novels of the 1930s. Yet just beneath this surface there are influences that include, in addition to Riesman and Fitzgerald, Bellow and Malamud as well as John Cheever, James Baldwin, Martin Buber, and Paul Goodman. At the same time, such lucidity—"The most purely readable prose in all American literature," according to literary scholar Michael Gorra—is bitingly sarcastic alongside tender observation. His portrait of Newark, especially the area near its vaunted downtown library is, to be sure, glowing—a loving portrayal of the city just before its rapid decline. ("I felt a deep knowledge of Newark, an attachment so rooted that it could not help but branch out into affection.") Roth shows a capacity to imagine the direction that Neil's life might well take if he were to marry Brenda in passages of considerable astuteness. Here he sits watching young mothers—some he recognizes from a few years earlier when they were students together at the same high school—chatting beside their babies in a suburban park, a dour forecast of his own possible future: "They looked immortal sitting there. Their hair would always stay the color they desired, their clothes the right texture and shade. . . . These were the goddesses, and if I were Paris I could not have been able to choose among them, so microscopic were their differences. Their fates had collapsed them into one."[28]

James Wood has suggested that the anger that would characterize so much of Roth's writing was not in evidence in the novella that gives *Goodbye, Columbus and Five Short Stories* its title but was a consequence of the attacks on him by Jewish readers in the wake of the appearance of that first book—it was, he says, only once he was charged with antisemitism by Jewish critics—furious especially at his story "Defender of the Faith"—that Roth would begin "spitting at decency."[29] Yet this assessment overlooks the bitterness that suffuses "Goodbye, Columbus," inspired, it seems, not so much by his experience with Maxine Groffsky and her family but by a turbulence independent of these experiences.

"Apparently, a lot of people felt bitten where there were no teeth, and they felt attacked where nobody had struck them over the head." This is how Roth summed up the criticism of *Goodbye, Columbus* a few years later—puzzled still at its ferocity. Surprised he may well have been, but rage would figure among his most persistent themes.[30] Brenda Patimkin would be the object of the full weight of such anger, in a story inspired by the devotion of a young, impressionable girl enthralled by him fresh out of high school. The fear—pervasive in "Goodbye, Columbus"—of being overwhelmed appears to have had more to do with the lure of Newark and its environs, which he now conflated with Groffsky: This a fear that could well suffocate him if he didn't manage to resist it. And perhaps he felt that he had to work all the harder to cut these bonds with Maxine, who was among the more disturbingly alluring reasons to stay put.

5

Apprenticeship

And still all you write about are Jews.

By THE SUMMER of 1958, Roth had settled on the stories to be included in the collection—the list, somewhat different from what had first been considered, with all except one about Jewish life. The final story added (this after he had already signed his contract) was "Eli, the Fanatic," just finished, a tale of a yeshiva misplaced in a suburb whose Jewish residents find its presence unacceptable, even abhorrent. Haunted as the story's characters are by the Holocaust, Roth finally managed here to blend his preoccupation with the uncanny into a tale that retained its concreteness and realism.

Only now, some five months after George Starbuck first invited Roth to send him a manuscript, was its Jewish content openly acknowledged. Roth proved cagey on this score, still acting as if he was unaware of the collection's Jewish preoccupations while nonetheless using them, at least obliquely, as a selling point. Warning shortly before the manuscript's acceptance that unless he received immediate commitment, he would start shopping the book around, he added a reminder of its salability, referring to how it could well be embraced by "that same group who buy Salinger by the thousands."[1]

Of course, Roth's disinclination to spell out the Jewish content of his writing was understandable. Once the manuscript circulated in the upper reaches of Houghton Mifflin—a publishing house not known at the time as receptive to writing about Jews—a memo to its general division head described the lead story "Goodbye, Columbus" as a tale of "two different sorts of Jewish family in the neighborhood of Newark," then adding, "it's not as depressing as this might sound."

Indeed, even those sympathetic to Jewish writing like Solotaroff acknowledged at the time the drab, uninspired markings of contemporary Jewish fiction: "So self-contained and peculiar, so drenched with nearly invariable shades of local color, that it can become almost inaccessible to the imagination."[2]

One of many striking differences between Roth's collection and other literary explorations of American Jews at the time was the sparsity of mention of enemies from without. Jews in this book are themselves the cause of their own misery, the result of their excessive eagerness to assimilate, their lust, or their outright bigotry. To understand a character like Epstein, who commits adultery with a neighbor, wrote Roth in the wake of a spate of criticisms, remember that the writer has no obligation to command any greater knowledge of Judaism than that possessed by Epstein himself, a small businessman of little learning: "A reader should not expect to find in the story knowledge on my part, or the part of the characters, of the *Sayings of the Fathers*. . . . The story is called 'Epstein' because Epstein, not the Jews, is the subject."[3]

Roth here is somewhat disingenuous: His distaste for Jewish foibles was particularly pronounced. "Eli, the Fanatic," for instance, was inspired by an article in *Commentary* (published in April 1949) describing a suburban flare-up of the sort depicted in Roth's story, but one that involved the protests of non-Jews, not Jews, as depicted by Roth. Roth took hold here of the basic contour of the episode, making Jews its culprits. And it was just this lack of sentimentality, this eagerness to confront the uglier side of one's own, that so impressed, and enraged, readers. With his rare fluency and capacity to capture colloquial prose, Roth was so strikingly different from the fablelike tenor of Malamud or the densely cerebral Bellow.

Slices of nearly all that would be included in *Goodbye, Columbus* had appeared in *Commentary* and the *Paris Review*. But the story eliciting the greater furor from Jewish pulpits, communal leaders, and others was "Defender of the Faith." It rankled not only because it told of Jewish military chicanery, but maybe more important because it had previously been published in the widely read *New Yorker*, not the sparsely circulated *Paris Review* or the Jewishly inflected *Commentary* published by the American Jewish Committee. Appearing in the *New Yorker* in March 1959 some two months before the release of *Goodbye, Columbus*, the story was heralded by others as Roth's finest work.

It tells of Sergeant Nathan Marx, who returns from European battle at the war's end to serve in a training company. Here he encounters three recruits—one particularly intrusive—who seek to play on Marx's sentimental side, insisting that Jewish convictions preclude Friday night duties and that they be given free time to attend a Passover seder. Critics of the story saw it as a tale of a conniving Jew, this especially egregious because the description of dodging military duty mirrored charges frequently leveled by antisemites. Roth dubbed the most manipulative of the shirkers Sheldon, a name that he often used to disparage: In *Portnoy's Complaint*, "I close my eyes . . . I see myself sharing a house at Ocean Beach with somebody in eye make-up named Sheldon."[4]

Sheldon is little more than a cipher—a smooth talker, a small-time manipulator. A better-developed character, largely overlooked by the story's critics, is Marx. Roth is interested in his inclination to sentimentalize—always a trait distrusted by the author—and to assign benign motives to the Jews under his command when little trust is warranted. It is the darker side of sentimentality that most intrigues Roth, who ends the story: "And then, resisting with all my will an impulse to turn and seek pardon for my vindictiveness, I accepted my own." Alfred Kazin admitted he was thunderstruck once he finished it: "A story with such extraordinary guts that I went around for days exhilarated by the change in the literary weather."[5]

Here, none of Salinger's coy obfuscation about the character's Jewish origins, no worry over the threat of antisemitism now sidelined in postwar America: a story replete with bad behavior but all misdeeds of Jews to one another.

Roth's book was immediately heralded by nearly all the leading critics of the day as a work of extraordinary talent. Almost immediately, Roth joined the pantheon of leading writers: When Sylvia Plath, then in England, sought to tutor herself in the writing of fiction (this just months after the appearance of *Goodbye, Columbus*), what she chose to read were Virginia Woolf's *The Years*, E. M. Forster's *A Passage to India*, and Roth.[6]

Goodbye, Columbus won the National Book Award for fiction—Roth was now twenty-six—alongside Richard Ellmann, the nonfiction winner that year for his magisterial biography of James Joyce, and the eminent Robert Lowell for his poetry. And despite the controversy in some Jewish circles surrounding it, the book garnered the Mark Daroff Award of the National Jewish Book Council. (The previous year's winner was Leon Uris's *Exodus*.) But so contentious was the choice that, by the next year, the criteria for winning books would include an affirmative expression of Jewish values.

Roth's winning the National Book Award was also deemed controversial beyond Jewish circles. When interviewed on his television program by Mike Wallace shortly after the award ceremony, Roth was badgered with questions about his unsavory characters, all of whom Wallace described as "unlikable." Wallace also pressed Roth on his lack of sympathy for the Beats like Jack Kerouac, viewing *Goodbye, Columbus* as out of kilter with its own times. Notes prepared prior to the interview reveal Wallace's distaste for Roth's book and his impression that the author himself was at least as unlikable as the characters he depicted with such disdain.[7]

Mostly, though, Roth was celebrated. But what Roth recalled—to the exclusion of almost all else—was the opposition. And he came to see the greatest single expression of such animosity—compared by him to a Kafkaesque trial or even excommunication—in his experience at a Yeshiva University forum in March 1962. The event would come to assume a tremendous importance for him, little less than, as literary scholar Timothy Parrish writes, "Roth's Proustian madeleine." As Roth would come to see it, everything he now wrote—above all *Portnoy's Complaint*, which appeared a decade after *Goodbye, Columbus* in 1969—was itself a response to that terrible, fateful night in 1962.[8]

In his autobiography *The Facts*, published nearly thirty years later, Roth would devote a chapter to this attack at Yeshiva University when speaking at a program there on the theme of "The Crisis of Conscience in Minority Writers of Fiction," this one of a series marking its 75th anniversary. "The luckiest break I could have had" is how he later characterized it, since it provided him with ample, if often excruciating, fictional material for years to come.[9] Certainly, though, he did not always feel this lucky. His decision to spend three years writing his novel *When She Was Good* he would credit to Jewish critics of *Goodbye, Columbus*, who had so enraged him that he decided to produce books without any Jewish characters.

Similar to his portrayal of Brenda Patimkin, in his reply to his experience at Yeshiva University fury would figure prominently into how he distilled the workings of the world inside his fiction and beyond it. Such rageful reactions were, he often insisted, merely staged for their effect—not because they revealed anything fundamental about his own responses but merely because he found it aesthetically useful. He often compared the use of rage in his fiction to the comedy of Jack Benny, whom he much admired, with Benny playing the role of a miser when in fact he was quite generous.[10]

Such demurrals aren't convincing, and there are few better examples of the role played by rage—"Yes, my blood has been drawn, my anger aroused, my feelings hurt, my patience tried," as Roth would put it—than his reaction to that night at Yeshiva. Recalling its humiliation, he remembered being confronted with questions like this one: "Mr. Roth, would you write the same stories you've written if you were living in Nazi Germany?" In *The Facts* thirty years later, he would lament that at Yeshiva "I was . . . being grilled. No response I gave was satisfactory and, when the audience was allowed to take up the challenge, I realized that I was not just opposed but hated."[11]

The evening's program featured Roth alongside the celebrated Ralph Ellison, author of *Invisible Man*, and Italian American Marxist novelist Pietro di Donato. Yet Roth was certainly right in seeing that the impetus for the event was his own work, with the questions raised regarding the responsibility shouldered by a minority writer inspired above all by his celebrated book.

Still, Roth's recollections are contradicted by a tape recording—long buried in Yeshiva's archives because Roth had threatened a lawsuit if it was aired or published—showing how contrary to Roth's version was the audience's reaction to him. They laughed heartily at his jokes, time and again applauded him, with nearly all criticisms shunted aside by appreciative listeners. The chasm separating what transpired that evening from how Roth would so emphatically recall it provides a clue as to how he would then and later refashion life into art.[12]

Roth's memory of the evening meshed with his overall sense

of oppression at the hands of Jews. Typical as he saw it was Eliyahu Ben-Horin's letter to the *New Yorker* in response to the appearance of "Defender of the Faith": "I had not read such an ugly piece of anti-Semitic literature in a long time."[13] But Ben-Horin was a leader of the far-right Zionist Revisionist movement—then a small, extremist minority, even in pro-Israel circles—and he would write comparably vituperative letters about a wide range of Jewish matters, including those much more closely aligned with communal life than Roth.

True, more mainstream Jewish figures would attack him too. The most egregious attack—something to which he would refer time and again—was the letter sent by Emanuel Rackman to the Anti-Defamation League, where the rabbi asked, rhetorically: "What is being done to silence this man? Medieval Jews would have known what to do with him." Rackman, a former US Army chaplain, later provost at Yeshiva University, and president of Israel's Bar-Ilan University, was clearly outraged by Roth's portrayal of Jews' avoiding responsibilities in the military. He was also one of the most vigorous proponents of the liberalization of Orthodox Judaism, with Yeshiva University then the mainstay of such efforts, and he likely felt Roth's provocative work would bolster resistance to change by religiously recalcitrant Jews. Rackman's attack would weigh on Roth for some time. In a talk Roth gave five years later at several university campuses, he declared: "If there are Jews who have begun to find the stories the novelists tell more provocative and pertinent than the sermons of some of the rabbis, perhaps it is because there are regions of feeling and consciousness in them which cannot be reached by the oratory of self-congratulation and self-pity."[14]

Roth remained furious, while never acknowledging the many complimentary voices aired in Jewish circles at the same time. Writing about "Defender of the Faith" (these letters forwarded to him by the *New Yorker*), J. W. Bloch wrote, "Am not accustomed to writing fan mail, but his story was so well drawn and beautifully told, I am tempted not to let this opportunity go by." Henry Gruenbaum, MD, offered: "It was one of the best stories about Jews which I have recently read, compared to which most other [*sic*] are pablum." Eileen Heymann wrote: "You have much courage, honesty, and creativity. . . . Yours is a truth that was needed at this time."[15]

Shortly after the Yeshiva University event, Oscar Cohen, the director of programs for the Anti-Defamation League, wrote to Roth praising the new novel *Letting Go* as a masterpiece and asking whether Cohen might soon visit him at Princeton, where Roth was teaching. (Decades later, Roth would say to his friend Benjamin Taylor: "Being denounced by the Anti-Defamation League was nothing compared to the firestorm Portnoy raised.") The distinguished Reform theologian Eugene Borowitz would soon compare Roth's understanding of morality to that of Martin Buber, saying that the best stories of *Goodbye, Columbus* were characterized by "prophetic denunciations of Jewish practice in the name of a higher, if unspoken, truth." Joachim Prinz, Newark's leading rabbi, took Roth under his wing, arranging for him to join a distinguished group of writers traveling to Israel in 1963 to meet with literary and political figures including Prime Minister David Ben-Gurion. Yiddish scholar Daniel Landes, a fervent admirer of Roth, announced that the imminent appearance of *Letting Go* was certain to be "a literary event of large magnitude."[16]

Instead, what Roth focused on, as he relates in *The Facts*, was "the full force of aggressive rage that made the issue of Jewish self-definition and Jewish allegiance so inflammatory. The group whose embrace had offered me so much security was itself fanatically insecure. . . . Fanatical security, fanatical insecurity—nothing in my entire background could exemplify better than that night did how deeply rooted the Jewish drama was in this duality."[17]

In the book's epilogue, he returns, repeatedly, to this event:

"I assure you that there is no equivalence between that and a *hundred* nights on the rack at Yeshiva." Or "Everything you are today you owe to an alcoholic *shiksa.* Tell them that the next time you're at Yeshiva. You won't get out alive." And he arrived at Yeshiva University ready to fight. In a letter to Solotaroff just before he left for the event, he said he had accepted the invitation "partly out of defiance . . . and it seems to me that someone ought to take the smug bastards out. I expect I shall have to take a lot of shit from the audience."[18]

Yet as the recording of the event reveals and contrary to Roth's assertions over the years, it was he, not the evening's moderator, who first referenced the Holocaust that night. And throughout, he was the star: Ellison was stately, articulate but demure; di Donato was muddled, airing mostly canned Marxist sentiments. It was Roth whom the audience responded to time after time with laughter and applause. No fewer than three times that night did the moderator David Fleischer, a professor of literature at Yeshiva, acknowledge his inability to persuade the audience of the importance of a minority writer's communal responsibility, saying that his effort was a distinctly minority view in contrast to Roth's. And he, too, made it clear that despite these differences, he was a warm admirer of Roth's writing.[19]

Roth garnered the hardiest laughter when describing a distraught letter from a Detroit man about his story of adultery, "Epstein." The letter writer asked Roth: "Is it conceivable for a middle-aged man to neglect his business and spend all day with a middle-aged woman?" When Roth, after a brief pause, said, "The answer is yes," he brought down the house. And in reply to Fleischer's questioning as to whether Roth felt a communal obligation to mute fiction that might prove inimical to Jews, Roth's replies were consistently applauded.[20]

Roth may have also misjudged the conservative makeup of the audience. Yeshiva University's archives contain a list of the spots where the event was advertised, which include more than a dozen in Greenwich Village like Café Bizarre, Jazz Gallery, Figaro, the Manzini Café, even the fish and chips shop on Sullivan. And ordered by the event's organizers for use by the audience—the auditorium in which the event was held was Yeshiva University's largest with a capacity of one thousand—were one-hundred skullcaps or yarmulkes worn by Orthodox Jewish men, with expectation that many of those attending wouldn't come with their own.[21]

"The story of Lou Epstein," Roth said that evening, "stands or falls not on how much I know about Jewish tradition but on how much I know about Lou Epstein." And—anticipating what he would say in his essay "Writing About Jews" published the following year and what would soon emerge as among his most persistent preoccupations—Roth recalled still another query from the same man in Detroit with reference to "Epstein": "Why so much *shmutz*?" Roth's response: "To which I have no answer. . . . It is a question that literature is always asking with wonder and awe." And he then added, "to have to deny the possibility of [Jewish] infallibility, to have to deny the actuality of *shmutz*, is to make Jews less than human."[22]

To be sure, there were attacks on him that night and on other nights, too. When the Yeshiva event ended, he was accosted by a cluster of hostile audience members (not recorded but described to me years later by those in the audience). And comparable criticisms persisted. Charles Angoff—an eerily prolific novelist, now forgotten—insisted in review after review of Roth's books that he had no talent, that he was almost inhumanly sex-obsessed, and that he had no understanding of Jewish life. Angoff went even further by declaring that Roth wasn't an artist at all, merely "a troubled man" who ought "to take some time off to collect himself"—preferably, he added, in an institution. Moreover, Saul I. Teplitz, a pulpit rabbi who officiated in Woodmere, Long Island, summed up Roth in a Reform movement periodical as believing "the world would be a much better and happier place without Jews." Similar attacks would continue for years. Portnoy, wrote another, is "one of the vilest men seen in the whole range of literature." "Tasteless, vulgar, and overrated," is how Harold Ribalow, a significant Jewish cultural figure at the time, later described Roth's writing.[23]

In the wake of all this, he tended to overlook as the years passed that at the time he admitted the hubbub surrounding his first book made him acutely aware of the importance of his role as a Jewish writer. He admitted, albeit somewhat hesitantly, at the 1963 writers' gathering in Israel, "I won't deny . . . that I'm passionately interested in [Jews] as they manifest themselves in the lives that I know—in Jewish life for which I have a good deal of feeling and (I hate to admit it) a good deal of affection."[24]

He would even then speculate about how he might come to occupy a central role in a budding Jewish literary renaissance. Soon after Solotaroff's description of Roth in an essay in the *Times Literary Supplement* on contemporary American Jewish literature—a few months before the appearance of *Goodbye, Columbus*—he suggested that Jews like themselves might well be at the forefront of a major shift in the writing of Jewish fiction:

> So, the function you served, old chap, was to point out to a large audience of literate people a big change that has occurred in the production of American literature. Boston had its day, then specifically Cambridge, and then in the twenties the Midwest, but now the producers are urbanites, and the verbal urbanites, the Jews. . . . Anyway, shy as I was some months ago about being grouped with a bunch of Jews as a Jewish writer, I suddenly find myself willing to believe that this is something.[25]

6

Marjorie Morningsickness

Side by side with an intensified interest in Jewish literary matters—Roth was now warring openly with the likes of Leon Uris, Harry Golden, and Herman Wouk, grading their sentimental take on Jews as "Marjorie Morningsickness"—his most dreaded foe at the time was the manipulative non-Jew to whom he was married.[1] Oddly, she was the same seductively dangerous gentile his father had long warned him about. For the remainder of his life, even after his retirement from writing, he would describe at length in memos to his biographers how Maggie had nearly destroyed him at just the moment he was first taking off as a writer. Roth acknowledged the rank ethnocentrism of this portrait while still insisting it was entirely accurate.

"Raving within and stolidly blond without" is how he describes Maggie, or Margaret Martinson Williams, in *The Facts*, where he speaks of her as Josie: "Josie would have seemed to my grandparents the incarnation not of an American prototype but of their worst dream. And just *because* of that, their American grandson refused to be intimidated and, like a greenhorn haunted by the terrors of a vanished world, to react reflexively and run for his life."[2]

This was certainly not how Roth felt when they met in the fall of 1956, when he was fresh out of the army and had returned to a lecturer's position at the University of Chicago. He had spotted her before and now pursued her vigorously. "A Clairol Girl with legs that meant business," is how Solotaroff captured her appearance. Roth's high school friend Bob Heyman remembered her as "amiable, attractive but also a little dumpy." Short, about five-one or five-two, she was sardonic, quick-witted, and funny. Writer Herbert Gold recalls meeting her in New York, where she told him that she had met a writer in Chicago whom she might well marry, unless, she added, she met someone better.[3]

She came to Chicago to study, but instead was hired by the university administrator Ruth Passin as an assistant. Her father, according to Roth, was a drunk, and her ex-husband, also a drunk who was eventually jailed for theft, left her with two children to raise. Soon, Roth was spending most of his spare time with her. During their first year together in Chicago, she had an abortion, a decision reached amicably. But as the year wore on, there were increasingly heated arguments punctuated by sex. And then, soon afterward, they married.

Roth would later insist that the decision was one of madness, though he acknowledged that he found Maggie charming even after their first breakup. Her obstinacy he first saw as a sign of strength and sound character, a refusal to bend to convention. The unruliness of her life, its messiness and lack of direction, he admired for its indifference to bourgeois normalcy. "She is a rare person, truly," he writes Solotaroff in the summer of 1958, "and if I were a little rarer I'd have not screwed up so often."[4]

Still impressed with her, he described with admiration a feisty exchange between Maggie and critic Leslie Fiedler at a gathering in honor of Fiedler where Maggie objected forcefully to his characterization of E. M. Forster as a homosexual: "Maggie, the rugged girl, pushed him on it and said in effect that he was full of crap." At much the same time and amid a snafu over the book's promotion at Houghton Mifflin soon after the appearance of *Goodbye, Columbus*—this one largely of Roth's own making—he wrote to assure his editor George Starbuck that while he did not fault him, the incident left him so exasperated that he was "unable to trust anybody but you. Oh: and Maggie, of course." His psychiatrist William Frosch told me the first time he spotted Roth—long before he would begin to meet with him professionally—was at a party at Roth's brother Sandy's apartment in New York's Stuyvesant Town, where Roth and Maggie were snuggled on a couch, so absorbed with each other that they appeared uninterested in talking with anyone else.[5]

Roth dedicated *Letting Go*, his first novel published in 1962, to Maggie; critics agree its most compelling character, Martha Reganhart, is modeled on her. "Maggie," wrote Bernard Malamud, who met her in the summer of 1962, "is a petite, well-formed girl who's been through a good deal and expects to be through a good deal more. There is a quality of strong will about her and reminds me of Martha Reganhart in *Letting Go.*" In a review of the novel, Stanley Edgar Hyman found Reganhart the most impressively drawn character: "bawdy and vulgar, honest and decent, funny and heartbreaking. . . . If *Letting Go* is at all poignant, it is poignant chiefly in that he had a chance to keep Martha and failed."[6]

Reganhart is also slatternly if disarmingly direct, with an inner life hopelessly messy, much like her bathroom cabinet, which disgusts Gabe, the novel's protagonist. But she is given the best lines in the book, certainly the most knowing comments on the chasm between knowledge culled from books and those drawn from life: "Are you coming to tell me about your fine conscience?" she asks Gabe, in reply to his efforts at seduction. "Those little pains don't even begin to count. Don't kid yourself . . . your conscience and [Henry] James' conscience both give me a pain in the ass, if you want the truth."[7]

Roth's University of Chicago friend Arthur Geffen told me he found her "a nice person, very scrappy, very game, quite smart." He recalls how shocked he was when they broke up. Roth's friends the writer Thomas Rogers and his wife Jacqueline also liked her very much. On the other hand, Gene Lichtenstein—who on Roth's urging hired Maggie in the summer of 1958 at *Esquire*, where he was an editor—found her dreadful. Still half a century later he shuddered when speaking of her. His then-wife, who shared an apartment with her during Maggie's *Esquire* stint, felt "browbeaten by Maggie," whom she described much like the hateful shrew Roth would capture in a full-fledged attack on her—including a beating—in his 1974 novel *My Life as a Man*.[8]

They married in 1959, and she accompanied him supported by fellowships to Rome and then to Paris, where he was at work on *Letting Go*. He had only agreed to marry because she announced that she was again pregnant and would abort only if they wed. (Maggie also converted to Judaism.) Only later did Roth learn that she had feigned pregnancy, buying urine from a pregnant woman in Tompkins Square Park near his apartment in the East Village. The hideous scene—so far-fetched, as he put it, that it could only be true—he built into novel after novel for years, later dwelling often on its perfidy in memos written to aid biographers at work on his life.[9]

"Country life is strange," Roth, now married to Maggie, wrote Solotaroff from Long Island, "M and I are constant companions, talking, walking, being bored and irritable, pleased . . .

side by side. We hardly see any people—none really until the weekends."[10]

Soon enough the relationship was imploding, and he found himself unable to admit to any of their better moments or their sexual attraction. Never did Roth convincingly explain his attraction. He suggested that she brought him closer "to a world from which I no longer wished to be sheltered and about which a man in my intended line of work ought really to know something: the menacing realms of benighted American life."[11]

She was, he insists, "nothing less than the greatest creative-writing teacher of them all, specialist par excellence in the aesthetics of extremist fiction." But Roth also said (this difficult to believe) that almost from the start he found her body repulsive: "Her short, heavy-legged body struck me as very nearly dwarfish in its proportions and was, from first to last, unremittingly distasteful. Her gait in particular displeased me: mannish, awkward."[12]

Nonetheless, he spoke about her with love in their first year or two together, or at least keen protectiveness. She proved a loyal companion when the two encountered an onslaught from Herman, pressing them unsuccessfully to leave their East Village digs for subsidized housing at Stuyvesant Town, or to replace Maggie's coat because her current one was, as he put it, "like a piece of shit." Roth told Solotaroff soon after their wedding that "every once in a while someone [will] say to me I made a wise choice marrying this little girl, and I'm shaken."[13]

He never explained a sexual attraction intense enough to have persuaded him to end his romance with Maxine Groffsky. And as Benjamin Taylor observes in his reminiscence of his friendship with Roth, *Here We Are*, there was good reason why she was driven to the point of fierce jealousy: "Philip was undomesticatable. She [Maggie] raged with cause. . . . She was a street fighter from nowhere possessed of a marital ideal with which her husband did not concur. The unholiness of their bond had as much to do with his profligacy as her possessiveness. His determination to make himself the nice-boy victim of a Medea or a Hedda Gabler or some other succubus remains hard to credit."[14]

Roth later acknowledged that, once he managed to break with Maggie in June 1962, taking refuge in Sandy's apartment, he "was wracked by severe nausea, vomiting, diarrhea, and chills." He found it so hard to leave her that they soon reconciled, with Roth making his final, excruciating exit some five months later. It was then that he contacted the first of the psychiatrists he would consult, overwhelmed by guilt for having abandoned her. Guilt about his treatment of her may well have followed him, too, in the wake of her death: Susan Braudy, who then dated Roth's friend Albert Goldman, recalls Goldman telling her that Roth had a dreadful argument with Maggie the night of her fatal accident in 1968, just hours before her car crashed into a tree in Central Park.[15]

In the end, why Roth found himself so smitten at first, remains unclear. In the final chapter of *The Facts*, Roth permits himself to ask just these questions: "Can *everything* about . . . [her] have been vengeful?" She was likely "both better and worse as a human being than what you've portrayed here."[16] Yet his notes to his biographers regarding Maggie were unambiguously negative. And Blake Bailey, who was willing at times to dispute Roth's accounts, so succumbed to this incontrovertibly miserable view of Maggie that he found it necessary to explain away the various insightful comments he quotes from her diary, which remained in Roth's possession: "In most cases I've tried to cull only the most telling, pertinent, and perceptive passages in Maggie's journal, and hence may have inadvertently misrepresented the basic tenor of what is, indeed, a pretty insipid piece of writing."[17]

"I read over a hundred pages of it when I visited the Roths in February or March," wrote Starbuck in early December 1959, describing his first perusal of *Letting Go:* "Its characters are young, confused, drifting in and out of the limbo between the Universities, the Artistic Life, the Steel Mills, and Daddy's Business. The hero's flaw and saving grace is that he is always escaping from his own failures and problems by compassionately, generously, and sometimes disastrously meddling in the problems of others."[18]

Starbuck's summary of the novel (then tentatively entitled "Debts and Sorrow") was astute. The dilemma at its heart, as he saw it, was the underbelly of altruism and its toxic impulses. Its protagonist Gabe acts not out of compassion—though this is how he prefers to see himself—but from a dimly comprehended set of assumptions regarding the true route to happiness. In rare moments of clarity, he admits that he is tired of meddling in other people's lives but then nearly always falls back into the same desultory patterns.[19]

It is a complex, overwhelmingly grim book. (Curiously, when Gene Lichtenstein, then fiction editor of *Playboy*, announced plans to publish a portion of it in the magazine, Hugh Hefner nixed the idea, insisting—astonishingly—it was too racy.)[20] By the time of its appearance in 1962, Roth figured among the country's most celebrated young writers. Yet he responded to fame with little obvious pleasure, mostly with impatience. To be sure, his relationship with Maggie was now already on the rocks. Roth later recalled that even during his sojourn in Rome with Maggie, the only pleasure he could recall were his cheap daily shaves at a nearby barber.

A glimpse of his argumentativeness in the months before the appearance of *Goodbye, Columbus* in May 1959 may be seen in the fierce negotiations with his publisher over his book's cover design as well as other matters. Countering a suggestion for a change in the title of *Goodbye, Columbus*, Roth sarcastically proposed the only alternative he would accept would be "The Revised Version of the Old Testament" or "Goodbye, Columbus:

A Gospel for Our Time." Irked by inadequate publicity at the book's release, he suggested an advertisement reading: "Whoever Knows New Jersey Will Have Trouble Putting Down One of the Most Acclaimed Books of the Year."[21]

Amid the eruption surrounding "Defender of the Faith," Roth sent a note to Houghton Mifflin's publicity department urging them to take full advantage of the controversy: "There is a debate going on whether I am Hitler reincarnate or not." Since he had all the mothers of Scarsdale irate, he wanted to "take advantage of it" since "where there's a row there's an audience." When Houghton Mifflin responded that publicity of that sort felt unseemly, Roth angrily insisted that he had been misunderstood. Soon he announced his intent to renege on the agreement with Houghton Mifflin and publish his next book with Random House, which had offered a larger advance. His behavior was described in an in-house memo as "deplorable."[22]

Years later, in *Exit Ghost* in 2007, it's possible Roth sought to capture what he was like at the time: "There it was: the tactless severity of vital male youth, not a single doubt about his coherence, blind with self-confidence and the virtue of knowing what matters most. The ruthless sense of necessity. . . . Those grand grandstand days when you shrink from nothing and you're only right."[23] This coincides with Alice Denham's impressions of him then. She described having sex with Roth in *Sleeping with Bad Boys:* "tall, dark and lean with tennis muscles. Wavy almost kinky black hair closing in on a high narrow forehead . . . [and] a sex fiend. He moved from tits to—aaaah!—so fast I was breathless. Speeded up like his talk and his head. But once he got there, he hung in long and steamy. Tepid men never move me. Philip was on fire."[24]

On fire elsewhere, too. Speaking at Stanford at a forum organized by *Esquire* soon after the appearance of *Goodbye, Columbus*, he explained how Bernard Malamud, Saul Bellow, and Norman Mailer had all gone wrong. The problem was that they engaged in escapist literature—doing so, it seems, because they were incapable of rising to the challenge of a contemporary America where reality had so outpaced fiction in its capacity to astonish: "It stupefies, it sickens, it infuriates, and finally it is even a kind of embarrassment to one's own meager imagination. . . . Who, for example, could have invented Charles Van Doren, Roy Cohn . . . Dwight David Eisenhower?"[25] It would take years for Malamud to forgive him.

Roth proved unyielding about the smallest affront: He refused to forgive then-prominent writer Herbert Gold for not including him in his 1961 collection *Fiction of the Fifties.* Never mind, Gold sought to remind Roth, that his best work had appeared too late for inclusion. Yet for years to come—long after Gold had lost standing as a fiction writer of importance—Roth would disparage him, insisting that Gold had never written a single coherent sentence. And Roth's painfully protracted wranglings over a film version of *Letting Go* continued for more than a decade. Peter Mark Richman, its prospective producer, would come to speak of Roth "as a man with the inner life of a roach."[26] To be sure, a copy of the second draft of the film treatment of *Letting Go* at the Academy of Motion Picture Arts and Sciences is awful, little more than a melodrama, bearing scant resemblance to Roth's novel.

All the while, accolades kept pouring in: a teaching appointment at Iowa, a two-year stint as writer-in-residence at Princeton, and a Ford Foundation grant to support his writing of plays at the American Place Theatre. There, he experimented with an early theatrical version of *Portnoy's Complaint* called "Good Jewish Boy," the unknown Dustin Hoffman in its leading role. Roth would eventually shelve the script.

By the mid-sixties his writing had appeared in *Harper's*, *Esquire*, *Mademoiselle*, *Saturday Review*, and *Cosmopolitan.* He published theatrical reviews for the just-launched *New York Review of Books. Seventeen* invited him to write a column on the value of reading novels: "They won't make you normal," insisted Roth, "according to the standards of 'normalcy.'" And without doubt, he continues, there is reason to believe that novels are actually bad for you: "They can leave you dissatisfied. . . . Upon finishing a book, you can't but dislike yourself—for being smug or narrow or callous or unambitious."[27]

Despite jaunty descriptions to friends of his social life, this was a particularly painful period for Roth, with Maggie frequently taking him to court, draining his meager resources. In letters to friends, Roth described—with faux offhandedness—dinners with Lillian Hellman and Edmund Wilson, referring to them breezily as "the usual crowd." In 1965, he enjoyed his one and only date with Jackie Kennedy. That same year, the *New York Times Magazine* listed him as one of America's one hundred "wealthiest, most famous, and most creative people." He ranked seventy-nine.[28]

A vivid portrait of Roth at the time can be found in an early draft of Alison Lurie's novel *Real People*, based on experiences in the mid-1960s at Yaddo, where she befriended Roth. Here, she introduced a character named Daniel Beck, inspired by Roth as she readily acknowledged in their correspondence. He is described as the author of a book called *Staying at Home* and "a rude if gifted child, with a beaky nose and overdrawn eyebrows." Seated at the breakfast table across from a literary critic, also a guest at the retreat, Beck declares that such people should not be permitted into an artist retreat: Letting a critic into a place like that is like "letting a hunter into a wildlife sanctuary."[29]

Roth, to whom she showed the manuscript, said that his criticism of the character, which was severe, had nothing to do with its resemblance to him, though he acknowledged that he might have scrutinized the depiction more closely as a result. The problem was entirely aesthetic: "He doesn't address people—he talks. Haven't you figured this out, kiddo?" Lurie dropped him from the finished novel.[30]

The correspondence with Lurie is packed with self-doubt—also intermittent bravado and an eagerness to help a new, promising, young, and unhappily married writer. He was, at the same time, wrestling with his own exasperating divorce negotiations, beginning therapy (at first, three times weekly), and writing—often unsuccessfully, as he admitted—*When She Was Good.* A persistent preoccupation is his unsettling feelings about "fags": He fears a new Yaddo resident with whom he shares a bathroom might desire him sexually and praises Lurie's ability in her Yaddo novel "to write from the point of view of a fag." Without any further explanation, he states in a letter to her written in fall 1964 that "I interpret all suffering first as homosexual, then I refine." And as soon as he began to flesh out the beginnings of *Portnoy's Complaint*, he wrote her—this in a letter he composed on the bus from Yaddo bound for New York City—that he had decided that the neurotic protagonist of his new book would have to be a homosexual.[31]

Starting in 1964 and for years to come, he would retreat to Yaddo, often for months at a time. It was there that, in 1968 and immediately after Maggie's death, he completed *Portnoy's Complaint.* Albert Goldman, who became a friend of Roth's in the mid-sixties, credited his special love for Yaddo, a former estate made into an artists' and writers' colony, to its function for him as "a surrogate home, a home without the annoyance of a family. . . . They get you up early, feed you breakfast, and pack you off to work in a little cabin with a lunch box full of cold chicken and a shiny apple."[32]

7

Hocker

Roth was acutely upset by the reception of *Letting Go.* Bailey captures well Roth's feelings about his first novel: "Roth would always look pensive whenever someone said hard words about *Letting Go,* as if the novel were a faded but beloved old girlfriend whom he hated for anyone but himself to mock."[1] Critical reactions were mixed: some warmly enthusiastic, many—including those who praised it—expressing surprise that this dark, dense story was where the author of *Goodbye, Columbus* chose to go after the rare fluency of the first book.

To be sure, several listed *Letting Go* as one of the year's best, outdistanced only by Vladimir Nabokov's *Pale Fire.* "The most interesting novel of the year," declared the *New Republic.* Stanley Hyman gave a mixed review, but credited Roth in closing with "the finest eye for details in American life since Sinclair Lewis." Roth, always sensitive to criticism, found that complaints about the book—perhaps especially because this was his first novel—rankled badly. As novelist Alan Lelchuk, a close friend for many years, recalled in a letter to Roth: "I still remember your story of getting off the train and reading the review of Letting Go in the Times, and almost falling, fainting."[2]

The book remains an impressive achievement: cluttered, packed with compounded, even diversionary stories, but brilliant in the portrayal of characters large and small. Among its more pronounced threads is its attention to the obstreperous behavior of Gabe's father, which likely connects *Letting Go* to the now-discarded Frankfurt manuscript. And it may well have been Herman's lifelong tendency to impose himself onto others, celebrated by Roth years later in his elegiac portrait in *Patrimony*, that was a driving force behind this obsessive, lengthy novel. It was unlike anything Roth would write again.

Late in Herman's life, on Christmas Day 1988, he wrote a letter to Sandy urging him to involve himself more actively in his son Jonathan's life; it captures Herman's unceasing determination to meddle (his word, drawn from the Yiddish, was *hock*), no matter the cost. Herman apologizes for the misspellings, saying that he was never a good writer and now suffered from failing eyesight. Still, the handwritten note continues for more than three pages, concluding: "I will always continue to Hock & Care. That's me to People I care for." He signs the letter: "The Hocker, Misnomer it should be the carer, Love Dad." Here's a bit of Herman's letter:

> I think there are two types of (among people) Philosophies. People who care and those that don't, People who do and people who procrastinate and never do or help. . . . [About Jonathan] I don't tell him once, I keep telling of Hocking, why because he forgets like a compulsive drinker, or drug taker, etc. Why do I continue hocking? I realize it's a pain in the ass, but if its people I care for I will try to cure, even if they won't . . . themselves. Including myself I have many

> battles with my conscience, but I fight my wrong thoughts and care for people in my way.[3]

Much like his father, Roth would interject himself into the lives of those close to him. He tirelessly championed obscure writers like Alan Lelchuk and Fredrica Wagman, covered the medical costs of several friends, and quite literally saved the Romanian novelist Norman Manea from destitution, setting him on a vibrant, late-life academic and literary career. He watched closely over the writing life of Harry Maurer, the son of his Bucknell friends. And there is the long list of beleaguered Czech novelists and others in Soviet-dominated Europe whom he would showcase in his remarkable project of the 1970s: Writers from the Other Europe. Roth wrote introductions to their volumes, pressed others to do the same, and negotiated contracts. He also rescued the masterful Bruno Schulz from oblivion, persuading John Updike to write the introductory essay for Schulz's last work, *Sanatorium Under the Sign of the Hourglass*, then barely known.

David Plante records in his diary that in the early 1980s, Roth, sitting with him in a restaurant in London, suddenly started to berate him: "'You're not taking care of yourself, David. You should join a club and go every morning for an hour's exercise. You're too young and good looking not to take care of yourself. And you should go to a hair clinic to get some treatment to keep your hair from falling out.' . . . He went on and on. I said, 'All right, all right,' thinking that, of course, I wouldn't do anything."[4]

Roth was also known to press, sometimes bludgeon, men close to him to leave their wives for the sake of their writing or artistic careers. He urged the artist R. B. Kitaj to do this and was upset when the advice wasn't heeded. Bernard Avishai describes similar conversations. Yet at the same time, his indifference to the discomfort, even the suffering, of those close to him stood out. Roth's treatment of Ann Mudge, his girlfriend in the mid-1960s—a beautiful, blond heiress who was deeply in love with Roth and whose relationship with him continued, on and off, for years—sometimes bordered on the sadistic. Arriving at her hospital room after a suicide attempt following one of their breakups, all Roth could think to say was, "I hope you don't think this is going to get me to marry you."[5]

The kernel of *Portnoy's Complaint* was already pulling at Roth. This was evident not only in his unfinished play at the American Place Theatre but also at wild dinner parties in New York with friends like Jules Feiffer, Barbara Jakobson and her husband John, as well as Robert and Barbara Brustein. Barbara Jakobson describes them concocting (sometimes in bed together—they started having sex soon after they first met at one of these dinners) elaborate schemes for Maggie's murder. "Being bad and funny were much the same thing in Roth's mind," observed Albert Goldman.[6]

While practicing routines that would eventually enter the talk-obsessed, self-consciously shapeless *Portnoy's Complaint*, Goldman's lover Susan Braudy recalls Roth bursting into Goldman's apartment, with the two immediately throwing themselves into "Jewish mannerisms much in the same way that a drag queen learns to swhish his hips . . . two overanalyzed, self-sensitized men [having] a campy, ironic rapport" while talking about Jewish mothers and fathers. Goldman tended to play a girl in these riffs, with Roth sometimes acting as the mother but picking up an umbrella with which he might perform masturbation. At times they were so hilarious that Braudy found it necessary to escape to the bathroom just to take a breath.[7]

Roth laid out what he was seeking to write, still very much in its embryonic state, at a writer's conference in Tel Aviv in fall 1963:

> I have been writing something else which is, as it were, more Jewish than anything that I have ever written before in my life. It is a kind of comic fantasy, which I think is very real,

> about an orphan who gets farmed out to lots of different Jewish families, and is brought up by a Jewish gangster and a Jewish milkman and about six different Jewish mothers. I had to settle on a number because it occurred to me that the true fantasy is to have someone brought up by six Jewish mothers, though I may have twelve or fifteen.[8]

He added, without further explanation, that the writers with the greatest influence on the text were, inexplicably, Henry James and Tolstoy.[9]

Roth described how teaching at the Iowa writing workshop inspired this novel. He found no fewer than five of his students, all Jewish males, who produced much the same story without direction from him. They contained what he was certain was nothing less than a "central Jewish fantasy": A young Jewish boy is possessed with unresolved feelings about sex in a family with a sister and a mute father: "The father never speaks in these stories; the only time he sees the young man is when he sits opposite him at the dinner table and silently stows away his meal, while the mother and the sister hover over his little flame, beating it and beating it and beating it. The only resolution is when he finds for himself his own redemptive *shiksa*."[10]

It was the following year, in September 1964, that Roth wrote to Alison Lurie saying that he now knew what his next book would look like: "I have an idea for a next novel. I got it all coming down on the bus from Yaddo. Fine novel full of things I know, and my dear I am going to write a novel from the point of view of a fag." On the cover page of the draft of the chapter that would be published in *Esquire* in April 1967—entitled "A Jewish Patient Begins His Analysis"—Roth crossed out with his black Sharpie the original title: "A Homosexual Begins His Analysis."[11]

Along with the early versions or, more accurately, the first intimations of *Portnoy's Complaint*, Roth worked mostly joylessly on *When She Was Good*. For a writer so often criticized for reverting to the same terrain (Newark), the same litany of themes (sex, its pull, its underbelly), Roth sought to experiment here with a vastly different form of writing. In *When She Was Good* he tried his hand at a laconic, humorless book: a steady, sober exploration of the dark side of righteousness and civility. "Not to be rich, not to be famous, not to be mighty, not even to be happy, but to be civilized—that was the dream of his life" is its opening sentence. There was, as critic Hillel Halkin observed, "nothing terribly wrong" with the novel—he viewed *Letting Go* in much the same way—but in contrast to the writing Roth would soon produce, what "they most lack is that feeling given us by the best writing that no force on earth could have prevented it from being written." Its characters are rarely more than monosyllabic, relentless in their commitment to dampen all desire, incapable of appreciating, as Roth pointedly underlines, "the most basic fact of human life, the fact that I am me and you are you."[12]

As always, Roth read widely—mostly in the evening after a day of writing—teasing out of books he loved insights that might sharpen his work. In a letter to Lurie in late 1964, he likened the tragic heroine of his book to "Anna K and Emma B," stating that he wasn't "comparing greatness, but ideas. . . . They set out to change things for themselves much more personally—with no moral bullshit. Quite the opposite. This is what makes them more womanly." He adds, puzzlingly, "There are two sexes, or ideal ones; women and Jews."[13]

Maggie haunts *When She Was Good*, much as she now haunted his life. He was convinced of her intent to ruin him financially, sapping him of all the promise he showed just a few years back. Having met her family and listened to her speak at length about this background—which he found so alluring, even darkly mysterious—he viewed *When She Was Good* as a guide to the gritty byways of midwestern gentiles. It is a relentlessly gloomy book, largely because its characters are so dimly self-aware, unable to absorb much if anything beyond the most immediate impressions—these ever clouded by drink. The novel's protagonist, Lucy, would die a terrible death just after she seeks to impose her belief in her own righteousness on all others in her life: "If only they'd say *no*. NO, LUCY, YOU CANNOT. NO LUCY, WE FORBID IT. But it seemed that none of them had the conviction any longer, or the endurance, to go against a choice of hers. In order to survive, she had set her will against theirs long ago—it was the battle of her adolescence, but it was over now. And she had won. She could do whatever in the world she wanted—even marry someone she secretly despised."[14]

At the book's core—a theme he would often explore in his books—was lament for the disintegration of family. The demons that overwhelm Lucy could have been held in check only by the force of family whose deterioration Roth meticulously charts. "Take away family, and what do you have? People just running around, that's all. Total anarchy," is how one reviewer summed up the book's message. "Just try to imagine the world with no families. You actually can't do it."

There were appreciative reviews, but the most prominent—and certainly those Roth most recalled—were the ones that tore it apart. "Pity the Poor Wasps" was the title of the review in the *New York Times Book Review*, where the novel was lambasted. "The kindest thing one can say about Philip Roth's new novel is that it is a brave mistake," wrote Robert Alter in *Commentary*. Roth had worked on the manuscript for four years, feeling confident that this might well be his breakaway book—the one that made him more than a writerly writer and finally a novelist with impact on the larger culture. He thought he had a real shot: The topic was gentiles, not Jews, whom he had watched carefully while in Iowa. He explained to Lelchuk that he would sometimes stare into the homes of his neighbors as they devoted themselves to the most mundane, thoughtless tasks—these performed with astonishing attentiveness. Roth describes a neighbor making fudge: "I say to myself, how nice. How nice that the pressure he places on life is so small. . . . That he can contain his passions and . . . uncertainties . . . [and] lust in that woman, that ordinary woman."[15]

One of the rare unambiguously enthusiastic responses to *When She Was Good* surfaced in the *Village Voice* two years after the novel's publication in the context of a review of *Portnoy's Complaint.* It was written by Sandra Hochman, soon a well-known feminist poet and documentary filmmaker. Hochman's review so pleased Roth that he reached out to her with thanks, helping her publish an autobiographical novel, *Walking Papers*, which he would describe as a "masterpiece." Hochman wrote in her review that the most pronounced feature of *When She Was Good* was its revelation of Roth's "genius when it comes to understanding and creating fictional women. Roth is a master at describing the neurotic female, the woman who searches but cannot find a way out of self-destruction." Later, when criticized for an inability to write convincingly about women, he would often cite Hochman on *When She Was Good*, with its portrayal of a woman set on imposing her sense of rightness, which, in turn, destroys herself: This the inevitable byproduct of consummate rectitude, forever freedom's severest enemy.[16]

8

Portnoy

> The suburban Jewish past of the characters in the fiction of Philip Roth is also a Jewish past, only as meager as the span of a generation or two and infinitely more distasteful . . .

Already in 1967, the same year *When She Was Good* came out, the first samples of *Portnoy's Complaint* were issued in wide-circulation magazines like *Esquire* and *Sport*, as well as the high-brow *Partisan Review*. Indeed, it was there, in that mainstay of the New York intelligentsia, that Roth signaled his departure from the magazine's austere norms with the chapter entitled "Whacking Off." Solotaroff's new paperback journal *New American Review* ran two excerpted chapters of the novel, the first almost two years before the book's appearance, the second numbering no fewer than twenty-eight thousand words.

By the time it was published in January 1969, *Portnoy's Complaint* was tipped as a phenomenal bestseller. The *Washington Post* predicted that, for a long time to come, "we will judge our friends by what they say" about *Portnoy*. Quoting lines from the novel, the *Houston Chronicle* said—barely a week after its appearance—had already become "a national sport." Few if any matched Albert Goldman's excitement, writing in *Life:* "A sav-

With the appearance of *Portnoy's Complaint* in January 1969 Philip Roth emerged as the rare serious writer who was also a bestseller. (Photograph by Barbara C. Sproul)

ior and scapegoat of the '60s," declared Goldman, "Portnoy is destined at the Christological age of 33 to take upon himself all the sins of the sexually obsessed modern man and expiate them in a tragicomic crucifixion."[1]

Roth acknowledged the debt he owed others—including

the by-now-obscure Wallace Markfield, the novelist and screenwriter Bruce Jay Friedman (author of the breakaway novel about Jewish neurosis *Stern*), and especially Isaac Rosenfeld, whose essays, short stories, and novels speculated, often hilariously, on the linkage between Jewish life and sexual inhibition. Particularly influential was Rosenfeld's 1949 piece in *Commentary*, "Adam and Eve on Delancey Street," with its insistence—half earnest and incredibly funny—that Judaism's prohibition against the mixing of meat and milk left a permanent scar on Jewish male desire. The essay's appearance in *Commentary* nearly brought down the then-liberal Jewish-sponsored magazine. *Commentary* was compelled to apologize for running it, with Roth seeing the episode as a precursor to the attacks on himself.[2]

"A clumsy beginner" is how Roth later characterized his early career, before he mastered his craft. For some two years, Roth had been (as critic Scott Saul put it) "hacking away" at *Portnoy's Complaint*. Here, much like *When She Was Good*, the book was the product of numerous drafts, some rather tepid, but what emerged from all this rewriting was a Portnoy that, while an "entrapped neurotic," Saul writes, "broadened Roth, allowing him to serve as the butt of the extended joke that Portnoy relates. For all his limitations, Portnoy does have the double consciousness to see that he is both the storyteller spinning out an elaborate joke and the protagonist laid low by its various punchlines."[3]

In the preface to the thirtieth anniversary edition of *Goodbye, Columbus*, Roth—speaking at first in third person and describing himself prior to *Portnoy's Complaint* as little more than an "embryo"—wrote that it was only once he made his way back to Newark, the origin of it all, that he finally found himself able to write an astonishing book:

> His particular skills . . . inclined him to reimagine as a species of folk fiction—as unguarded short stories, spontaneously

> told, that somehow stretched over the bones of the folktale a skin of satiric social comedy—what not that long before had been the undifferentiated everydayness of Jewish life along the route of Newark's Number 14 Clinton Place bus. In this way, without knowing it, he proceeded to make identical the acts of departure and return and to perpetuate those contradictory yearnings that can perplex the emotions of an ambitious embryo—the desire to repudiate and the desire to cling, a sense of allegiance and the need to rebel, the alluring dream of escaping into the challenging unknown and the counterdream of holding fast to the familiar. Altogether unwittingly, he had activated the ambivalence that was to stimulate his imagination for years to come and establish the grounds for that necessary struggle from which his—no, my—fiction would spring.[4]

It is the Freudian couch that Roth chose as the focal point for life's drama. With the best remembered of all lines in the book, its punch line on the final page, where the psychoanalyst (hailing from Central Europe, the birthplace of psychoanalysis), who has remained silent throughout the entire monologue, issues the only words in the entire book by anyone except Portnoy himself: "So [said the doctor]. Now vee may perhaps to begin. Yes?"

Roth's primer in psychoanalytic parlance was long in coming, with seven years spent in the presence of Hans J. Kleinschmidt, described later by another of his patients, the writer Adam Gopnik, as "a German Jew of a now vanishing type—not at all like the small, wisecracking, scared Mitteleuropean Jews that I had grown up among. He was tall, commanding, humorless. He liked large blooming shirts, dark suits, heavy handmade shoes, club ties." Gopnik credits Kleinschmidt with considerable, if ponderous, insight laced with anecdotes, often inappropriately intimate, about his many famous literary and artistic patients. Regarding Roth, Kleinschmidt so stretched the limits of confidentiality that he published a summary of his analysis, only lightly disguised, in a psychoanalytic journal. Still, more astonishing is that Roth continued to see the analyst after discovering the article. And long after their sessions came to an end, in the 1990s, Roth made a point of having lunch with him once a year until Kleinschmidt was too ill to meet. When Ross Miller started work on Roth's biography in 1996—this the first of several efforts at the writing of Roth's life—Kleinschmidt was among the first Roth urged him to interview.[5]

In Kleinschmidt's lightly disguised description published in the journal *American Imago*, Roth is depicted as a southern playwright suffering from dreadful guilt over leaving his wife—this, of course, a strikingly different version than Roth's own obsessively repetitive account. Indeed, Barbara Jakobson remembers her surprise at Roth's reaction to news of Maggie's death: She bought champagne to celebrate but recalls his dark disapproval of her excitement, which looked nothing less than "sanctimonious and rabbinical." Kleinschmidt captured much the same: Guilt, he said, weighed terribly on him, exacerbated by a lifelong fear of abandonment traceable to childhood when his mother locked him out of the house, leaving him for hours in the freezing cold with him beseeching her to allow him to come in. Soon this would be translated into fear of castration, an enduring source of terror exacerbated by a calamitous episode that left him "ashamed, angry, betrayed, and speechless" when, at the age of eleven, while he was shopping with his mother for clothes, she spoke openly in a store about the size of his tiny penis.[6]

Narcissism would emerge, according to Kleinschmidt, as his defense against this anxiety prompted by his mother (whom he had imagined in his childhood to be so ubiquitous that, in disguise, she was also his teacher flying home right after class to serve him milk and cookies). By the time he reached adulthood, he managed to slake his anger with the use of sex, cheating on his wife almost from the start of their marriage, although now desperately in need of her in the wake of his abandonment. His affairs helped, if only temporarily, to restore an ever-tenuous self-esteem. "His way of bypassing painful feelings and of avoiding any true confrontation with emotional reality was to libidinize both anger and anxiety," as Kleinschmidt wrote. At best, it is only a "pleasurable anxiety" achieved with reliance on "polymorphous sexuality," including "voyeurism, exhibitionism, fetishism, isolation, and masturbation."[7]

Kleinschmidt's sessions, with their assistance in permitting him to air these childhood traumas and the interplay of insight and folly in Freudianism, was the stew out of which emerged the novel that made Roth a household name. This was a standing, Roth often insisted, he wished he had never achieved, but one he would come to miss and wish to retrieve once it disappeared, which, of course, it was bound to.

Which Freud Roth absorbed remains unclear—the Freud as understood by Lionel Trilling, then the country's most influential critic, or that of Norman O. Brown, the Nietzsche-inflected author of the widely discussed *Life Against Death* published in 1959, with its insistence on the primacy of body over mind? Kleinschmidt was undeniably far closer to Trilling: "He believed," writes Gopnik, "that the only thing to do with the knowledge of murderous rage within your breast was not to mythologize it but to put a necktie on it and heavy shoes and a dark-blue woollen suit. Only a man who knew that, given the choice, he would rape his mother and kill his father could order his spaghetti *vongole* in anything like peace."[8]

Yet Patrick Hayes, among Roth's finest literary interpreters, reads *Portnoy's Complaint* as deeply influenced by Brown's Nietzschean Freud, with the novel's call for the liberation of instinctual life as exemplified by Portnoy's much-disparaged lover, nicknamed The Monkey, a brilliantly conceived exemplar of physicality. Crucial, as Hayes sees it, is her ability to absorb the beauty of Yeats's poetry—to "Feel feeling!" as Roth puts it—the poet's words capable of making her "pussy all wet." "Sweetheart! You understood the poem!" exclaims Portnoy, "And with your cunt, no less."[9]

No matter how Roth read Freud, it remains clear he wrote his novel with the master's *Collected Papers* close at hand as an indispensable source, if also perhaps a foil. It served him here no less than did James's *Portrait of a Lady* in the writing of *Letting Go.* David Rieff—long a close friend of Roth's and his editor at Farrar, Straus and Giroux—recalls Roth being a quick learner, assiduous if also keenly selective in his reading; in all the years they knew each other, Rieff never remembers Roth reading or so much as mentioning Nietzsche.[10]

Still, Freud, as well as Norman O. Brown and Lionel Trilling, were all in there—others, too—stretching the narrative, deepening it without the need to reference them. Misconstrued by many as something akin to an extended Henny Youngman routine, *Portnoy's Complaint* more closely resembled, according to Albert Goldman, the comedic world of adolescent Roth and his buddies, with its audacity, ferocity, originality, and sheer fecundity. That its themes were so repetitive made their creativity all the more impressive, as the novel vented and ridiculed—as Goldman saw it—"the feared, admired, and despised *goyim* and . . . the Jewish family and society that surrounded them. . . . The Jewishness of [Roth's] humor lay precisely in its obsessional concern with the fact of Jewishness . . . screaming out the curses of a particularly hysterical and obscene self-mockery."[11]

Roth rejected all comparisons with comedians like Youngman or Lenny Bruce, seeing these as demeaning while counterposing instead the great Jewish "comedian" Franz Kafka. He preferred to compare the novel's achievement to that of Sherwood Anderson, William Styron, or Saul Bellow, while also pleased to acknowledge the book's therapeutic impact in providing readers with permission to say things aloud that they never could before. Zadie Smith, later a close friend of Roth's, summed this up well: "Roth's gift with Portnoy was large precisely because it had no aspirational element and no precise directions. Like any good gift, the less strings we find attached to it the better. The offer was not 'You, too, can be like Portnoy.' The offer was, 'Portnoy exists! Be as you please.' . . . He's written things down that seemed unsayable, impossible, and in taking this freedom for himself, intentionally or not, passed the freedom down."[12]

At the epicenter of *Portnoy* is the mother, and—despite Roth's demurrals—the portrait draws on his mother Bess: "Mine remember, patrols the six rooms of our apartment the way a guerilla army moves across its own countryside—there's not a single closet or drawer of mine whose contents she hasn't a photographic sense of." True, Sophie Portnoy possesses none of Bess's self-restraint, her ability to superimpose limits with the use of little more than a passing gesture, no more than a word or two. But it is the mother, not sex, that is the novel's primary focus, with its cry of protest, its desperate call to be left alone.

The book, writes Hayden Carruth in the *Philadelphia Inquirer*, never uses humor "simply for its own sake: The more one listens to his memories, however, the more one feels that the clown's mask reveals a deeper neurosis."[13]

And the stultifying rules, as often as not illogical—like the strict prohibition against the eating of pork, which pertains everywhere except, apparently, Chinese restaurants—are omnipresent; they are an insurmountable barrier against the prospect of simple mindless pleasures, which, as Portnoy sees it, is a universe enjoyed never by Jews but exclusively by gentiles. He longs for a world where there is no obstacle against simply being bad—no barrier to, say, hunting deer, or eating lobster, drinking whiskey, or flunking tests—without shame. To be bad and enjoy it, this is Alexander Portnoy's greatest wish:

> Look, am I exaggerating to think it's practically miraculous that I'm ambulatory? The hysteria and superstition! The

Roth and his mother, Bess, at his fortieth-birthday party.
(Photograph by Barbara C. Sproul)

> watch-its and the be-carefuls! You mustn't do this, you can't do that—hold it! don't! you're breaking an important law! *What* law? *Whose* law? They might as well have had plates in their lips and rings through their noses and painted themselves blue for all the human sense they made! Oh, and the *milchiks*, and *flaishiks* besides, all those *meshuggeneh* rules and regulations on top of their own private craziness! It's a family joke that when I was a tiny child I turned from the window out of which I was watching a snowstorm, and hopefully asked, 'Momma, do we believe in winter?' Do you get what I'm *saying*. I was raised by Hottentots and Zulus! I couldn't even contemplate drinking a glass of milk with my salami sandwich without giving serious offense to God Almighty.[14]

Far worse, to be sure, are the preposterous underpinnings of Christianity, where they take a Jew and turn him into a God after he is dead and then accuse Jews of having done away with him.[15]

Ribald, wildly anarchic, it is also a poignant book full of a longing for redemption—this synonymous, as Portnoy comes to see it, with mediocrity: the capacity not to strive for excellence at home, school, work, bed, or marriage. For all its limitations, mediocrity is immeasurably superior to ceaseless ambition, the need always for superlative achievement. Portnoy is keenly aware of the chasm, separating the (quite modest) sins committed by his parents and the unquenchable rage they've engendered. But despite all the energy and intelligence he devotes to understanding this dilemma, he fails altogether. Now in his thirties, a figure of some stature in the New York City government, he finds himself simply tongue-tied, incoherent when confronted with the simple question asked by his mother: What are the horrible things that she has done to him? "I believe she considers the question unanswerable. And worst of all, so do I. What *have* they done for me all their lives, but sacrifice? Yet that this is precisely the horrible thing is beyond my understanding—and still, Doctor! To this day!"[16]

He dreams of returning home, yearnings especially acute toward the novel's end, when he fears The Monkey has killed herself because he brought a prostitute into their bed for a threesome. He wishes desperately to re-create the bland normalcy of childhood or, at least, an unblemished adulthood like his father's, from which, of course, he fled years ago:

> I love those men! I want to grow up to *be* one of those men! To be going home to Sunday dinner at one o'clock, sweat socks pungent from twenty-one innings of softball, underwear athletically gamy. . . . Yes, home I head for resuscitation . . . and to whom? To *my* wife and *my* children, to a family of my own, and right there in the Weequahic section! . . . A future, see! A simple and satisfying future! Exhausting, exhilarating softball in which to spend my body's force—that in the morning—then in the afternoon, the brimming, hearty stew of family life.[17]

This "brimming, hearty stew of family life," its allure, the inconceivability of return of the sixties. Portnoy enjoys little of his promiscuity, and it is inconceivable that his yearning will ever be satisfied. Built squarely into Roth's portrait, as he explained it at the time to Alan Lelchuk, was an already attentive reading of Kafka: "an angry little man . . . a guy who stands in front of you at the bank . . . he's giving the teller a hard time and he won't leave until he gets his way . . . he never tires, he's indefatigable . . . right down to the door of the Castle . . . which he never enters."[18]

Few at the time watched Roth with greater acuity than Albert Goldman. On the staff of *Life*, his portrait in the magazine on the cusp of the book's appearance was among the most enthusiastic and keenly perceptive, scorning "the scandal fuming up from the book's pungent language, a veritable attar of American obscenity; and from its preoccupations, foremost among which is the terrible sin of onanism." Goldman identified as Roth's greatest achievement his capacity to produce "the final perfection of . . . the comic art of this Jewish decade," a blending of the genius of the Marx Brothers, *Catch-22*, Lenny Bruce, Freud, and much more into a profound study of the Jewish family transcending ethnic boundaries.[19]

Goldman was a cultivated man and a professor (trained at Columbia by Trilling), in love with classical music, and widely read. A learned scholar of the art of plagiarism (the topic of his Columbia dissertation), he indulged in it himself, forfeiting the prospect of a permanent university appointment. A friend of his, James Wolcott, told me that Goldman introduced Roth to New York nightlife, leaving its mark on the writing of *Portnoy's Complaint.* Still, when introduced by Goldman to "real swingers, you could see his nostrils quiver."[20]

A rock music critic of great talent, his portrait of the origins of rock and roll in Solotaroff's *New American Review* is masterful. Goldman was the author of a widely praised study of Lenny Bruce. His later, no less extensively researched books on Elvis and John Lennon were nonetheless hotly contested, with music critic Greil Marcus describing the Elvis biography as an exercise in "cultural genocide."[21]

What Roth would not know (it seems unlikely that he was ever aware) was that Goldman kept what he described as a "Rothlog": dictating it into tapes, then arranging for its transcription. He started it when he wrote his essay for *Life* in February 1969 and added to it, on and off, until shortly before his death in 1994. No more detailed portrait of Roth exists for the period from the late 1960s until the mid-seventies:

> Walking the streets of the area with Phil reminded me of the old days in Yorkville. He sees the eastern European stores through the glamorizing medium of obsessed fantasy. Its [*sic*] as if he were in Hungary, Czechoslovakia or Poland. Pointing to a delivery truck, he says: "There's the sort of name I

> like for a novel: Lemish!" Then we go to Paprik Weiss and buy a couple of pastry brushes that are made with white chicken feathers. Clit tickler they are in Philip's mind. He even buys one for me. What a big deal to buy anything for another person. Cheap to the bone.[22]

Goldman's friendship with Roth tapered off eventually, and never was he among Roth's small number of intimate friends. Perhaps the distance was a result of Goldman's eventual drug use or the appearance of *The Professor of Desire* published in 1977, whose sardonic portrait of David Kepesh drew heavily on Goldman. But for a period of some five or six years, Goldman was close enough to scrutinize Roth relentlessly, and the Rothlog is a remarkable study of admiration and keen perceptiveness:

"He was smart, funny and clever, outrageous and edgy," recalled Barbara Sproul about Goldman; Sproul, whose romance with Roth started around the same time in the late sixties, told me: "All these qualities cloaked a serious morality. . . . He challenged Philip who was an even 'gooder' boy." In his log, Goldman hints at its excision of their wildest moments together. In an outline of a book proposal written in 1992 drawing on his friendship with Roth, Goldman notes that he expected to include "sexual and other adventures not in the log."[23]

Preparing for his exuberant celebration of *Portnoy's Complaint* in his *Life* article, Goldman's notes describe his intent to capture "Philip as a personality." He adds that Roth is "always hidden behind the literary mask." To achieve this for him is crucial: "Consider the energetic level Philip obtains. Hysterical. Lap up humiliation; like he laps that girl's pussy."[24]

Goldman's sense of Roth is one where his literary genius is interlaced with the same obsessive preoccupations that he cannot permit himself to act on, but consigns to his prose with rare determination, self-denial, and extraordinary intelligence. This, arguably, is the most significant of his many gifts. Goldman describes the glee with which Roth buys a couple of pretzels from a New York street vendor, crying out that he loves them mostly because they're so dangerous, so full of germs. All this Roth builds into his remarkable prose constructed with consummate discipline, a keen awareness of his literary strengths as well as his limitations. Goldman writes in a log entry in 1970:

> The strongest sense you get in talking to Philip Roth about these projects is the creative mind is constantly coming up with ideas. The real artistry is not in the writing, not in the conceiving, but almost, you might say, in the editing. Philip is a very good editor of Philip. He goes through all the different ideas his mind throws up and he carefully selects the right one, ejects the wrong ones. He is very canny, very smart, very shrewd, and he knows what's good and bad. It's like there are two Philips: there's the creative Philip that throws all this shit like crazy, manic style; and there's the very cold, calculating Philip who sits down and says that's bullshit, that's cheap, that's trash. . . . The two operations of the creative mind—the mining and the refining.[25]

Assessing Roth here, weighing his many strengths and not inconsiderable weaknesses—his fears, paralyzing inhibitions, and fierce competitiveness—Goldman declares in 1975 that finally he is convinced that he has earned Roth's admiration with his much-acclaimed Lenny Bruce biography. And now—in large measure for the first time since his glowing *Life* portrait—Goldman comes the closest to summing up as fully as he would Roth's unnerving complexity:

> You don't know anything about Philip until you grasp the idea that he has this sort of gleaming, mad, glazed-eye fascination with the moral incongruity of contemporary civilization. It's sort of gleeful—where someone else would say, oh that's disgusting or sick or appalling or depressing—he has a gleeful exhalation in completing out-of-joint we are morally

[*sic*]. It's just now that he's beginning to get that into his writing. In the time that I've known Philip well in the past 5 or 6 years, that has been the most striking feature of his mental makeup—exulting in someone else's fuck-up. A sort of male exhaltation [*sic*] he gets when he sees these incredible moral incongruities these abysmal blindnesses.[26]

9

Grand Old Man of Letters

THE UNPRECEDENTED ATTENTION lavished on *Portnoy's Complaint*, suddenly a fixture of contemporary culture, elated and overwhelmed Roth. The book sold 400,000 copies in hardcover alone. By 1971, 3 million copies were in print, and it was eventually translated into thirty-one languages. "It was," as critic Adam Kirsch sums it up,

> an unrepeatable feat for a literary novelist, the result of a perfect cultural storm. The rise of the sexual revolution made Roth's gleeful descriptions of masturbation feel cutting-edge, while the collapse of censorship laws made them publishable. America's fascination with Jews and Jewish humor was at its peak. . . . 1969 was just about the last moment when literary fiction was prestigious enough to make a novel like *Portnoy's Complaint* a major event—debated on talk shows, parodied in *Mad* magazine—yet popular enough to make it a bestseller.[1]

The appearance of the movie version of "Goodbye, Columbus" in March 1969, a month after the release of *Portnoy's Complaint*, confirmed Roth as a celebrity. The movie, starring Richard Benjamin and Ali MacGraw, was praised by critics and a success at the box office. It also managed to upend still regnant censorship restrictions, with sticky negotiations between Paramount and the Motion Picture Association of America's production code overseers continuing, on and off, for some two years. Censors objected to its use of the term "penis" and the length of its nude scenes.

Geoffrey Shurlock's tenure as chief censor of motion picture production ended abruptly after his unsuccessful campaign to cut the following words—as enumerated in a letter he sent to Paramount in February 1968—from the *Goodbye, Columbus* script: damn, hell, son-of-a-bitch, oral love, and crap. "The discussion of the pill and of the diaphragm . . . seems overly frank and too explicit," Shurlock wrote, and he listed scenes that must be cut: nude lovemaking, use of contraceptives, and "one girl to other, 'What were you doing all summer?' Reply, 'I was growing a penis.' "

A memo sent to Paramount two months before its release warned that unless its sex scenes were altered, "we could not give the picture any other rating than an X." In the end, the MPAA was thwarted by Paramount—the film, largely unaltered, was granted a PG rating—delivering a blow to censorship restrictions in place since the 1930s.[2]

Suddenly Roth was a household name: Jacqueline Susann, author of *Valley of the Dolls*, announced on Johnny Carson's *Tonight Show* that she'd much like to meet him but would never shake his hand. *Mad* magazine featured news of Blanda Pretenkin's upcoming wedding to "one of the richest Jewish men in the world today."[3]

Roth escaped New York City to Woodstock, eventually buying a stately home in Warren, Connecticut. His literary stature suddenly was immense, and he now would casually poke fun at the vast ambitions of some of his closest friends, like William Styron, who were set on producing nothing short of The Great American Novel. Roth belittled the aspiration while determined to achieve much the same. He would give that title to a wild, playfully erudite excursion into baseball mythology he would publish in the early 1970s. He also wrote a rambunctious Nixonian spoof. Both were efforts at subverting, or at least testing, the limits of the literary stature he had worked so strenuously to achieve, which was, in its own way, the intent of *Portnoy's Complaint*, too.

Barbara Sproul—a twenty-three-year-old doctoral student in religious studies he met at a dinner party—was now his primary romantic partner. Beautiful, gentle, and thoughtful with a touch of mordancy, she would both encourage his work and warn him not to take himself too seriously. Eventually, she would coin the term "GOMOL" (Grand Old Man of Letters), intended as a warning for him not to fall into this seductive trap. What he produced during the happiest years of their relationship—they broke up in 1974—were the most playful of his books, all attributable, it seems, to her wry, discerning influence. He would dedicate *The Great American Novel* to her, the novel packed with references to ancient mythology, *Moby-Dick*, baseball trivia, and much more of what they pored over together in their playfully erudite love.

"I'm always sort of surprised," Roth remarked to Lelchuk, "when I'm taken seriously and then I'm hurt when I'm not."[4] Now, in the wake of *Portnoy's Complaint*—and later, too, with the writing of other rambunctious novels like *Operation Shylock*, published when he was sixty—he would test this hunger for validation, knowing full well what he was doing while fearing the results.

Already he was experimenting in the way that famed literary critic Janet Malcolm—once a close friend of Roth's but a fierce detractor by the time she wrote these lines—describes Roth's labor on a never-completed novel about the Viennese physician and Freud mentor Josef Breuer and Lou Andreas-Salomé. There, Malcolm says, "We find a kind of Rosetta Stone of Roth's 'art.' We find here his, on the one hand, characteristic well-made sentence (he was a sort of idiot savant of grammar and syntax) and, on the other, his wild and skewed vision of life, his way of taking perfectly ordinary events like people sitting in a café drinking caffè latte and making something monstrous and strange out of them."[5]

By the summer of 1969, soon after the appearance of his bestseller, Roth completed a draft hundreds of pages in length built of "three layers of self-consciousness about being the author." This would be the core of *My Life as a Man.* Eventually he would fill fourteen boxes with drafts of the book. Roth greatly valued the work—seeing it as little less than a masterpiece—and was visibly upset with Hermione Lee when she admitted that she didn't like it.[6] Alongside these works, at roughly the same time, he penned the wildest, least realized of all his published writings: an exploration of an incorrigible American huckster, "On the Air," first conceived of as a full-length novel.

Yet Roth poured his greatest energy now into the writing of *The Breast*—widely considered among the worst of his books—a study of his character Kepesh coming to terms patiently, even realistically, with having metamorphosed overnight into a mammary gland. Roth said that it owed its inspiration to his own overnight transformation in the minds of many into a sexual bandit with the appearance of *Portnoy's Complaint.* Essayist Hillel Halkin called the books Roth wrote in this period "the worst of all his twenty books to date," but added that he was convinced that all were the consequence of a post-Portnoy effort to "maintain the pretense that his fictional interest extended beyond the immediate world of a single Newark-born Jewish writer."[7]

The unabashed impertinence of these books also owed something to his then-close friendship (as well as an exercise at mentorship) with novelist Alan Lelchuk, with whom, when he was away from his typewriter, he spent much of his time at Yaddo. "Scrappy," "rude," "rough" was how he described Lelchuk's writing—and the man himself. Lelchuk courted Roth hungrily, while Roth admired the younger man's bravado and the late-night hours Lelchuk expended on sex, indifferent to the strictures Roth imposed on himself.

"I think it as good a piece of fiction as anybody has produced in a long time. . . . The body of the thing is so rich and such a joy," Roth wrote Solotaroff, seeking to dissuade him from turning down a part of Lelchuk's first novel, *American Mischief*, sent to *New American Review*.[8] Roth saw Lelchuk as a novelist of talent who shared an array of common interests: an intense if sardonic take on Jewishness, wide reading, and cynicism laced with an insatiable hunger for fame. "I think he is writing a brilliant novel," Roth writes Solotaroff from Yaddo. "He is a good friend, and a good solid practical mind."[9]

Starting already before the appearance of *Portnoy's Complaint*, Roth would lean heavily on Lelchuk for promotional needs. Lelchuk was the questioner for a faux interview in the *Atlantic*, throwing mostly softball questions with the goal of promoting Roth's *The Great American Novel.* Lelchuk was also on hand to help prepare Roth for a more intellectually robust interview about *The Breast* in the *New York Review of Books* in fall 1972.[10]

In turn, Roth gave Lelchuk's inaugural novel *American Mischief*, published in 1979, an immense promotional push, calling it—in an essay devoted to a small cluster of little-known but exceptional writers—"a brilliant and original comedy." This contributed to "enormous prepublication ballyhoo," raising expectations far too high, as noted in the book's *New York Times* review. The reviewer, a harsh critic of *American Mischief*, added

Novelist Alan Lelchuk was one of Roth's closest friends in the late 1960s and early '70s. (Photograph by Barbara C. Sproul)

that Lelchuk's theme—the incompatibility of domestic happiness and intense sexual experience—was far better handled by Roth, whose "wit and narrative crispness," he wrote, were sorely missing in *American Mischief*, which lacked "insight or control." The *New Yorker*'s reviewer L. E. Sissman was still more pointed in its criticism of Roth's vigorous promotional activity: "Mr. Lelchuk has been badly served by his promoters, his seconders."[11]

It took Lelchuk a long time to face the strain and eventual disintegration of their friendship. The first instance of a rupture may have occurred after the publication of *The Professor of Desire*, which drew on Lelchuk—alongside Albert Goldman—for one of its most unseemly characters, as Lelchuk immediately recognized. "Is it really the untamed animal in him that causes this carnivore to tear at the meat between his teeth and with such stupendous muscle power? . . . Where did he first eat flesh, in Queens or in a cave? One night the sight of Baumgarten's incisors severing the meat from the bone of his breaded veal chop sends me home later to my bookshelves to take down the collection of Kafka's stories and to reread the final paragraph of 'The Hunger Artist.' "[12]

Roth did not send Lelchuk the manuscript of *My Life as a Man*. He stopped inviting him to book parties and took little interest in Lelchuk's new fascination with Israeli literature. Nonetheless, Lelchuk continued to court Roth, trying to evoke whatever warmth might remain in their now-fraying relationship, referring to Roth in letters as Southpaw or Skipper and reminiscing about their bachelor days together: "The freedom, the women, the travel, the dope." Things badly deteriorated when Lelchuk criticized Roth's treatment of Anne Frank in *The Ghost Writer*, describing it as "a mistaken strategy." But in the same letter, Lelchuk beseeched Roth to write an introduction for a book written by his wife. Later, Lelchuk, still trying to reignite Roth's interest, tells him of his latest risqué encounter: "A few afternoons ago an old student of mine, now 29 with 38D's, stopped for coffee, with her groom-to-be, a nice young Jewish man in the 'music copyright business' in Atlanta. When I showed her where the bathroom was, at the far end of the house, she squeezed my hand, pulled me inside, and put her tongue down my mouth. They are to be married in late October."[13]

The friendship long over, Lelchuk published the novel *Ziff: A Life?* in 2003, a blistering attack on Roth—not his talent, but his character. The story is told by a once-promising, now largely neglected writer who teaches at a tony northeastern college (Lelchuk spent much of his adult life at Dartmouth), suddenly invited to write the biography of Ziff, a famed novelist, once a close friend. Ziff takes full advantage of the endeavor—behind the scenes he probably initiated it: a plot to snag finally the Nobel Prize. The would-be biographer is convinced he has now discovered a huge array of Jewish-related philanthropic activities set in motion by Ziff, who, as a result, quiets opposition, finally winning the Nobel. Lelchuk's protagonist, Levitan, is left out in the cold: a pathetic figure straight out of one of Malamud's most dismal stories, a portrait of tragic entanglement with an exceptionally charming, cruel, sorely missed buddy. In an afterword, Ziff writes Levitan, offering an introduction to the editor of the travel section of the *New York Times*, where he might manage to place some of his future jottings.[14]

One of very few criticisms of Roth leveled by Barbara Sproul—who remained a loyal friend long after the end of their romance—was his "weakness for sycophants" by which she meant particularly Lelchuk, whom she had always disliked. Responding in a memo to Bailey in 2015, Roth came to his defense, speaking of the "lively aggressiveness" that drew him to the younger writer. There was in Lelchuk's writing, raw as it was, "a force worth cultivating," and Roth recalls finding him "argumentative, audacious, brash, and throughout a companionable, good-natured friend." He added that he was drawn to Lelchuk because of this: "Intensity. That was my weakness. There also, unfortunately, was my strength."[15]

The friendship with Lelchuk was forged in the late 1960s and early '70s, with all its political and cultural combustibility. Roth would now, in the wake of *Portnoy's Complaint*, find himself thrust into the limelight with his newfound celebrity and sudden wealth: The size of his advances was frequently noted in reviews of *Portnoy's Complaint*, sometimes with the implication that all that cash explained why he now succumbed to writing pornography.

True, Roth was attracted to this anarchist zeitgeist. But he remained then and later contemptuous of its anti-intellectualism, teasing, sometimes even lambasting, friends like Jules Feiffer about their immersion in the counterculture's wilder excesses. He remained an admiring reader of gurus like R. D. Laing and Paul Goodman but never emerged like them as one of the counterculture's heroes. He was too buttoned-down, too assiduous a worker, too straitlaced to succumb to bohemia. Asked by Mike Wallace in a television interview soon after his National Book Award for *Goodbye, Columbus* what he thought of Jack Kerouac, Roth said he thought little of him. Rowdy with his closest friends, rambunctious on the page, Roth seemed to strike Wallace as stiff and unattractive, an earnest, even dull intellectual.[16]

By far the most calming of all influences now—perhaps the most deeply satisfying relationship with a woman he would ever enjoy—were his six years with Barbara Sproul. "She's this young, beautiful PhD in Theology from Columbia," writes Goldman, "who is a master photographer and a master cook and a master suck and a master sailor and a master flyer." Goldman observed a "slightly sarcastic edge to her all the time. . . . Quite cheerful, she seemed very self-possessed, and she seemed to be sort of indulging Philip—'there he goes off again on his bullshit again, his ego trip, but I'll get him.' "[17]

As Sproul put it in a conversation with me, "I was cute, and I was smart." Her parents—who despised each other—ran a New York ad agency, and she grew up on a one hundred–acre waterfront farm in Guilford, Connecticut. She was raised mostly by a nanny, her parents showing up mostly on weekends. "I had parents who weren't interested in being parents."[18]

When she was eleven her brother died in a car accident.

(The boy driving the car, a friend whom she recalled fondly, would kill himself out of guilt some six months later.) Her mother abandoned her, and her father committed suicide when she was twenty-one. "One of the interesting things that separated me from Philip was death. A virgin when it came to death." Sproul insists she never felt sorry for herself: Her nanny, who raised her, was a "great spirit" who grew orchids in the basement. Sproul grew up confident: "Farms teach you a great deal about life and death." A gorgeous young woman—as well as being wise, sardonic, and a devoted idealist—she maintained a matter-of-fact demeanor. Goldman described Sproul in these terms: "She doesn't strike me as being female in the fundamental sense, just in the sense of being pretty, having a perfect figure. . . . And she's very compulsive, orderly, neat, highly strung girl who oddly, Philip feels is good for him because she knows where the pencils are kept or something."[19]

Escaping to Yaddo from the hubbub surrounding *Portnoy*, Roth admitted to Sproul soon after his arrival that "everything suddenly feels wrong about my life down there now [in New York]. Except for you; and 'you' seem like something I can fuck up down there if I don't watch out." He adds that he now hoped to achieve a life of calm, which he feels Barbara can help provide as long as he doesn't once again permit his work to overtake all else: "You are a love-girl, a sweet radiant love-girl, and you're smart and wise to know that spirit is there, with us. I think that's what makes me patient now, and so calm about sex, so willing to wait. And you're generous about this holy pain-in-the-ass called Phil's Work."[20]

Already at the start, Roth identified how Sproul's needs could well spell trouble. There were signs of imperfection, a reliance on therapy, the impact of her dreadful past. He wrote Lelchuk a few years later, in 1972, still concerned that "Barbara Sproul, the unadulterated living animal some five feet seven inches tall, has her symptoms weekly (today it is spasmodic ovary) but otherwise we are getting used to each other, and she's changing her little ways."[21]

For her part, she was smitten above all, as she later recalled, by the intensity of his love for the written word: "I remember asking him one night why he had underlined a specific sentence in a book . . . and he looked it over and said 'because it is beautiful.' . . . I hadn't known anything of such perspectives before and had a wonderful time learning and expanding what I understood. . . . I loved his commitment to literature, his seriousness about his own writing and that of others, his tough mindedness, his humor."[22]

And she added, ruefully, "The sex was okay too." Soon after they met, Roth wrote her from Yaddo, astonished at the sexual abandon of this theology scholar: "That was an intense erotic voyage we made together. I woke Monday morning feeling you beside me in the bed a full-grown animal, together. It was marvelous."[23]

Meeting him in late 1968 just on the cusp of the hubbub surrounding *Portnoy's Complaint*, she worried—long afterward, too, once their sexual relationship had ended—about the prospect of fame's corrosive influence. His books written in the immediate wake of *Portnoy*, likely influenced by Sproul, were all aimed at deflecting such expectations, in doing anything but replicating the grand style of the previous generation of literary lions. Joel Conarroe—a close friend of Roth's, later president of the Guggenheim Foundation—described a conversation with him about these matters in the mid-1970s: "Phil then spoke about the differences between the generations. These writers, now in their sixties, were all prima donnas (Philip didn't use that word), touchy, interested in fame only in the sense of wanting to be on Mount Olympus. . . . The writers in their forties—Updike, Roth, Oates, Price, Gardner, Barth, etc.—seem more than anything else to work extraordinarily hard, to turn out book after book, and to live in more or less remote places."[24]

Decades after their breakup, Sproul would send Roth this cautionary poem that she wrote—still a close friend, still clearly concerned:

A GOMOL is an interesting beast
A Grand Old Man of Letters,
The Most of Most, not least of least
He certainly has no betters

His early works, once free and gold,
Are now thought staid and classic
Enshrined in hazy memory's gold,
Leatherbound but Jurassic

It's thirty years since he complained
And jerked off into liver.
Since then some twenty books have rained
A veritable prose river. . . .

You're not a GOMOL yet my dear,
You still defy description.
Too fresh, too hot, those lines that sear—
Too vibrant for conscription.[25]

He now worked most persistently on *The Breast*, rewriting parts of it, rearranging it up until the time of its appearance in 1972 for Lelchuk's interview in the *New York Review of Books*. In the interview, he declared that contrary to what some believed he never intended the novel to be an extended joke. "I resisted comedy or farce in large part because the possibility was so immediately apparent," said Roth. He saw it much like Kafka's "The Metamorphosis," where the author made clear from the start that the experience was no dream but that the catastrophe occurs to him in a very everyday world of families, jobs, and bosses.[26]

Roth was convinced this was his best book, selling it for nearly a quarter of a million dollars (despite being fewer than a hundred pages), with a still larger sum for paperback rights. He

Barbara Sproul, with whom Roth enjoyed one of the longest, happiest relationships in his life. (Photograph provided by Barbara C. Sproul)

was stunned at its bleak reception. Both reviews in the *New York Times* were dreadful, with novelist John Gardner stating that while bad, this book was Roth's best. To be sure, Margaret Drabble acknowledged that reading it made her return right away and reread Kafka, but most characterized it as slight, little more than a comedic short story, a bore. Critic Jonathan Yardley insisted that the book's failure was truly unfortunate since its author possessed more "perception, inventiveness, humor, and sheer talent" than nearly any young writer in the country. "One senses reading it a great talent going to waste."[27]

"*The Breast* has nothing to do with black humor," Roth wrote in response to this cascade of criticism. "Its intent is realism. Its effect is tragedy."[28] Indeed, in one of the book's more striking passages, Roth has Kepesh convinced—whether comforted or terrified by this thought, it remains unclear—that he may not actually be a breast but is insane, the condition brought on by excessive reading of Gogol and Kafka. It could well be literature that is to blame, softening and eventually perverting the mind.

Then, on the heels of these mostly bad reviews—and in response not only to *Portnoy's Complaint* but to the audacity of following it with something like *The Breast*—came the most devastating attack on his work ever written. And it was all the more shattering because it was written by someone Roth long revered. "Sooner or later," Roth wrote in *The Anatomy Lesson* more than a decade later and still smarting, "there comes to every writer the two-thousand, three-thousand, five-thousand-word lashing that doesn't just sting for the regulation seventy-two hours but rankles all his life. Zuckerman now had his: to treasure in his quotable storehouse till he died, the unkindest review of all, embedded as indelibly (and just about as useful) as 'Abou Ben Adhem' and 'Annabel Lee,' the first two poems he'd had to memorize for a high-school English class."[29]

10

"Thinness of Culture"

The attack in December 1972 on *Portnoy's Complaint*—along with nearly all else Roth had written—was the work of Irving Howe, a father figure of sorts in the firmament of tough-minded Jewish criticism. And it hit all the harder because of its appearance in *Commentary*, which had nurtured Roth's early work. Howe's essay "Philip Roth Reconsidered" was prefaced in the same issue with a bitter sally from its editor Norman Podhoretz, who announced grimly, "I have no doubt that the general direction Roth has traveled as an artist from *Goodbye, Columbus* in 1959 to *The Breast* in 1972 is down."[1]

Howe had praised Roth's first book. Now, he took back nearly all the good things he once said while savaging essentially everything Roth had produced since: Roth's are caricatures, not genuine portraits, "impatient, snappish, and dismissive." Throughout—starting with his first book, then in *Letting Go* as well as *When She Was Good*—he reveals "a swelling nausea before the ordinariness of human existence. . . . Men grow paunches, women's breasts sag, the breath of the aged reeks, varicose veins bulge." His is a cold, vindictive imagination replete with an impatient cruel contempt, "an unmanageable frustration with our common fate."[2]

Portnoy's Complaint was Howe's major target, adding that little more can be said about *Our Gang* or *The Breast* than that these slight, readily digestible, "boring," and "tasteless" morsels were created to satisfy uncritical, readily grateful consumers. Howe acknowledged that with the appearance of *Portnoy's Complaint*, there is no doubt that Roth occupies, as many have observed, a position "close to the center of our culture." But this is precisely the problem and nothing for Roth to feel pleased about, since the culture to which Roth panders is an empty shell: hedonistic, sexually obsessed, a travesty across the political spectrum.[3]

There may well have been more than a hint of jealousy in the attack, as Bernard Avishai, a friend to both Howe and Roth, sensed. (Avishai met Roth soon after the Howe essay was published.) Howe—a leading figure in the smallish but intellectually commanding world of anticommunist socialism and editor of *Dissent* magazine—was perhaps irked by having been left in the dust by the young, whose own inclinations were now more attuned to voices like Roth than to a politically principled and sober cultural critic like himself. Besieged throughout the 1950s by communists, Howe now may have felt that his time had finally arrived, and yet suddenly he was overtaken by Roth's nihilistic, dangerously infectious imagination.[4]

Howe acknowledged that there were glimmers of talent in one or another of the stories in *Goodbye, Columbus.* Elsewhere, however, he pointed out only the vulgarity of standup comedy, a vapid tendentiousness, and, above all, "thinness of culture." This a body of work characterized by "unexamined depression . . . an assault without precise object, an irritable wish to pull down the creatures of his own imagination which can hardly be explained by anything happening within the stories themselves." Amid this barrage, it was the charge that Roth's work reflected a "thinness of culture" that left the deepest scars.[5]

Of course, Roth had experienced fierce denunciations before by prominent figures in Jewish culture. But criticism from Howe was different. This was the author of the blistering essay "The Age of Conformity," one of the most brilliant assaults on the dangerously quiescent, ascendant liberalism that also deeply concerned Roth. There, Howe saw as jarringly alarming—much like Roth—the dominant "zeitgeist, that vast insidious sum of pressures and fashions." What Howe had long meant to him, as Roth later captured in his novel *The Anatomy Lesson*, was as an exemplar of an "aggressively marginal sensibility, the disavowal of community ties, the taste for scrutinizing a social event as though it were a dream or a work of art."[6]

Nothing would soothe Roth. William Styron sought to do so, with no apparent success, reminding Roth of the many attacks on him. "A writer has to be extraordinarily good to arouse that kind of spleen," he wrote. Styron recalled that, a few years earlier, he received in the mail an entire book published by a trade house, devoted exclusively to an attack on his novel *The Confessions of Nat Turner*, "damning me for a racist, a perverter of the truth, a distorter of history."[7]

And then, a year later, Howe approached Lelchuk to ask whether Roth might sign a letter in defense of Israel—at the time being widely criticized in the wake of the 1973 war. This so enraged Roth that he sent off a five-and-a-half-page typed diatribe to Howe, wherein Roth rehearsed a defense of *Portnoy* characterizing Howe's request: "When I [Howe] or Kazin or Bellow come out in support of Israel, that's not news . . . but if Roth came out with his forthright statement that would be news of a kind" precisely because he is "a Jewish author who dislikes Jews."[8]

No attack would ever bruise so deeply or resonate for so long—until, that is, the appearance years later of Claire Bloom's memoir of their married life, *Leaving a Doll's House.* And despite the vats of reading that shaped his work and his time at the University of Chicago, Howe's essay highlighted the unsettling truth that Roth was a New Jersey boy who grew up with few books at home and who had completed his formal education without much formidable scaffolding and without knowledge of a foreign language. Now Roth was rubbing shoulders with the crème of New York Jewish intelligentsia like Philip Rahv, Alfred Kazin, Norman Podhoretz, and Clement Greenberg, as well as Updike and others.

Soon afterward—and not long after a trip to Prague on which he accompanied Sproul, long an active member of Amnesty International who introduced him to the city—he wrote his essay "Looking at Kafka." He began to forge close ties with Ivan Klima, Milan Kundera, and other Czech intellectuals and novelists, soon launching the Penguin paperback series imprint Writers from the Other Europe, a veritable publishing house.

Of course, well before his trip to Prague, Roth had been intrigued by Kafka: his family drama, the explosive relationship with his father, and the subtle workings of his fictional realism. Predating Howe's attack was his awareness of Kafka's uncanny ability, as Roth put it, to allow "an obsession to fill every corner." He claimed that this insight had helped him when he was at work on *When She Was Good.* Kafka's impact on *The Breast,* which appeared in 1972, was obvious. Still, it was only once he went to Prague and met local writers both favored and hounded by the regime, becoming aware of the role still occupied by literature in this ornate and crumbling city barely five hundred miles from the Galicia of his ancestors, that his absorption was jump-started. As biographer Ira Nadel put it, Roth would now feel "rooted in the Jewish past of European persecution." This considerably deepened in the wake of Howe's attack on his cultural arsenal. Indeed, according to Ivan Klima (eventually one of Roth's close friends), no other Western writer had mastered Kafka's writings more thoroughly than Roth. And he began to devote considerable energy to shepherding many of the most impressive East Central European voices onto the world stage, while also teaching Kafka at the University of Pennsylvania—this a compelling retort to the most devastating of Howe's accusations. Who, indeed, could accuse the novelist with the finest understanding of Kafka outside Prague of having a thin cultural repertoire?[9]

Still, Roth's touchiness regarding such matters remained a source of discomfort, often anguish. (He acknowledged to friends that he expended far too much energy worrying about what critics like Alfred Kazin might think of his work.) And while his engagement with Central European writers, most of them Jews, was undoubtedly born out of a commitment to the importance of their voices, it was also prompted by a desire to confront and dispel the nagging sense of inadequacy about his own cultural buttressing: Despite a lifetime of assiduous reading, he remained largely self-taught.

He later described to Claudia Roth Pierpont, author of *Roth Unbound: A Writer and His Books*, the palpable connection he felt from the moment of his first arrival in Prague to "a place which in earlier days must have been not too unlike those neighborhoods in Austro-Hungary Lemberg," the birthplace of both branches of his family. Klima said that unlike any other American he had met, Roth avoided small talk, insisting straightaway on discussing only what most interested him, which was Jewish identity and the Second World War. And Prague served to deepen his understanding of repression, particularly its impact on Jews, which he had previously written about almost exclusively in terms of the distress Jews enacted on other Jews. It was in Prague, writes Pierpont, that he discovered "historical weight, unjust opposition, burdens of conscience, looming threats of exposure and disaster"—these among the more pronounced themes of his future work.[10]

Roth now started laboring on what would emerge as his Zuckerman Trilogy, launched with the most lyrical of all his books, *The Ghost Writer*, dedicated to the dean of Czech writers Milan Kundera. It served as a reminder, as critic James Wood astutely put it, that his was not always the raucous voice of Portnoy but that he was capable of "high minded restraint . . . tiny rounding of each fine phrase."[11] *The Ghost Writer* presents a young, uncertain hero who has just finished the first of the stories that will presumably go into a future book. Roth may have intended the book as something of an apology for *Portnoy's Complaint*, a signal that he was able to write something altogether different, and it was indeed. Nearly all the protagonists of his subsequent novels would be writers.

Roth saw the new book as closely linked with his first: He made certain that *The Ghost Writer* appeared on the twentieth anniversary of *Goodbye, Columbus*. And in a preface to the Modern Library edition of *Goodbye, Columbus* published in 1995, he admitted that—much like Nathan Zuckerman in *The Ghost Writer*—it was his dream from the start to enter that "republic of discourse" populated by the likes of Freud, Martin Buber, and Ralph Ellison (among at least twenty others named). Not included in the list—though, he might well have been under different circumstances—was Irving Howe.[12]

Working once again, as nearly always, and producing numerous drafts of *The Ghost Writer*, a work comparable in its beauty to that of the Russian master Ivan Turgenev, he published in 1974 *My Life as a Man*, a massively overstuffed and awkwardly paced novel (this perhaps intentional). It was composed of a range of voices, with different narrators telling much the same story: leaning on similar details but rendered with starkly different intonations, some straightforward if furious, others arch and almost baroque.

As he described in an interview with Joyce Carol Oates soon after the book's appearance, "I'd been writing, abandoning, and returning to [it] ever since I published *Portnoy's Complaint.* Whenever I gave up on it I went to work on one of the 'playful' books . . . all the while that *My Life as a Man* was simmering away on the 'moral' back burner."[13]

The book's overlapping, vastly different narrators are all writers or educators. And this is the first time Roth comes close to describing his own day-to-day routine. The novel's first section, "Salad Days," blends an amalgam of Kafka to now-vintage Roth (the father a brutish boss, the son overcultivated) with nearly all other biographical details (schooling, college, army, backaches); it is a summation of Roth's life with all its soon-familiar signposts. The adolescent Nathan devours Wolfe's *Of Time and the River* and joyously discovers somewhat older literary ancestors in the first English-language paperback edition of Isaac Babel. Soon enough, literary influences overwhelm him. In the space of little more than a page or two, we find our hero reading Mann, Kafka, Gogol, Freud, more Wolfe, Henry James, Melville. He seeks to romance a young love with the use of literary analysis: "Ah, Miss Oakes, if only I hadn't been so overbearing! Memories of my behavior make me cringe. I told you about Isaac Babel and about my wife with the same veins popping."[14]

Using Freud to attack the reductionism of his psychotherapist—here loquacious in contrast to Portnoy's—he argues against a diagnosis of narcissism:

> And if I may, sir—his *self* is to many a novelist what his own physiognomy is to a painter of portraits: the closest subject at hand demanding scrutiny, a problem for his art to solve—given the enormous obstacles to truthfulness, *the* artistic problem. He is not simply looking into the mirror because he is transfixed by what he sees. Rather, the artist's success depends as much as anything on his powers of detachment, on

> *de*-narcissizing himself. That's where the excitement comes in. That hard *conscious* work that makes it *art!* Freud, Dr. Spielvogel, studied his own dreams not because he was a "narcissist," but because he was a student of dreams. And whose were at once the least and most accessible of dreams, if not his own?[15]

Two matters are of the greatest of interest to him here, argued Hillel Halkin: how a novelist draws on personal experience in creating fictional characters, and how the way in which we write fiction is analogous to how we sustain our own lives. It is a book made of a multitude of voices—those of literary heroes, relatives, lovers, and the fiercest of all: an unforgettably monstrous wife. Roth integrates into the text verbatim entries from Maggie's diary. He blames the era, the 1950s, for his early marriage (to a woman whose body he insists he deplored from the start), with its celebration of premature adulthood and his conviction at the time that to be a good writer it was essential to experience life well beyond the Jewish family cocoon. "I wanted something called 'a woman,'" he writes. It is a complex book made of fragments, something of a prelude to *The Counterlife*, published more than a decade later. No other work of Roth's would ever as astutely probe the slippery byways of autobiography: It was far more revealing than *The Facts* and, as he admitted, as close to the truth as he would ever write.[16]

"Yes," he told Claire Bloom, to whom he dedicated the book, speaking of how Maggie tricked him into marriage by lying about her pregnancy: "the urine incident is grisly, I thought so when I first heard about it in what is so innocently referred to as 'real life' and spent nearly ten years trying to find a way of including it in a novel." It was only once he recognized, he says, that it "should be a novel about trying to write that novel" that he was "able to finally face the thing in a book."[17]

He had long pondered (as he described elsewhere, ever since

the writing of *Portnoy's Complaint*) how to capture Maggie's treachery. Everything he wrote starting from that point on was an attempt at "blasting my way through a tunnel to reach the novel that I couldn't write."[18] And depicted here, too, was him beating her—indeed, his wish that he had beaten her to death. It is these passages that first gave rise several years after *Portnoy's Complaint* to charges of Roth's misogyny. Few took up these charges just yet—the feminist movement was at an early stage in the mid-1970s, only beginning to enter the cultural mainstream. But critical feminist readings of Roth would later consolidate into one viewpoint: "If in Bellow misogyny was like a seeping pile," wrote Vivian Gornick after the appearance of *My Life as a Man*, "in Roth it was lava pouring forth from a volcano." And with no personal knowledge of Roth, she added that the women in his fiction are "monstrous because for Philip Roth women are monstrous." Nothing he could do—whether ignoring such criticism or highlighting the complex treatment of Lucy in *When She Was Good* or eventually Drenka in *Sabbath's Theater*—managed to quiet such denunciations.[19]

No one, critic Morris Dickstein wrote, in an overwhelmingly negative review of *My Life as a Man*, "contributed more to the confessional climate" of the age than Roth, with so much of his writing harnessed to his own life and that of those around him. And Roth proved himself surprisingly candid when drawing on the pitfalls of his own life. Already in *The Breast*, appearing two years before *My Life as a Man*, Kepesh's young, beautiful, eminently reliable woman-friend Claire—a "cool, imperturbable girl" modeled on Barbara Sproul physically and intellectually—was described as no longer exciting him sexually: "the strong lust her physical beauty had aroused in me during the first two years of our affair had been dwindling for almost a year now." Her beauty—Kepesh describes her as "a green-eyed blonde, tall and lean and full-breasted"—has ceased to overpower him, and there is nothing he can do to rectify this.[20]

Roth and Sproul had a longstanding living arrangement: separate apartments in New York and a beautiful Connecticut house purchased by Roth (soon after publication of *The Breast*), which Barbara discovered for him and carefully furnished and where she tended its beautiful garden. His relationship with Sproul remained Roth's main romantic involvement, even while he continued to enjoy sex with others. Barbara Jakobson—a close friend of Ann Mudge's—described to me a decades-long, on and off, sexual involvement. (She explained that during her marriage, which eventually dissolved, she gravitated sexually almost exclusively to writers or artists, both because of common interests and because they could be available in the afternoon, since she made it a point to be home for dinner.) Sproul recalled that, when at Roth's New York apartment, she spotted in the bathroom women's underwear and asked Roth where they had come from. He responded that he had no idea.[21]

The relationship with Sproul was as secure and affectionate as any Roth would enjoy. "BS's [Barbara Sproul's] qualities, as we know both, are hard to find," wrote Lelchuk soon after the breakup, "great sexpots and intelligent beauties don't usually turn into competent and kindly companions. The combo is generally ruined along the way."[22]

They separated in 1974 because of Roth's unwillingness to consider their having a child together. Their sexual relationship had by then cooled—Roth laments this in *My Life as a Man*—but they might well have continued for a while, at least, had Sproul not pressed the issue. They saw Kleinschmidt together, wrestled with the matter for months, with Sproul puzzled by how emphatic he was: "I don't understand—much of anything, of course—but now I don't understand how we couldn't be us. I don't understand how you could be afraid of me."[23] Roth explained that the decision was the only reasonable response to Barbara's desire for children and marriage, which, after his first ghastly experience, he would never repeat. Sproul insists that marriage was the last thing on her mind, and worked hard to salvage what they had. As she wrote Roth:

> You kid me about adoring you just because I'm used to you. Perhaps so; but you can fool me. But, while you think in terms of dependence, I don't. Each to his own in terms of neurotic backgrounds. Mine never let me get dependent on anyone, like to or not. No, that's not it for me. I really do love you, parts of you, all of you, traits, mannerisms, jokes, habits, things, styles. The works. It gives me pleasure, amusement, comfort, joy, strength, purpose, and all the rest.[24]

Sproul would later acknowledge to herself a certain relief that the relationship had ended—much like other women linked with Roth who described the same feeling: As much as they loved him, his presence was the source of ongoing, not infrequent anxiety, apparently the price for intimacy with a tightly wound artist.

The breakup left Roth feeling bereft too, unable to concentrate, grimly depressed. His Connecticut life with Sproul had brought him into regular, pleasurable contact with an array of neighbors. One of them was the iconoclastic painter Philip Guston—a large, playful, intermittently joyous and gloomy man whom Roth grew to like greatly. Joel Conarroe—a man of immense warmth and a dean at the University of Pennsylvania, where Roth then taught a seminar—was a frequent guest, as were William Styron and his wife, Rose, who lived nearby. There were also Lelchuk and the Princeton sociologist Melvin Tumin, later an inspiration for Coleman Silk in Roth's *The Human Stain*. It was a small, intimate cluster of friends that Sproul had nurtured with good humor, food, and warmth.

In stark contrast to the Connecticut home, his apartment

on West 81st Street in New York City, sublet for a time by writer Jack Miles (soon a good friend), was barren of nearly everything but books: It was formally furnished with synthetic logs in the fireplace and an all but empty bedroom. The apartment was comparable, Miles wrote to Ross Miller, to the dire place where Alexander Portnoy might suffer from impotence.[25]

Roth would soon find solace right upstairs from his apartment, with a woman fifteen years his junior and married. She was also stunningly beautiful and a talented writer. The relationship with Janet Hobhouse—later a biographer of Gertrude Stein as well as a short story writer and novelist—was brief and intense and inspirational. Hobhouse wrote the sharpest of all biographical sketches of Roth in *The Furies*, an unfinished memoirlike fiction, the character Jack standing in for Roth in her description of their affair. Essayist Daphne Merkin ruefully described Hobhouse's *Furies* as made up of sentences "somewhat baroque . . . owing more to Henry James than Raymond Carver, looping back and zigzagging all over the place."[26]

The romance started, Hobhouse says, with a casual meeting at the mailbox, moving slowly to "flirtation, courtship, seduction"—for him, seduction was "everything." What Hobhouse says drew her the most was, curiously enough, the "depressive minimalism of his life"—the rituals that governed his routine, the tidy sparseness of his living arrangements, his collegiate dress, the sum total of his "spartan life." Soon Roth ended the romance, after discovering that Hobhouse was using prescription drugs for depression. He managed to all but disappear, though he continued to live just downstairs. He would now chat amiably with her when they ran into each other at the mailbox, suggesting that she and her husband might consider having another child while clearly indicating that he hoped she would not take advantage of their "brief though delightful liaison."[27]

> There was something wound and ready to spring about him, physically, though it was all driven by his brain, from the shoulders that bent toward you when he listened—and he always listened like someone decoding, sensing, processing vulnerability, a place to enter, to overpower—to the thick tight hair that covered that cranium like excess energy. Humor could make him lean less hard at you, disarm him for a moment, but that respite of laughter was only a momentary purring because the language itself—of humor—was really a tribute to his own authority there, the place where he famously triumphed, won all the speed prizes, set the rules.[28]

It is a beautifully wrought, affectionate portrait, if also chilling: "The great man tired of it all, longing for his peace and routines, bored with the performing and the showing and the colors . . . boredom with the little bird in all her feathers and delightful youth—too much of that youth."[29] Yet, as we have seen, the friendship didn't come to an end there. Roth eventually reemerged as one of Hobhouse's most attentive friends when she was diagnosed with the cancer that eventually killed her. Once she died, he mourned her, admitting to some that he regretted his offhand treatment of her years earlier.

Visiting her grave, which he had located and paid for, he would speak to her, as he told his University of Chicago friend, the writer Richard Stern. "I tell her things I don't anyone. I ask her advice and I get it." Maletta Pfeiffer—Roth's lover for nearly two decades and the model for the erotically alert Drenka Balich in Roth's *Sabbath's Theater*—described for me the intensity of this preoccupation, saying that he frequently would stand over Hobhouse's grave and urinate, just like Mickey Sabbath—overwhelmed and eager to speak once again, to link himself somehow forever with her.[30]

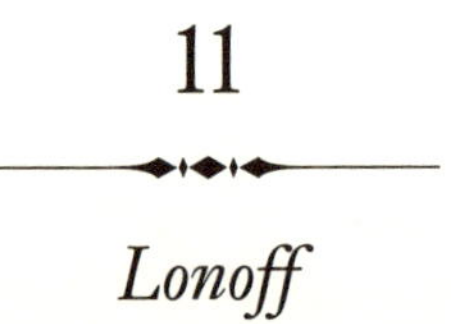

11

Lonoff

> But these Lonoffs—such a suffocating investment in temperance, in *dignity*, of all damn things.

Roth had long seen Kafka in a category all his own. During his own dry spell in his thirties after *Goodbye, Columbus*—particularly after the Yeshiva University episode—Roth spoke of his great admiration for Kafka's capacity to live with his overpowering obsessions, then infuse them with "grave comedy." This introduced him to a useful fictional roadmap at a time when Kafka had largely come to replace Marx as an intellectual beacon for much of American intelligentsia. It was now that Roth wrote—then put into the drawer—the start of the first of his major works on the underpinnings of twentieth-century America, a text originally set in Prague: this the start of his novel *American Pastoral*, completed decades later.

He made himself into little less than an indispensable link between Prague and the Western literary world, engaged as he was in a feverish range of activities—wholly uncharacteristic in view of how meticulously he protected his writerly schedule. Roth was the presumed author (it was actually written by Sproul) of a detailed report for Amnesty International on the wretched condition of the Czech literary milieu. Simultaneously he launched a complex, remarkably successful system of financial support for beleaguered Czech writers, sustained financially by contributions solicited personally by Roth from a wide range of Western intellectuals—including Howe. And then, with remarkable speed, he launched the series Writers from the Other Europe.

His descent deep into Kafka he announced with one of the finest of his interpretive essays doubling as a short story: "'I Always Wanted You to Admire My Fasting'; or, Looking at Kafka" was published in 1973 amid Roth's immersion in Kafka and was released side by side with his raucous *The Great American Novel.* Both showcased Roth's dexterous talent and his capacity to make whatever he touched his own, infusing both with his fluent, unobtrusively knowing voice.

Roth begins by examining Kafka's photograph: "a black towel of Levantine hair pulled close around the skull the only sensuous feature," with a nose "long and weighted slightly at the tip," adding "the nose of half the Jewish boys who were my friends in high school." And then moves to the horrors at the edge of any description of Kafka with the implosion of his world: "Skulls chiseled like this one were shoveled by the thousands from the ovens: had he lived, his would have been among them, along with the skulls of his three younger sisters."[1]

Roth now muses about how inconceivable it would have been for Kafka to escape in any way other than death at the age of forty-one. And yet, as Roth reminds us, this is just what he quite nearly managed to do in the eleven months before he died: He met Dora Diamant (a girl of nineteen), moved in with her in Berlin far from the family home, agreed to have some of his writings appear in book form, started to learn Hebrew while also attending classes on Judaism, and—most amazing of all—asked Dora to marry him. Roth sums up this oddly happy turn in Kafka's terror-ridden life: "As Franz Kafka awoke one morning from uneasy dreams he found himself transformed in his bed into a father, a writer, and a Jew."[2]

Kafka's writing now shifts in response, says Roth, to these surprising turns: In contrast to the "piercing masochistic irony" of the author of "The Judgement" or *The Trial*, more recent stories were informed by a surprising degree of "personal reconciliation and sardonic acceptance." He speaks here of Kafka's story "The Burrow," which Roth describes as "an unromantic and hardheaded fable about how and why art is made, a portrait of the artist in all his ingenuity, anxiety, isolation, dissatisfaction, relentlessness, secretiveness, paranoia, and self-addiction."[3]

The piece then takes a jarring turn, with Roth ushering Kafka into a story of his own, the European master now "spellbound in the family circle" (Max Brod's memorable description). Roth begins by relating how starting at the age of nine, he was compelled to attend Hebrew school for a wretched hour every weekday afternoon, languishing there instead of playing on the baseball field. It was during just these walks to Hebrew school with equally despondent friends that he would sharpen his comedy routines with their focus aimed squarely at their hapless Hebrew school teacher Franz Kafka, dubbed by Roth Dr. Kishka. He chooses the nickname because of "his sour breath, sharply spiced with intestinal juices by five in the afternoon." Roth makes it clear that his encounters with Dr. Kishka are what gave him his start as a comedian as well as a writer: "A coddled child, I do not yet think of myself as persuasive, or, quite yet, as a literary force in the world. . . . Already at nine, one foot in college, the other in the Catskills. Little borscht-belt comic that I am outside the classroom, I amuse my friends . . . on the dark walk home from after-hours Hebrew school with an imitation of Kishka, his precise and finicky professional manner, his German accent, his cough, his gloom."[4]

Soon enough the young Roth comes to recognize that comedy alone isn't sufficient, learning how it is that Kafka, having escaped the fate of most of Europe's Jews, lives alone in a rented room on one of Newark's shabbiest streets. The boy persuades his mother to invite Kafka for a meal. His father makes sure that Roth's unmarried Aunt Rhoda—a woman still terrified of "the facts of life"—joins them. Soon the two are dating, and on Kafka's urging Rhoda joins a theater troupe set to perform Chekhov at Newark's YMHA. As the relationship deepens, Rhoda blossoms and Kafka suggests they spend a weekend together in Atlantic City. It's there that he proposes something sexual to Rhoda, which she deems so unspeakable that the relationship ends then and there.

Years pass, Roth finds it intolerable living at home, fighting incessantly with his father, whose love smothers. He goes off to college, and in a letter his mother attaches a brief obituary announcing the death of Dr. Kafka, who, as Roth writes, "leaves no books, no *Trial*, no *Castle*, no Diaries." How bereft we would all be, Roth concludes. This a fate still stranger than a "man turning into an abominable insect. No one would believe it, Kafka least of all."[5]

Prague would now reappear in book after book, starting with *The Professor of Desire* in 1977 and coinciding with an increasingly intense preoccupation—inspired by his new Czech friends—with the wages of history and politics. His writing now took on, as Claudia Roth Pierpont has observed, a heightened historical weight, a preoccupation with "unjust oppression, burdens of conscience, looming threats of exposure and disaster, difficult claims of loyalty . . . even some no-nonsense anti-Semitism." Earlier his feelings about antisemitism—always overt and intense—had been seen by him as a wretched phenomenon of the past, a relic of the bygone days of the Second World War. Dismissing talk of anti-Jew hatred in an exchange with his mother in *The Ghost Writer*, Zuckerman responds to the charge that the dark Jewish past might well presage something about the present, too: "Ma, you want to see physical violence done to the Jews of Newark, go to the office of the plastic surgeon where the girls get their noses fixed. That's where the Jewish blood flows in Essex County, that's where the blow is delivered."[6]

It was Klima and others in Prague who alerted Roth to antisemitism's still-disruptive fury. Indeed, eventually he would conclude the so-called Zuckerman saga—*The Ghost Writer*, *Zuckerman Unbound*, and *The Anatomy Lesson*—with a nod to the madness of contemporary Czech literary life: *The Prague Orgy*. This faux-jokey portrait of East Central European artistic hopelessness included some of his most evocative writing on the relentless pull of the European past:

> I board a trolley by the river, then jump off halfway to the museum where Bolotka is expecting me to pay him a visit. On foot, and with the help of a Prague map, I proceed to lose my way but also to shake my escort. By the time I reach the museum the city seems to me a city that I've known all my life. The old-time streetcars, the barren shops, the soot-blackened bridges, the tunneled alleys and medieval streets, the people in a state of impervious heaviness, their faces shut down by solemnity, faces that appear to be on strike against life—this is the city I imagined during the war's worst years.[7]

Klima was only one of several survivors befriended by Roth. Almost immediately after the appearance of *The Counterlife* in 1986, Roth arranged to spend time in Turin with Primo Levi, interviewing him for the *New York Times* and soon acknowledging that he felt brotherly love for Levi.

Roth also set in motion plans for the Romanian writer Norman Manea, another survivor, and his wife, Cella, an art restorer, to settle comfortably in New York, where Manea was hired to teach at Bard, with no more than rudimentary English. Roth provided the down payment for their Upper West Side apartment. In a relationship forged by mutual love for Jewish humor, the three would now function as something of a family, with nearly every New Year's Eve spent in one another's company. And when Manea was warned he was on the verge of diabetes, Roth paid for a residential weight-loss treatment in North Carolina, a program built around the consumption of rice. But after a week, Roth phoned to say that he was so depressed without Manea's presence that he needed him to return home. And then every day for nearly a month, Roth would come to the Maneas' one-bedroom apartment to enjoy dinner together. Arriving at the building, Roth would announce himself to the doorman as Dr. Rice.[8]

Klima felt certain that no other American author captured the fate of writers in his country with greater persistence or earnestness. In *The Professor of Desire*, the most powerful sections were devoted to Prague, though Roth feared, as he told Claire Bloom, even after he had completed the book, that "something is missing in its center." He admitted this to her in a letter dedicating the book to her now that she was his primary love.

Reviews of the novel were mostly unforgiving. And just as Roth was beginning work on *The Ghost Writer*—it would appear two years later—he admitted to Solotaroff that he felt more misunderstood as a novelist, more isolated than ever before:

> It's getting stranger and stranger old friend. I mean the sense of being so entirely on one's own wavelength. Of course it's always been like that, but there was one's indestructible innocence and comforting saying it ain't so, it ain't so. What makes it all the odder is that the sense of strange isolation has probably been so enormous—but side by side—with it the miracle (for me) of coming upon a woman of whom I feel closer and more in tune than I have with any woman before in my life. I am dumbstruck by my luck.[9]

Bloom and Roth met at the home of mutual friends, then chanced to meet on Madison Avenue in spring 1975. By fall

1976, they were deeply in love. Finally, he felt certain he had met a true soulmate—a woman of independence with her own celebrated career, a lifelong reader of serious literature, and just the sort of partner for whom he had been searching all his life.[10]

Roth later told David Plante that he fell for Claire long before he met her because of the "beautiful aura" she exuded in the movie *Limelight*, released before Roth was twenty. Hence the relationship began—at least, as he would later reconstruct it—as something of an abstraction. He found himself powerfully drawn to her, as he told Plante, "because she was connected to what I thought was interesting work in an interesting world."[11]

In January 1976, Roth was addressing letters to Bloom "Dearest pal." By early April, it was "Dearest Claire." By then, he had made it clear that he was enraptured: "What else? Just that I think of you, miss you, and find myself pleased enormously when out of nowhere I am recollecting something you said or did." Soon enough his letters would become far more explicit. Anticipating a visit soon, he writes on June 9, 1976: "Without your sweet ass and other parts—including head—it is awfully difficult for me to fall asleep, awakened with a matutinal erection this morning, a lot of good it did me."[12]

By the month's end he admits, "I see myself fucking you in every posture conceivable. . . . I should be working, and I will, but felt you might want to know that I am pining in all ways and will gladly do it in the road, in the garden, in the salad dressing, in the tub, in the basement, the attic, and woods, the car, the trunk of the car, even if your heart and cunt should desire it, in the glove compartment. I'm yours."[13]

Maletta Pfeiffer recalls her first meeting with Bloom in the summer of 1977—Pfeiffer and Roth had already embarked two years earlier on their decades-long relationship—and what she witnessed was that with Claire, Roth's darkness "lifted . . . they were playful together. They were affectionate and would sometimes hold hands." Roth described to Pfeiffer how "dazzled" he was by Bloom, how impressed by her knowledge of English literature, including her suggestions for new books that he now read. Together they read Henry James and Edna O'Brien. Claire, as Pfeiffer recalled, revived the house's beauty, much of it lost once Sproul left the scene. She now "brought life and domesticity and made the house feel warm. Claire filled the living room with fresh-cut flowers. Philip hired a gardener. Now there were large flower beds around the house. The gardener even put in a vegetable garden with asparagus."[14]

At work on *The Ghost Writer* late in 1978, Roth wrote Joel Conarroe: "I think (secret, this) that Lonoff is growing into a book. I am not writing anonymously, I can tell you that, but with great fluency and pleasure." And Roth found himself now chewing over Michel Foucault's onslaught—at the height of its influence—regarding the myth of authorship.[15]

The Ghost Writer would emerge as one of Roth's most admired books, its first chapters previewed in consecutive issues of the *New Yorker* and among the most lucid of all contemporary explorations on how and why novelists write.

Much like "Goodbye, Columbus," it, too, is the story of a guest in a stranger's house. In Roth's first novella, Neil Klugman is an aimless, bookish man, perhaps on the cusp of a literary career but this at best only hinted at by Roth. Now just a few years older, the Nathan Zuckerman of *The Ghost Writer* is well on the way toward a promising career with a clutch of much-praised short stories under his belt. Yet he is wracked with self-doubt—seeking desperately a patron, maybe even a father different from the unsatisfactory parent he already has. Zuckerman's talk is peppered with self-deprecating asides, though he knows that he has moved into the literary stratosphere.

While in *My Life as a Man* the obsession is the protagonist's dreaded wife, here it is the interplay between life and art, with the book's characters handled with a tenderness rarely on display in Roth's writings at this time, its scaffolding spare, parablelike. Here, too, there is ample evidence of Roth's capacity for jaundiced, even savage characterization. Abravanel—in early drafts, the name of the book's protagonist but eventually a brilliantly observed portrait of Saul Bellow—exudes a "charm . . . like a moat so oceanic that you could not even see the great turreted and buttressed thing it had been dug to protect."[16] There are also sardonic glimpses of Bernard Malamud and Henry Roth—author of the brilliant, long-neglected 1934 portrait of Jewish childhood *Call It Sleep*—as well as Norman Mailer and Isaac Bashevis Singer.

Lonoff himself, it was widely believed, was meant as a glimpse of Malamud, with the befuddled protagonist-biographer from his novel *Dubin's Lives* (published the same year as *The Ghost Writer*) torn between fealty to his wife and the allure of a younger lover. All these forebears may well have left their mark, but Emanuel Lonoff, the writer at the center of *The Ghost Writer*—now obscure, overweight, hidden away with a hopelessly bored wife—most resembles Roth's own sense of how he himself might look in the future. Claire Bloom is no doubt accurate (their relationship was at its height when he was working on the book) when she rejects in her memoir the idea that Lonoff is modeled largely on Malamud or Bellow, insisting that "the writer on whom the portrait was most clearly modeled was Roth himself."[17] Here is a Roth who has subsisted long in isolation deep in the wilderness, who is fat (much like Mickey Sabbath, as portrayed years later), who is caught up in a domestic miasma he can already envision despite his current happiness.

Ever since *Goodbye, Columbus*, all his books save *Portnoy's Complaint* had disappointed him, and he could imagine how he too—much like Lonoff, who has also retreated into "the goyish wilderness of birds and trees where America began and long ago had ended"—might well face eventual literary oblivion. And spending year after year turning sentences around, he could well imagine his own physical transmutation from a Valentino look-alike (as Lonoff is described based on one of his first book flaps) into flabby middle age. Blending irony with a banter typically associated with the likes of Jimmy Durante (who surfaces in the book, too), Lonoff's most memorable monologue is this dour and astute description of a writer's daily drudgery:

> Meanwhile, he was saying to me, "I turn sentences around. That's my life. I write a sentence and then I turn it around. Then I look at it and I turn it around again. Then I have lunch. Then I come back in and write another sentence. Then I have tea and turn the new sentence around. Then I read the two sentences over and turn them both around. Then I lie down on my sofa and think. Then I get up and throw them out and start from the beginning. And if I knock off from this routine for as long as a day, I'm frantic with boredom and a sense of waste."[18]

Roth's books had in recent years nearly all started with longish sentences strung together with the apparent intention of overwhelming the reader with the narrator's uncontainable vitality: "First, foremost, the puppyish, protected upbringing above his father's shoe store in Camden. Seventeen years the adored competitor of that striving, hot-headed shoedog . . . " (*My Life as a Man*). "Temptation comes to me first in the conspicuous personage of Herbie Bratasky, social director, bandleader, crooner, comic, and m.c. . . . " (*The Professor of Desire*).[19]

The Ghost Writer's opening is altogether different: little hint of excess and no evidence of Roth's expository heroes—nothing of Dostoevsky or Céline:

> It was the last daylight hour of a December afternoon more than twenty years ago—I was twenty-three, writing and publishing my first short stories, and like many a *Bildungsroman* hero before me, already contemplating my own massive *Bildungsroman*—when I arrived at his hideaway to meet the great man. The clapboard farmhouse was at the end of an unpaved

> road twelve hundred feet up in the Berkshires, yet the figure who emerged from the study to bestow a ceremonious greeting wore a gabardine suit, a knitted blue tie clipped to a white shirt by an unadorned silver clasp, and well-brushed ministerial black shoes that made me think of him stepping down from a shoeshine stand rather than from the high altar of art.[20]

Nathan Zuckerman arrives at Lonoff's door a troubled young man. In fact, he is in a desperate state, though he reveals none of this openly, all hidden beneath layers of well-honed civility, the courteousness of a well-parented Jewish boy. "You're not so nice and polite in your fiction," Lonoff tells him just before they part, "You're a different person."[21] Nathan is miserable because he fears that his relationship with his father will never recover from his having published a short story built around a sordid family tale. In search now of a surrogate father, he pins his hopes on Lonoff, speculating whether it's possible that the sequestered genius of contemporary American fiction might take him under his wing—claiming him as kin or heir or something of the sort.

Set decades after this visit to Lonoff, Zuckerman—employed here by Roth as a central character for the first time—is reminiscing from his perch as a celebrated author, fearful that eventually he too might, despite his present popularity, become no less obscure than Lonoff. *The Ghost Writer* came in the wake of another dry spell, punctuated by publication of *My Life as a Man* and *The Professor of Desire*—both mostly panned by reviewers and overwhelmingly ignored by readers. Here, too, Roth is engaged in measuring himself against the austere standards of writerly responsibility, with the unruly, unseemly success of *Portnoy's Complaint* (owing at least some of its spectacular achievement to the fact that it was so blatantly unseemly) deemed an act of unforgivable betrayal.

"I know of no other novelist," wrote critic Martin Green

around the same time, "who makes the discussion of books such a valuable part of his story's action—with critical comments quite substantial in themselves and yet not an obstacle to the flow of dramatized life."[22] This is apparent throughout Roth's works, with King Lear resonating in *Sabbath's Theater*, Howard Fast's *Citizen Tom Paine* and Arthur Miller's *Focus* in *I Married a Communist*, Henry James's *Portrait of a Woman* in *Letting Go*, and Conrad's *The Shadow Line* in *Exit Ghost*.

Nowhere is this quality more persistent than in *The Ghost Writer*. Its centerpiece is *The Diary of a Young Girl* by Anne Frank, whose inner workings Roth explores with insight and originality. His description of the book's significance—as text and still more as metaphor—anticipates the work of the best analytical work of critics like Francine Prose and Ruth Franklin. "How," asks Green, "can a writer be so in tune with Mann, Woolf, James, and still be so raucous and raunchy in word and deed? Even more, how can any writer pass so surefootedly and unembarrassedly from one to the other?"[23]

The Ghost Writer is a book about books. In the novel, Roth links Kafka to Anne Frank: "Everything he dreamed in Prague was, to her, real Amsterdam life," he writes in his notes. Here he links Anne Frank to *Little Women* and Lonoff to Isaac Babel and Chekhov. "Well, 'connected' of course isn't the right word," says Zuckerman. "Neither is 'influence.' . . . You are Babel's American cousin." The chapter entitled "Nathan Dedalus" is a nod to Joyce and, arguably, also a reply to Foucault, with its reminder of how Stephen Dedalus's muse could surface only once he rejected family, country, and faith. And while Zuckerman finds more German philosophy on Lonoff's shelves than he had expected, the impact of philosophy on Roth himself is scant. Roth admitted in a taped conversation with Alan Lelchuk in the late 1960s, "I don't have critical language. . . . I'm not a penetrating thinker." He added he could speak about ideas only through a fictional prism.[24] Still, hovering at the edge of *The Ghost Writer*'s pages are echoes of Foucault, not dissimilar from the role of Riesman or Trilling years earlier in the shaping of "Goodbye, Columbus."

What most urgently preoccupies Zuckerman in *The Ghost Writer* is what it feels like to be on the cusp of one's first glimmers of literary success, while also searching for a new father, also a wife, perhaps also a path toward reconciliation with Jews who have recently attacked him for his writing. Here as elsewhere, Roth is wrestling with how to maintain devotion to one's own while living as a free and independent artist.

Zuckerman sets his sights on Lonoff precisely because in short story gems of his—like "Revenge," "Lice," "Eppes Essen" (meaning "something maybe you'll eat")—he discovers characters who find themselves forever paralyzed "by the ruling triumvirate of Sanity, Responsibility, and Self-Respect" while seeking to replicate the expansiveness of Babel's Jew battling on horseback with Cossacks. Yet for Lonoff (much like Babel), even when his characters do battle, there remains, as Roth observes, the ever-paralyzing inhibitions of "the timetable, the rainstorm, the headache, the busy signal, the traffic jam, and, most loyal of all, the last-minute doubt."[25]

Lonoff's staying power in the face of obscurity overwhelms Zuckerman. When Lonoff tells him that there are no fewer than twenty-seven drafts of his short story "Life Is Embarrassing," he is filled with awe, especially once Lonoff adds: "To get it wrong . . . so many times."[26]

Blissful in the presence of a literary genius who takes him seriously, Lonoff describes his incapacity to extricate himself, even momentarily, from his writing desk while ignoring his wife, whose name ironically is Hope. Soon Zuckerman is introduced to a young beauty in the house—all face and hair, all but bodyless—named Amy Bellette, whom Zuckerman will soon decide might be masking her true, astonishing identity: She, he at least tentatively concludes, is the real Anne Frank, which leads him to muse about how their encounter might solve all his dilemmas with his glimpse of a life spent at her side, a gloriously studious life producing his masterpieces while beloved by his parents once again: "Beyond the cushioned windowseats and the colorless cotton curtains tied primly back I could see the bare limbs of big dark maple trees and fields of driven snow. Purity. Serenity. Simplicity. Seclusion. All one's concentration and flamboyance and originality reserved for the grueling, exalted, transcendent calling. I looked around and I thought, This is how I will live."[27]

At dinner, Lonoff toasts Zuckerman, calling him "a wonderful new writer." Lonoff's wife—who carries herself with something of "the obedient air of an aging geisha"—suddenly announces that Lonoff must toss her out and claim Bellette, whom he clearly desires but denies for himself. Responding to the declaration that his needs are of no consequence since his self doesn't really exist, Hope (here arguing with both Lonoff and Foucault) responds without equivocation: "But your self does exist. It has a perfect right to exist—and in the everyday sense!"[28]

The interplay between self and text was central to Roth as he wrote draft after draft of *The Ghost Writer.* Throughout he pondered, as he told Ted Solotaroff in the mid-1970s when just starting work on the book, that the trouble with leading writers of the recent past—he calls them Mailer's generation, including William Styron or Nelson Algren—is that "They live like writers, but don't think like writers, to think through writing. On the other hand, there is Gass, Barth, Barthelme, Coover, who seem to think only through writing, or rather think about writing in a compulsive and consuming way which excludes 'real life.'" He now adds provocatively: "Two different schools of *goyim.* It is the Jews (a rough and leaky generalization—get ready) who seem to me to work from the middle area of consciousness and self-consciousness. No?"[29]

Never in drafts of the book is there any mention of Foucault. Still, as Patrick Hayes convincingly argues, he is one of the book's more intrusive ghosts. Hence, Roth's insistence that a writer's most humble desires remain no less compelling than the demands of art, with Zuckerman turning to James's "The Middle Years" soon after masturbating in Lonoff's study. Here he also tries to write a letter to his father, seeking to make him understand the harsh, intrusive, sometimes nasty obligations of the artist. Standing on top of a volume of James to better spy on Lonoff and Amy, who are speaking of forbidden passion in an upstairs room, Zuckerman hears her beseech him to run away with her somewhere, perhaps to a villa in Florence. Lonoff rejects the idea, assuring her that she'll always be fine if only because "You're the great survivor."[30]

Here, as Roth sees it, literature—independent of lived life—is naturally upended by a moment so real and enthralling that fiction can't expect to compete: "Oh, if only I could have imagined the scene I'd overheard! If only I could invent as presumptuously as real life! If one day I could just *approach* the originality and excitement of what actually goes on!"[31]

What Roth rehearses here is a retort to literary theorists with their insistence that the content of literature exists independent of a writer's life. This, he says, is nonsense: the prospect of capturing extraordinary moments like the conversation between Lonoff and Bellette—with its passion, poignancy, and prospect for betrayal—is just what a writer must always seek to accomplish. Here, too, he recalls his anguish as a young man confronting how to write about matters certain to upset his elders, whom he continues to fear may never forgive his transgressions. How to survive such antagonism, including the possibility of being disowned?

It is now that Zuckerman chances upon a solution: the notion that Amy Bellette—consummate survivor, as described by Lonoff—is the most famous survivor of all. He imagines their falling in love and informing his father he has found a bride. And when his father asks whether she is Jewish, Zuckerman's reply will redeem him forever, this the most definitive proof that he remains the truest, most devoted of Jewish sons: "I met a marvelous woman while I was up in New England, I love her and she loves me. We are going to be married." "Married? But so fast? Nathan, is she Jewish?" "Yes, she is." "But who is she?" "Anne Frank."[32]

It was the novel's third chapter, entitled after much rewriting "Femme Fatale," that caused Roth by far the greatest grief. He composed three drafts written over the course of a single year. In the first, Roth has Amy Bellette acknowledge that she is Anne Frank, saved from death, her fate unknown to her father as well as the rest of the world. Already at work on this section while writing *My Life as a Man*, he admitted to Solotaroff in July 1973 that "The Ann [*sic*] Frank section doesn't work in the book. . . . So it's going to be on its own, someday." It was only once Roth decided that what worked best was for this to be the product of Zuckerman's imagination that *The Ghost Writer* coalesced. Before then, as Roth imagined what transpired, Frank survives, spends a dismal time as a ward in England ("a silent, dark, emaciated girl"), and learns quite by accident that her diary has been published and that her father is alive. At a performance of the Broadway version of the diary, she decides to keep her fate a secret. The role of the Holocaust in contemporary culture—Roth completed the writing of the novel just as the television series *The Holocaust* was aired to great acclaim—cannot, she realizes, become her responsibility: "The improvement of the living was their business, not hers; they could improve themselves, if they should ever be so disposed; and if not, not. Her responsibility was to the dead, if to anyone—to her sister, to her mother, to all the slaughtered schoolchildren who had been her friends. There was her diary's purpose, there was her ordained mission: to restore in print their status as flesh and blood . . . for all the good that would do them."[33]

News of her survival would only serve to undermine the book's impact. He comes to understand that the diary—despite how the public preferred to see it—was in its final version the work of a sexually alert adolescent, a young woman, savvy and ambitious. And with a thinness of Jewishness for which she was nonetheless hunted down: "once a year the Franks sang a harmless Chanukah song, said some Hebrew words, lighted some candles, exchanged some presents—a ceremony lasting about ten minutes—and that was all it took to make them the enemy."[34]

The book's ghosts? Anne Frank, surely. A ghost the world happily if also thoughtlessly embraced. And Henry James, too—amply haunted by ghosts of his own—is here to inspire, if also eventually to abandon. There is also Isaac Babel, having insinuated himself into the bloodstream of American Jewish literature: "Jewish writer . . . with autumn in his heart and spectacles on his nose," with Roth inspired to add, "and blood in his penis."[35] And, of course, the ghost of young Zuckerman writing twenty years later, probably soon after the publication of his raucous, famous novel of the late 1960s, the product of a sensibility starkly in opposition to Lonoff's spartan coda.

The Ghost Writer was justly celebrated as a masterpiece. Never would this book be likened, as would often be the case with his writings, even in celebratory assessments, to "loose baggy monsters" (Henry James's phrase). Here his touch was delicate, intricate, with the book's four chapters blended seamlessly. A slim book packed with a vault full of insights about the workings of artistry, the reception of the Holocaust, and—once again—the relationship between life imagined and life lived.

With the use of Nathan Zuckerman, who surfaced first in *My Life as a Man* and would reappear in another seven books, Roth managed the breakthrough he had wrestled with over the course of a long, exasperating decade. He was now the author of an extraordinary book about books, at once lucid and wise, lyrical and hilarious. And after thinking long and hard since the

1950s about how to write about Anne Frank—the defining Jewish totem of his age—he had finally done so with wisdom and freshness.

Why stick with Zuckerman for so many more books, the last of these—*Exit Ghost*—published in 2007, shortly before he stopped writing altogether? Tarnopol, among the first, he dispensed with quickly. Kepesh, introduced alongside Tarnopol in *My Life as a Man*, returns a few times but always as a consummate isolate, the least humane and most single-minded of all his protagonists: a man devoid of shame, unrestrained by his selfishness.

In stark contrast, Zuckerman is from the start an achingly divided soul, eager for escape from the endless obligations meted out to him at life's beginning yet unable to shunt them aside, sensing their disarming resilience. "Never again to feel such tender devotion—and a desire to escape," Roth jotted down in a draft of what would be the second of his Zuckerman novels, *The Anatomy Lesson*, deleting this line from subsequent versions. No other protagonist of his suffers from these same dilemmas, these at the core of his fictional genius.

In an interview, Roth explained the choice: "From all turbulence, from all his deeds and misdeeds and the distraction of the pursuit of happiness . . . whose personal trials and historic travails come to possess his imagination entirely and feed on the strength of his mental energy." And fittingly, Roth ends the last of his Zuckerman novels, *Exit Ghost*, acutely aware that this long, arduous fictional journey is "Gone for good."[36]

12

"Fuck the Middle Ground"

He knew about solitary confinement from writing alone
in a room virtually every day since his early twenties;
he'd served nearly twenty years of that sentence,
obediently and on his best behavior.

Judith Thurman met Roth soon after the appearance of her justly celebrated *Isak Dinesen: The Life of a Storyteller* in 1982. He wrote her, as he often did when impressed with someone's writing, to acknowledge his admiration if also seeking to explore the prospect of Claire Bloom in a starring role if the biography was ever filmed. (Shortly afterward, *Out of Africa*, based on the biography, was made with Meryl Streep as the lead.) Thurman and Roth would soon become close friends, lovers briefly. Thurman, a splendid essayist as well as biographer and a great admirer of Roth's work, had a deep attachment for him until the end of his life without the need to sideline his clamorous complexity.

It was Thurman who suggested to me that to best understand Roth—particularly when his decisions seemed contrary to what appeared to be most advantageous to him and his coveted reputation as a writer—it was useful to consider Henry James's story "The Figure in the Carpet." This a tale of a feverish, self-seeking book reviewer eager to discover the secret behind the allusive prose of Hugh Vereker, who wants his (well-sequestered) imaginative life to be understood while exasperated with the incapacity of readers to do so. As Vereker explains: "By my little point I mean—what shall I call it?—the particular thing I've written my books most *for*. Isn't there for every writer a particular thing of that sort, the thing that most makes him apply himself, the thing without the effort to achieve which he wouldn't write at all, the very passion of his passion, the part of the business in which, for him, the flame of art burns most intensely? Well, it's *that!*"[1]

Roth's choice to follow up on *The Ghost Writer* with the ribald *Zuckerman Unbound*, featuring a phalanx of sketchily conceived characters—a gorgeous movie star who abandons Zuckerman after a night together to return to her true love Fidel Castro, and a doppelganger with onanistic tendencies—astonished many of his readers, including some close to him.

Solotaroff admitted he was upset with Roth for the decision to publish this jokey, patchy novel in the wake of the triumph of *The Ghost Writer*. Roth responded sharply, rebuking his old friend for advising that Roth should try to situate himself in comfortable "middle ground," the space between the rancor of *Portnoy* and the sublimity of this last book: "The middle ground. FUCK THE MIDDLE GROUND. You don't stand on the middle ground, you crazy Jew bastard. That's why we've come as far as we have. The rest of them back in Essex County straightening teeth. That's the middle ground." Roth described his current project as "a trilogy about dybbuks, doppelgangers, and ghosts. And Newark."[2]

Why he wrote this book, Roth continued, would become apparent only once his next volume appeared. *Zuckerman Unbound*, now finished, left him with, he said here, a feeling comparable to that of a jumbo jet amid "a great sense of motionlessness, nothing moving, but you're moving, six hundred miles an hour no less, and nobody's doing a thing, the plane is just flying—and boy, that's what it was like coming down the home stretch with this book. So nobody's going to tell me anything this time I know. Signed your old and grateful and tired and new new Roth."[3]

The friendship would survive this snag. But Roth's thankfulness to the critic Edward Rothstein, for a warmly appreciative essay about *Zuckerman Unbound* in *New York Review of Books*, went far deeper than mere gratitude. Roth made clear to Rothstein that not only had the critic managed to understand the complex undercurrents of this book—intended as half-baked and packed with nagging doubts about the value of art—but, indeed, the essential components of Roth's sensibility. Roth had set out in the novel, as Rothstein intuited, to measure the salience of art against the turbulence of life, which Roth felt Rothstein appreciated more astutely than nearly any other reader he ever encountered: "*Zuckerman Unbound* is not a sequel to *The Ghost Writer*. The order is reversed. *The Ghost Writer* is the book Zuckerman himself will write, seven years after the pathetic end of this work." Growing directly out of the debacle described in the earlier book, *The Ghost Writer* would come to constitute "Zuckerman's attempt to return to his literary origins, to reestablish his relationship to his past, to understand the making of Art from Life, and revise his vision of his father, and his own moral struggles."[4]

Roth sets out to appear in *Zuckerman Unbound* as a novelist who has lost his way. Pepler, his doppelganger, is sketchy, and the famous actress, a "billboard beauty," Zuckerman himself a "narcissistic cipher." But what Philip Roth is doing, says Rothstein, is something truly substantial: He is telling the story of a book misread, with its own author "chaotically mixing the real with the imagined." All is turned upside down, with *Zuckerman Unbound* intended as "almost sheer artifice."[5]

"The desire to be freed becomes its own enslavement," writes Rothstein. "The prisoner is always lost, always turning back to early family scenes. No matter which way he turns he is face to face with his past, and his fate. . . . The labyrinths of enslavement are narcissistic variations on Kafka's enclosed worlds," with Zuckerman here, as well as in *The Ghost Writer*, left to confront these dreadful dilemmas with the use of literature.[6]

The new novel, says Rothstein, is meant to be incomplete, leaving Zuckerman in a state of desperately wanting more: "his unbinding . . . is not yet completed." Once again, much like Roth's decision to follow *Goodbye, Columbus* with *Letting Go*, then *Our Gang*, *The Breast*, and *The Great American Novel*, Roth—who enjoyed both the attention and the money earned from *Portnoy*—remained intent on shaping his own idiosyncratic writerly path. Criticism from the likes of Irving Howe could recast this trajectory but never the literary marketplace. Capable of drawing a surprisingly large reading audience—though rarely large enough, as it happens, to recoup his advances—he was nonetheless contemptuous of satisfying their inclinations. His heroes, as he often put it, were people in trouble, unwilling or unable to fit in: How, indeed, does a Breast fit in? Or, for that matter, much later Seymour "Swede" Levov of *American Pastoral*, whose downfall is precisely the result of a tireless, lifelong pursuit of compromise and ever-yielding patience, with his tragic fate the price of just such niceness.[7]

It was shortly after the appearance of *Zuckerman Unbound*, while awaiting the publication of *The Anatomy Lesson* in the summer of 1983, that Roth met Ross Miller, eventually the first of his authorized biographers and, long before that, among the most trusted of his friends. Others close to him, like Bernard Avishai, eventually felt a greater distance, at least for a time. Roth's eagerness for companionship was now stoked by mounting disappointment with Bloom, beginning already in the early 1980s—Roth now splitting his time between Connecticut and a flat he shared with Claire in London. He was particularly impatient with what he perceived as an obsequious relationship with her daughter Anna (from Bloom's marriage to Rod Steiger), as well as her anxiety regarding an acting career—once stellar, now skirting to its end because of her age. Roth would soon tell his writer friend David Plante that he was convinced Bloom would kill herself if he ever left her, something he was already thinking about doing.

Miller, a literature professor at the University of Connecticut, was the nephew of playwright Arthur Miller. Well read, self-assured (or at least prone to giving this impression), a scholar of modest achievement, he would emerge as a fixture in Roth's life for the next twenty-five years.

Roth met Miller at a mutual friend's home, and they hit it off immediately. Soon they were spending many hours together at Roth's home in Warren. Miller lived no more than an hour's drive away, and he knew books well. He provided access to the university world, revealing it to a delighted Roth with sardonic, offhanded irreverence. Commenting on a review by Yale scholar Harold Bloom of Roth's *The Prague Orgy*, published in 1985, soon after *The Anatomy Lesson*, he wrote Roth: "It does smell a bit of old farts (the inevitable result of hanging around a university campus)."[8]

Miller could be funny, quick-witted, and congenial; for years to come, he would be an unceasing source of encouragement to Roth. Like Roth, he was unhappy at home, and like Roth, he had little regard for Arthur Miller's work. Long an obsession of his, Ross Miller was certain that his famous uncle possessed far less talent than his own father, Kermit, whose life was stymied by the burden of the family business. Still late in life, Ross would complain—he did so to biographer John Lahr, at work on a book on Arthur Miller published in 2022—of the shameful excuse given by his uncle for missing his bar mitzvah: Arthur claimed that, as an artist, he was too busy to take the time to come. By the time Miller met Roth, Ross was at work on a memoir (never published) called "Relations," attacking his uncle, whom he held responsible for destroying his father's life: "A mutual cannibalizing of each other's experiences that is both the source of Arthur's art and the slow paralysis of my father's ambition" is how he summed up the backdrop to his uncle's dubious achievements.[9]

Shuttling back and forth between London and the United States, Roth, often alone in Connecticut or with Bloom in England or elsewhere, was increasingly reliant on Ross's company. For years before Roth eventually dropped him as his authorized biographer—furious about his lack of initiative and dismissive comments about Roth to friends and relatives—he considered Miller one of his closest local friends, alongside the physician C. H. Huvelle and writer William Styron. Roth described Miller in a letter to Joel Conarroe as "Very quick, smart, well-read, and with good, strong, reliable taste."[10]

From the start, Miller lavished Roth with fulsome compliments. Reassuring him soon after their meeting regarding *The Anatomy Lesson*—which Roth was still writing, as he wrestled with doubts—that it was "moving and emotionally real." He added that, in contrast to the first two Zuckerman books, both devoted to "construction of self," this one was built around life's "reconstruction"—namely, "the stuff of adulthood." "There is a terrific heat to this work," he wrote, "communicated above and beyond the words. I value it enormously." By the summer of 1985, Roth was sending him tapes of *The Counterlife*.[11]

All the while, as described in great length in *The Anatomy Lesson*, Roth suffered from frequent, excruciating back pain of the sort that would afflict him, on and off, for the rest of his life. There was also a diagnosis of severe arterial disease in 1982, with the medicine prescribed rendering him for a time exhausted as well as impotent, and an emergency operation for peritonitis. Put on a salt-free diet, Roth would eventually undergo quadruple bypass surgery, then a terrible, prolonged bout with Halcion withdrawal.

Roth built much of this into *The Anatomy Lesson*, set amid

the Watergate hearings of 1973. It is a study of self-imposed incarceration with the text haunted once again by Kafka: "If you can't get out of yourself," he writes in a letter to Updike after a beautifully wrought review of *The Anatomy Lesson*, "you can't be a writer because the personal ingredient is what gets you going, and if you hang on to the personal ingredient any longer, you'll disappear right up your asshole." Much of *The Anatomy Lesson* is Roth's response to Howe's dreadful review, nearly ten years in the past. As Updike enthusiastically describes the book, it "unrolls with a meditated savagery both fascinating and repellent, self-indulgent yet somehow sterling, adamant, pure in the style of high modernism, that bewitchment to all the art-stricken young of the Fifties."[12]

It is a story of loss, a lament for the disappearance of "His health, his hair, and his subject": "gone—his birthplace the burnt-out landscape of a racial war and the people who'd been giants to him dead. . . . Without a father and a mother and a homeland, he was no longer a novelist. No longer a son, no longer a writer."[13]

It was now not only the burned remnants of Newark that Roth sought to leave behind. His next book, *The Counterlife*, which he had already begun writing in 1984, he viewed at the time as no less than an effort at leaving fiction behind altogether. "I'm <u>not</u> thinking about myself! Fifty-one years I've spent thinking about myself. Here I don't think about myself. It's all I've ever wanted!" Roth may well have felt pressed to explore other inspirations in the wake of Martin Amis's take—cruel yet the judgment of someone he could not readily dismiss—that he had "lost the capacity to surprise." Plante records in his diary in late November 1984, during a trip they took together to Israel—one of several Roth took to research the new book—that his intent was to abandon literature. "It is shit," he declares to Plante, "it's shit literature!" His intent was to produce finally something "equal to the experience," with its focus on Israel that now, in the 1980s, was akin to Prague of the '70s, a place where "everything matters."[14]

For years to come, Roth would list *The Counterlife* among his nonfictional books, as truthful as anything he had produced, notwithstanding the incompatibility of the various narratives. To his beloved Bucknell teacher Mildred Martin, he characterizes it "as perhaps the best book I'll ever be able to write."[15]

Plante describes in his diary in one of hundreds of handwritten volumes produced over the years—now housed in the Berg Collection of New York Public Library—a late 1984 trip he took with Roth to Israel. A talented miniaturist as well as a novelist and diarist, Plante's tripartite volume *Difficult Women: A Memoir of Three*—with its biting, wryly affectionate depictions of writers Jean Rhys, Sonia Orwell, and Germaine Greer—remains a classic of sorts. Roth admired Plante as a writer, particularly his capacity, alien to Roth's own temperament, to manage to unreservedly adore. And Plante felt just this way toward Roth.

Roth comes to Israel and to his prospective book set there, as Roth explains to Plante, because "my life as it is offers me nothing to write about." He speaks with Plante "with pain, of our paucity of reality." It is with eagerness, with a kind of longing, that he talks of "the real experiences of the people we meet" in Israel. Captured by Plante is Roth's acute anxiety as he begins to weave together the disparate parts of *The Counterlife*, eventually among the most tightly wound and complexly assembled of his books. Here, too, as Hermione Lee has observed regarding Roth's approach to his books, "In the limbo before starting each book he would be subdued and despondent; as the work took shape, he would seem much more ebullient and outward looking."[16]

At lunches with Plante before their travel, Roth confessed feeling miserably estranged from Bloom, with whom he had less and less to speak about. But he seemed still more perplexed as to where to go as a writer. "I've written," he says, "about sex, about women, about being a Jew. I want some new subject." Plante admitted surprise and admiration for Roth's candor, his willingness to acknowledge some of the most unpleasant aspects of his character, even estrangement from his own work. Stymied after having written two chapters of the new book—at this juncture the story of a "goy" who travels to Israel—Roth now invited Plante to travel with him to Israel in November 1984 to watch Plante's reactions while gathering material for the book.[17]

Once the book was completed, Roth openly acknowledged these motivations: "As a writer I'd mined my past to its limits. . . . I wanted to hear a new voice . . . to break away."[18] At about the same time, Roth was informed of heart problems. He now introduced fear of dying into nearly every conversation, as his Connecticut lover Maletta Pfeiffer recalls.[19] This, too, may well have prompted him to accomplish something he felt was truly extraordinary: a book on a major scale of the sort he long aspired to achieve but never felt he had sufficiently mastered.

"Jewishness comes up in every conversation I have with him," recorded Plante in his diary in May 1982, "and always within five minutes."[20]

Roth wrote Bloom from Connecticut in the summer of 1976: "Tonight after dinner I took a walk in the last light. A skunk crossed my path. Or, as the skunk would have it, a Jew crossed my path. We gave each other plenty of room—given the folklore about each of us, we were wise to."[21]

Roth cultivated his Jewish identity ever more attentively during his years in England beginning in the early 1980s. And he was known to argue, sometimes vociferously, at dinner parties when confronted with sentiments he judged too anti-Israel, this despite his own dovish inclinations. Perhaps in response, he now grew a thick beard and befriended the expatriate painter R. B. Kitaj, whose fierce Jewish preoccupations would eventually crystallize into his own curious, obsessive book *First Diasporist Manifesto*.

Roth would come to be convinced that British antisemitism was pervasive, if also often sequestered behind glacially polite deportment. But it detonated when Israel was deemed in the wrong. Proof of the resilience of such bias, as he saw it, was the pertinence of Shylock in the English imagination—this a milieu disdainful of displays of emotion, yet all but encouraged it where antisemitism remained. He writes Kitaj ("Dear old Jew" is how he addresses him), soon after his return home, regarding his London life which "I've come to loathe . . . full of loneliness and cultural deprivation that nearly drove me mad in the end."[22]

At the same time, Ira Nadel's observation regarding Roth's time in England may also be true: Here, suggests Nadel, "Roth felt uncomfortable because he was generally comfortable. 'Nothing drives me crazy here,' which itself may well have encouraged him to focus his attention on British 'hypocritical politeness' regarding Jews."[23]

His sense of displacement, of irreversible foreignness, he captures in *The Counterlife*'s depiction of Zuckerman's funeral, where his brother Henry is accosted by a disgruntled man of fifty who looks, sounds, and acts much like Roth himself: "tall, thin . . . wearing gold-rimmed bifocals and a gray hat, looking from the conservative cut of his clothes as though he might be a broker—or perhaps even a rabbi."[24] He has none of the smooth, easy mannerisms of the English wellborn. Without bothering with an introduction, he launches into an attack on the eulogy just delivered by Zuckerman's editor, followed by a lengthy disquisition on how he had long assumed Zuckerman would die of something excruciating, a humiliating disease like cancer, not a death on the operating table: "The cancer deaths are horrifying. That's what I would have figured him for. Wouldn't you? Where was the rawness and the mess? . . . I really had him down for cancer. The works. The catastrophe-extravaganza, the seventy-eight-pound death, with the stops all pulled out. A handful of hairless pain howling for the needle."[25]

Roth's turn to Israel in *The Counterlife* and then *Operation Shylock* was a startling choice. Scarcely had the country preoccupied him before. Roth had spent time there in 1963, invited to attend a gathering of Jewish writers, American and Israeli, and his presence had sparked considerable interest because of the controversy surrounding *Goodbye, Columbus.* But he came away with little more than a photograph of himself beside Israel's prime minister David Ben-Gurion (that his parents proudly displayed in their living room) and eventually a description of Alexander Portnoy's sexual impotence when confronted with the prospect of sex with two Israeli women—one looking strikingly like his mother.

"The Holy Land is real and full of Jews," he writes Ted Solotaroff on his return from the visit. "The cops are Jews, the fags are Jews . . . so are the truck-drivers and the dishwashers. And the place is full of dummies and blonds with big tits." Israel had been a topic of passionate—in Roth's mind, laughably excessive—preoccupation for his father, who championed it with a fervor comparable to his loathing for Lyndon Johnson or Reagan. Before Roth went to Israel to research *The Counterlife*, he had visited the country with Claire Bloom, accompanying her on performances, but he seemed to have been little impressed with it (though he gained good friends there, including journalist Amos Elon and Bedouin expert Clinton Bailey). The extent to which he had valued Israel previously he likely put into the unfettered mouth of Cousin Essie in *The Counterlife:* "You know why I give to Israel? . . . Because in Israel you hear the best anti-Semitic jokes."[26]

The primary reason to focus his attention now on Israel, or so he told Plante, had little to do with the country itself. It had far more to do with the prospect of a drastic change regarding his future as a writer. *The Counterlife* is a sustained exploration of what it means to turn around one's life: "I think what you've done is colossal," Zuckerman tells his brother Henry, who has suddenly abandoned his life as an upper-middle-class New Jersey dentist for that of a West Bank settler deep in the hills of Judea. "An exchange of existences like this—it's like after a great war. . . . I don't minimize the scale of this thing."[27]

He read little about Israel before, according to David Rieff, his editor at Farrar, Straus and Giroux, who worked closely with Roth on *The Counterlife*. Roth greatly admired his good friend Bernard Avishai's book *The Tragedy of Zionism* and had many conversations about Israel with Clinton Bailey as well as Amos Elon, Yael Dayan, novelist Aharon Appelfeld and a small cluster of others. And it was now that he started voraciously reading about the country, parceling out his time with the greatest care. "When he wasn't writing or fucking he was reading" is how Rieff has described him. "He read like a professional, only reading what he had to. Only much later, once he retired, would he permit himself to read Lucretius."[28]

Clinton Bailey in particular served him in these years, observed Rieff, as little less than his Virgil, his horse whisperer. He gave Roth a vibrant insider's guide to the byways of Israel, its Arabs, and the interplay between Judaism and Zionism. Bailey, who had served as an adviser for the Israeli government, recalls having rehearsed with Roth some of the ideas that went into the most ribald section of *The Counterlife*, where Zuckerman encounters an erstwhile yeshiva student—a fervent fan of Zuckerman's writing—intent on sabotaging the airplane carrying the writer back from Israel to England to bring an end to the Jewish obsession with the Holocaust. Roth and Bailey met at a dinner party in Jerusalem, saw each other often during a research stint of Bailey's in Oxford, and remained in touch throughout the writing of the novel. They grew particularly close sharing, as Bailey described it to me, the pleasure and fascination both had for extramarital affairs.[29]

Crucial to Roth's decision to bring Zuckerman to Israel was his awareness that "I lead a tidy life, but I have a strong taste for disorder and its enticements, and there's plenty here." From the start he found himself uninterested in the viewpoints of left-liberal friends, like those of journalist Amos Elon, fascinated instead by those on the radical right. These he thought were better attuned to the sort of chaos he sought to explore. Plante describes Roth's excitement after meeting a Hebron fanatic: "He said he was exhausted but fired up from what had been the most exciting day of his life. An extraordinary man, a very right-wing man, had taken him to a settlement then, with a gun in the glove compartment, had driven him around the West Bank in his car."[30] The experience shaped his description in *The Counterlife* of the far-right figure Mordecai Lippman, who has captured the heart of Henry Zuckerman: "He hasn't only a Jewish gun, he has a Jewish mouth—remnants even of a Jewish brain. There is now so much antagonism between Arab and Jew that even a child would understand that the best thing is to keep them apart—so Mr. Lippman drives into Arab Hebron wearing his pistol. Hebron!"[31]

He would find calmer, less obviously unreasonable figures on the political right disappointing. Israel Harel, a leader of the religious Zionist settler's movement with whom he spent a day at the West Bank settlement Ofra, failed to impress him because he didn't sound like a wild man. "He had a sense of humor, was totally without self-consciousness," writes Plante in his diary—these qualities Plante saw as beguiling; Roth did not. Impressions of Harel would never make their way into *The Counterlife*. In Tel Aviv he meets with another right-wing politician who, like Harel, disappointed him: "I want the mad fanaticism of the man I saw yesterday on the West Bank."[32]

The need to lose oneself, Zuckerman muses in the book, is no less essential for a writer than for anyone else: "Certainly a life of writing books is a trying adventure in which you cannot find out where you *are* unless you lose your way." And Henry's decision to embrace one of the rawest forms of Judaism may have had, suggests Roth, less to do with its beliefs than with the overpowering prospect of uprooting him from a preexisting, stifling past that he now found "old, suffocating, self-strangulating." Judea—with its rocks, and fanatics, and endless rancor—was his brother's mode of escape.[33]

Roth's description of a West Bank fanatic provides a particularly vivid example of why *The Counterlife* works as well as it does in its interplay between the counterintuitive and the concrete. In a book that has its hero, Nathan Zuckerman, die on the operating table while seeking to remedy his impotence, then, in a separate thread, go to Israel to confront his brother—suddenly a fanatical Zionist—and later contemplate life in a bucolic corner of the English countryside beside a comely wife and child, it is also a fiction of consummate realism.

The portrait of the fanatic in the Hebron Hills, Mordecai Lippman, Roth insisted was based on the far-right lawyer Elyakim Haetzni. Still, many of the meticulously outlined details in this section of the novel are identical to Jewish Hebron's charismatic leader Moshe Levinger. Indeed, it may well be the most perceptive description of this volcanically intelligent, explosive figure ever written, starting with his appearance: "Lippman's very looks seemed to be making a point about colliding forces. His wide-set, almond-shaped, slightly protuberant eyes, though a gentle milky blue, proclaimed, unmistakably, STOP." Before the start of the Friday night Sabbath meal, he shows Zuckerman the books his German-born parents brought to Palestine (Levinger's parents moved from Germany in the 1930s); the depiction of Lippman's charming, if also fiercely determined American-born wife is a persuasively lifelike portrait of Miriam Levinger, a heroine of Israel's far right:

> And the voice that dominated now was [his wife's] Ronit's, leading with her folksingerish, fervent soprano. Singing in the

> Sabbath, Ronit looked as contented with her lot as any woman could be, her eyes shining with love for a life free of Jewish cringing, deference, diplomacy, apprehension, alienation, self-pity, self-satire, self-mistrust, depression, clowning, bitterness, nervousness, inwardness, hypercriticalness, hypertouchiness, social anxiety, social assimilation—a way of life absolved, in short, of all the Jewish "abnormalities," those peculiarities of self-division whose traces remained imprinted in just about every engaging Jew I knew.[34]

When in my early twenties, I had a Sabbath meal at the Levingers' table. I recall still with unease Miriam Levinger's contempt for everything associated with the diaspora—including me—and remember her husband declaring many of the same words that Zuckerman recounts in *The Counterlife:*

> This is the Middle East, these are Arabs—paper is worthless. There is no paper deal to be made with the Arabs. Today in Bethlehem an Arab tells me that he dreams of Jaffa and how one day he will return. . . . That's what this man was telling me—he will go back, even if it takes him the two thousand years that it took the Jews. And you know what I tell *him?* I tell him, "I respect the Arab who wants Jaffa," I tell him, "Don't give up your dream, dream of Jaffa, go ahead; and someday, if you have the power, even if there are a *hundred* pieces of paper, you will take it from me by force."[35]

Whether or not Roth encountered Levinger, his capacity to capture the likes of him with such vibrant accuracy—and after only the briefest, most fleeting experiences with the Israeli right—is further proof of his uncanny ability to describe the outer limits of rage and to do so with skill and intimacy.

This raw West Bank reality is contrasted starkly in the novel's final chapter, "Christendom," with life for Zuckerman back home in England, where he and his wife are building a house beside a quietly flowing river with its towpath and ageless greenery. In the explosive end to the novel, it is Zuckerman who comes to recognize that this peaceful life is a farce, a denial of the inescapably bracing if terrible lessons he learned at the austere Judean encampment: namely, that Jews are to history what Eskimos are to snow. To remind Jews of this, and for Jews to "protect themselves against the pastoral myth of life before Cain and Abel," is itself the timeless wisdom of circumcision: "Circumcision is everything that the pastoral is not and, to my mind, reinforces what the world is about, which isn't strifeless unity. . . . The heavy hand of human values falls upon you right at the start, marking your genitals as its own."[36] Agor—the name Roth gives the West Bank settlement he visits—is a dreadful, spare, intellectually grim reality, but worse still, insists Roth, are the vapid promises of a strifeless idyll beside an English towpath.

The Counterlife is, among its many other compelling features, a study of theatricality, what it means to live with life's multiple masks, none simply a sham yet none the whole story. Janet Malcolm—one of the most bitingly perceptive English-language critics of her time—began reading *The Counterlife* soon after its appearance, having just met Roth at a dinner party. (Their meeting led to a friendship of several years.) She wrote him, "Maybe the most brilliant of your books," adding that she was now prompted to read all of the Zuckerman books in succession—this, "an important literary experience for me, and, as you know better than anyone, such experiences are as rare and precious as falling in love, and sort of come down to the same thing."[37]

Divided into five sections, *The Counterlife* is, as Roth saw it, Pentateuch-like in its ambition to depict a kaleidoscope of familial and tribal responses to life's provocations. Unsurprisingly, after being lavished with praise from Robert Alter (who had often criticized Roth's more "manic" work, as he put it in a letter to Rieff), he was scandalized. Such praise, he insisted, constituted little less than the "deballing" of Zuckerman. "That's what their fucking approval is all about," he wrote. "I only earned the right to write it because I wrote the other books. Without smelling the shit, you don't have the right to come on sane and brainy and generous. . . . I could have been doing this from the beginning. But nothing would ever have been at stake."[38]

Here, once again, is Roth's stunning capacity to turn talk—this novel too is built around persistent talk—into something insistently dramatic while acknowledging its limitations. He seems willing to challenge himself on all fronts, to lay bare all his limits as a writer, son, and Jew. The chapter on Nathan's brother's retreat into the hills of the West Bank has him declaring this to Zuckerman: "Beyond all your profundities, beyond the Freudian lock you put on every single person's life, there is another world, a larger world, a world of ideology, of politics, of history—a world of things larger than the kitchen table! You were in it tonight; a world defined by *action*, by *power*, where how you wanted to please Momma and Poppa *simply doesn't matter!*"[39]

13

Facts

The Counterlife won the National Book Critics Circle Award (as well as a National Jewish Book prize), celebrated even by postmodernists like William Gass, usually critical of Roth's work. And while Roth recoiled at the sudden embrace by Robert Alter, whom he typecast as a critic of conventional Jewish taste, he nonetheless felt he had finally produced a book he was entirely pleased with.

He also declared to friends—this in 1986—how pleased he was, at least for now, with Claire Bloom, confident that theirs was a lifelong union. True, he continued to detest her daughter Anna (he'd been friendly with her for a while but eventually was bitterly estranged). Yet the relationship with Bloom now felt resilient, as he actively helped guide her career as she entered middle age.

There were, of course, other women. Among the more important was Minette Marrin, a BBC radio writer-producer, whose voice—alongside Janet Hobhouse's—would help inspire the sound of Zuckerman's English beauty Maria in *The Counterlife* ("She speaks in the most mesmeric tones, . . . the voice that I have to caress me"). And his relationship with Barbara Jakobson, begun when Roth was in his late twenties, continued; long married to a successful stockbroker, Jakobson found Roth the funniest man she had ever met. She likened him in a conversation with me to a lifelong soulmate, the two meeting regularly in Connecticut when Claire was away. Also New Jersey born, she felt a deep kinship to Roth and remained proud, well into her eighties, to have been one of the few Jews he found sexually alluring. It was as a sister that he portrayed her in *My Life as a Man:* "Electrolysis on the upper lip and along the jawbone, plastic surgery on the nose and chin, and the various powders and paints available at the drugstore have transformed her into a sleek, sensual type, still Semitic, but rather more the daughter of a shah than a shopkeeper. . . . This woman today is the gregarious glamor girl of America's most glamorous city."[1]

And starting in 1976, at much the same time as he embarked on his courtship of Bloom, Roth began a relationship—the longest and, by his own account, his most sexually explosive—with Swedish-born physical therapist Maletta Pfeiffer: tall, blond, large-breasted, keenly sexual, while also tender and motherly. Eventually she would inspire two characters in *Sabbath's Theater*, most memorably Drenka: "her shape . . . reminiscent of those clay figurines molded circa 2000 B.C., fat little dolls with big breasts and big thighs unearthed all the way from Europe down to Asia Minor and worshiped under a dozen different names as the great mother of the gods."[2]

Jakobson told me of Roth's great fear that Claire might discover their liaison, attentive publicly to the societal norms that he fiercely excoriated in his fiction. He long admired those like his father—the sort of men so often celebrated in his books—capable of remaining stalwart family men, steady in their devotion to wife and daily grind and who returned home after a long day's work tempted by neither drink nor extramarital sex. But, of course, he also keenly distrusted monogamy as unnatural, the staging ground for repression or dissimulation. Nonetheless, when soon after the appearance of *The Counterlife* Roth arranged to interview Primo Levi for the *New York Times* (they had recently met in London), he described Levi admiringly, if also inaccurately, as happily married. This aspect of Levi's life clearly moved him, seeing it as an all-but-impossible feat that made Levi all the more admirable.

Indeed, in the *New York Times* essay, Roth lavished considerable attention on how Levi lived so amicably in the same apartment of his childhood, in a Turin neighborhood of "bourgeois solidity," an area much resembling New York's Upper West Side, sharing the flat with his wife as well as his mother. His mother-in-law lived nearby, his son was next door, and his daughter a few blocks away. "I don't personally know of another contemporary writer . . . [so] intimately entangled. . . . He may well be the most thoroughly adapted to the totality of the life around him." Rooted firmly in place, in family, and labor, Levi appeared to Roth as a blessed man—indeed, something of a "holy man," as Roth may well have described him.[3]

Enthralled by Levi's workday employment at a paint factory until his retirement, Roth requested a tour of the plant, much to the Italian Jew's bemusement. Levi had left his management role years earlier, as soon as he was financially able to do so. And when Levi said to Roth that once liberated from Auschwitz he threw himself into work largely because of a crippling shyness around women, Roth contradicted him, insisting that Levi was downplaying what was undoubtedly a noble effort on his part to reclaim the real meaning of the word *Arbeit* from the horrific cynicism attributed to it at Auschwitz. To this Levi disagreed: "I think that *at that time* work was for me a sexual compensation rather than a real passion." Roth did manage

Roth found in Primo Levi a kindred spirit, a brother of sorts.
(Courtesy of the Philip Roth Personal Library, Newark Public Library)

to extract an acknowledgment that his time at the factory "kept me in touch with the world of real things."[4]

Overlooked by Roth was the discomfort shown by Levi whenever the topic of his invalid mother—by now, paralyzed by a stroke—was raised or, for that matter, his cool, at best correct relations with his wife. Family home life, Levi admitted to Roth, deprived him of adventure of the sort he had experienced in "the awful mess of a Europe swept by war." His time in Auschwitz and his perilous travel home after liberation he remembered in "Technicolor": "Family, home, factory are good things in themselves, but they deprived me of something that I still miss: adventure." What the two seem to have most appreciated regarding each other was their elusive, undeniable Jewishness. When Roth queried whether, despite Levi's obvious "rootedness," he felt something akin to a "grain of mustard" because he was a Jew, Levi turned the tables deftly: "If I may return to the question: don't you feel yourself, you, Philip Roth, 'rooted' in your country and at the same time 'a mustard grain'? In your books I perceive a sharp mustard flavor."[5]

Months later, when Roth learned of Levi's suicide—some continued to believe it might have been accidental—Roth felt certain it was intentional, and he was devastated. Perhaps it was this he was thinking of when he wrote this much-cited passage several years later in *American Pastoral:* "You get them wrong before you meet them, while you're anticipating meeting them; you get them wrong while you're with them; and then you go home to tell somebody else about the meeting and you get them all wrong again. . . . It's getting them wrong that is living, getting them wrong and wrong and wrong and then, on careful reconsideration, getting them wrong again. That's how we know we're alive; we're wrong."[6]

Knee surgery in March 1987, shortly before Levi's death, left Roth in great pain, for which he was prescribed Halcion, already banned in England because of its potential side effects. Its impact on Roth was horrible: he suffered well into the summer, asking Rieff to watch over him when in a New York hotel as he found himself contemplating suicide. Bloom was, it seems, too self-absorbed or too overwhelmed to care properly for him, and she herself depicted this dilemma not altogether differently in her memoir *Leaving a Doll's House.* Whatever the circumstances, Roth requested that Bernard Avishai come help him, the first night together with Conarroe. Avishai, who himself had gone through a terrible experience with Halcion, remained with Roth for two more days, locked in a room in the Connecticut house as Roth experienced excruciating withdrawal.[7]

Avishai lost his father to suicide (and his mother to psychosis) and managed in adulthood, as he came to understand it, to find a fatherly protector in Irving Howe and something of a brother in Roth. Much as Roth joked with Albert Goldman years earlier, he and Avishai often acted the role of faux-Yiddish comedians (without, however, Goldman's quirks or jealousy). Avishai sensed that Roth saw him as someone who managed to combine rebelliousness with solidity—as well as a sexual constancy—qualities that Roth admired while also upending them time and again in his own life.

A deeply thoughtful intellectual, if also sufficiently impetuous to take risks (his 1985 book *The Tragedy of Zionism* derailed a promising university career), he was supported by Roth in his decision to leave his first wife and marry the literary scholar Sidra DeKoven Ezrahi—a beautiful woman whom Roth greatly admired. Roth believed, saying this to Avishai, that he had finally found a comparable combination of qualities in Bloom, a woman of great achievement with a life of her own, who showed herself no less voracious sexually than she was intellectually.

Roth's close friendship with Avishai, much like his other relationships with men as well as women, waxed and waned. "The Zuckerman years, that is when I knew him best," Avishai told me.[8] The friendship, which later reignited, tapered off for a time when Roth discovered Ross Miller, whose support proved invaluable. Roth, now cured from his dependence on Halcion, patched together almost immediately the first bits of his next book, *The Facts: A Novelist's Autobiography*, written quickly and published just a year later. This was his first sustained work of nonfiction.

To Miller—as with Bloom, lovers, editors, and others—Roth read aloud sections of the new book that, as he expressed in its first pages addressed to Nathan Zuckerman, was an exercise in turning himself "into but the boy I had been when I went off to college. . . . I suppose I wanted to return to the point when the launch was the launch of a more ordinary Roth and, at the same time, to reengage those formative encounters, to reclaim the earliest struggles, to get back to that high-spirited moment when the manic side of my imagination took off and I became my own writer."[9]

And much like the backdrop to *The Counterlife*, Roth admits here, too, that he found himself exhausted by fiction's "masks, disguises, distortions, and lies," abandoning in this book "imaginative fury" for the prospect of revisiting life as it was actually experienced.[10]

The book's description of Roth's family was "surprisingly (suspiciously) mellow" as a reviewer in the *London Review of Books* put it.[11] This then followed up by tales mostly of unhappiness. True, he acknowledged, his years at Bucknell and then the University of Chicago were some of his happiest, but these were followed by persecution of his work by Jews, early literary promise all but snuffed out by a witch-demon, and the circus surrounding the reception of *Portnoy's Complaint*, with the widespread belief that its masturbatory confessions were autobiographical.

Reviews of *The Facts* were mostly desultory: "This is a miserable and frequently distasteful collection of facts"—the stingingly harsh critique perhaps a byproduct of exasperation with a writer whose books often veered off jarringly in unexpected directions.[12] Certainly, *The Facts* is an odd book, with chapter headings jauntily named after television shows like *All in the Family;* even the book's title is likely meant as an allusion to a catchphrase from the then-popular police drama *Dragnet.* Stranger still was its lengthy epilogue attributed to Zuckerman himself, not Roth, where his best-known protagonist beseeches the author not to publish it.

There is, to be sure, much poignancy here, especially the portrait of Herman, a prelude to Roth's *Patrimony,* written shortly afterward. But largely absent is the vitality of his other books, except in the lengthy retort at the book's end where Zuckerman lays bare—more bitingly than the book's severest critic—its weakest underpinnings.

Enumerated in the epilogue's more than thirty pages is the text's timidity, its evasions, and above all the unlikeliness that the author of *Portnoy's Complaint* emerged out of the peaceful family depicted here. The near absence of his mother in the book is coupled with this absurdly brief portrait: "This image of an utterly refined, Jewish Florence Nightingale . . . seems to me particularly striking for all it appears to omit." The paucity of anything beyond the barest hint of adolescent struggle is said to be simply unbelievable: "Because if there wasn't a struggle, then it just doesn't seem like Philip Roth to me. It could be anybody, almost."[13]

Questioned here—and something Roth found intolerable, well into old age—is why he had been so smitten with his first wife. And isn't it likely that Maggie was less heinous than he tended to portray her? "There were obviously times . . . that you enjoyed her and found her appealing." And criticized harshly is Roth's treatment of his lover of the 1960s, Ann Mudge, one of many crucial to his life story but rendered here incomprehensibly. By far the most incoherent of all, declares Zuckerman, is Roth himself: "the least completely rendered of all your protagonists."[14]

Once their friendship ended, Miller would level similar criticisms. Roth complained bitterly about this betrayal, complaints included in the many hundreds of pages of memos sent first to Hermione Lee, then to Blake Bailey. The similarity between the details in the final chapter of the book—"a long epistolary epilogue that lifts *The Facts* into the liberating uncertainties and revisionary cross-references of fiction," as John Updike put it—and the charges eventually aimed against Roth by Miller is striking. It serves to make Miller's claim, related to friends after his break with Roth, that he was the actual author of the book's epilogue less preposterous than it might first appear.[15]

Yet there is little likelihood that Roth, no less obsessive than his character Lonoff regarding the precision of all he wrote, would publish sentences written by someone else. (So assiduous was Roth that all he wrote, starting with *The Anatomy Lesson* in the early 1980s, was polished—this including even memos to his biographers produced after his retirement—by a superb copyeditor, Roslyn Schloss.) And nothing published by Miller contains the verve or narrative power of this chapter. It is conceivable that some of the ideas in the epilogue were the result of conversations the two had at the time, which Miller might have construed as authorship of a sort. Roth wrote the book mostly while in England, and Miller, who was in regular letter communication with him at the time, may have forwarded some of these ideas, but it's inconceivable that anyone except Roth wrote it.

The most delicate issue raised in the book's epilogue concerns Roth's reticence about his mother, Bess. Her death at seventy-seven of a heart attack in 1981 he admits never ceased to overwhelm, but he fails to say much more than this: "Even though it might not be apparent to others, I think that subterraneanly my mother's death is very strong in all this."[16] He begins the celebration of his father in *Patrimony*, at which he was at work at the same time, with Herman's desolation over the death of Bess, but there, too, she is little more than an apparition—her absence intensely mourned, yet shadowy.

It was nonfiction, he told himself, that interested him after the completion of *The Facts* and *Patrimony*. Roth includes in notes he prepared while working on *Operation Shylock*, published shortly afterward in 1993, the assertion that his most recent books should be seen as "autobiographies in four acts." In longhand, he describes them as exercises in rebellion, the result of a new loathing for the fiction that has so defined his life and fame. "Don't want to be a writer & haven't wanted to for years." Here he adds that he remains unconvinced his breakdown resulted from Halcion, suggesting instead that it may have been a consequence of repulsion to his former life: "The work itself. The stupid celebrity. The readings, misreadings."[17]

Deception, published in 1990, a year before *Patrimony*, is an exploration of the basic rudiments of nonfiction. It is also intended as a study of the fetishism of talk as well as the relationship between fiction and adultery. Built of pre- and postcoital conversations, explored are themes close to Roth's heart: betrayal, secrecy, Jews, England, Jews in England, the chasm between a love affair and marriage.

It is not sex, which occurs offstage, but rather the inappropriateness at the heart of all good fiction that surfaces here as a persistent preoccupation. "Swift, elegant, disturbing" is how novelist Fay Weldon summed it up in the *New York Times.* "He is very brave," she pronounced Roth; "this literary navel-gazing is a risky occupation."[18]

That it enraged Bloom when he gave her the finished manuscript was unsurprising. She vomited on its pages when she saw herself identified as the dull woman the narrator had married (Bloom and Roth weren't yet wed at the time), which Roth agreed to remove while insisting that it was all a fiction. Bloom charges, "You do not go off to your studio to work—you go off to your studio to fuck! You are having an affair with someone in your studio." Roth responds, "The only woman in my studio is the woman in my novel."[19]

When interviewed by a reporter once the book appeared and pressed to say whether the women depicted in *Deception* were modeled on real liaisons, he grabbed a newspaper and, after scanning it quickly, blurted out the first female name he spotted: "Sarah Lyall. Suppose I say to you it's Sarah Lyall. Once you know that, what do you know? All you know is gossip, which is to know nothing."[20]

Perhaps not quite nothing. The inspiration for the novel's enticing woman was Minette Marrin—former BBC *Saturday Review* host and longtime columnist for London's conservative newspaper the *Telegraph*. A controversialist among UK feminists, a self-proclaimed Tory in an intelligentsia overwhelmingly left leaning, she was a blond woman of considerable fluency and wit. At the end of his many meetings with her in his rented studio, as Roth told Blake Bailey, "I would feverishly try to remember and write down the most elegantly succulent of her loculations." It was Marrin who was his inspiration for the novel's best lines. Take, for example, her retort to Roth's insistence that in his book she doesn't "exist as only you." Her reply: "Then who was that in your studio with my legs over your shoulders?"[21]

And it is likely that it was Marrin who subjected Roth, as described in the book, to a mock-feminist tribunal. "Can you explain to the court why you hate women?" Roth is asked here—he later said it was inspired by Margaret Atwood's feminist dystopian novel *The Handmaid's Tale*.[22] Knowing that the interrogation could well have been a version of a playful if also unsettling conversation with Marrin goes some distance toward deepening our sense of how the text functions in its exploration of the tenuous line separating truth from fiction.

This notebook-turned-novel of sorts may be closer to a play, as novelist Fay Weldon described it in her *New York Times* review, and could also be said to presage, with uncanny prescience, Twitter's mode of communication. As essayist Sean Hooks argues, "In many reckonings of 2020 . . . *Deception* feels amazingly apropos. The times are dramatic *and* we dramatize them. . . . It seems like all life is now is dialogue—smartphoned blurts, 'rude truths' . . . and disembodied voices." Roth, he says, was—eerily, brilliantly in this respect—much ahead of his time.[23] Still, there is no evidence that Roth witnessed this communication as troublesome, though the shallowness of these relationships built out of passing moments of rapid half-sentences might be seen as the antithesis of true communication.

14

"He Understood . . . Only What He Understood"

A QUADRUPLE BYPASS in the summer of 1989 (Roth had a brief, joyous sexual relationship with his nurse) and Herman's steady physical decline all coalesced in the writing of *Patrimony: A True Story*—the least if also the most predictable of all his books. Now, physically invigorated and working with the most formidable of American literary agents, Andrew Wylie—who, starting with *The Facts*, would negotiate prices for Roth's books unlike any he had enjoyed in the past—Roth produced a book in the wake of Herman's death of consummate realism as well as tenderness. Drawing on careful notes he took about Herman's illness, he wrote a memoir detailing his father's decline and its impact on himself too, an uncompromising work overflowing with love and devotion yet somehow devoid of sentimentality. And tinged also with more than a dose of mercilessness.

By now he was no longer living half a year in London, having returned full-time to the United States. Roth's distaste for England had to do with Bloom's daughter Anna, whom he despised and viewed as monstrously egotistical. (This, no doubt, was much akin to how she viewed Roth.) He insisted that he now found even America's vulgarity enticing, especially those same impossible Jews who had made his first steps as a writer so miserable. They, especially, he missed: "Complaining Jews who get under your skin," as he describes these feelings in *Deception:* "Brash Jews who eat with their elbows on the table. Unaccommodating Jews, full of anger, insult, argument, and impudence."[1]

It was now he turned his attention to his father. "My old father still lives at the boil," says Roth to his lover in *Deception.* "He's got an opinion about everything and often it's not mine. I sometimes have to suppress being a fourteen-year-old with my father. Rather than waiting to die, sitting with my father I sometimes feel as though I'm waiting for life to begin."[2]

Literary critic Sidra Ezrahi once observed that the feature that most distinguished Roth's writing was what he knew to leave out. And what she meant is especially applicable to *Patrimony:* details. Although *Patrimony* is packed with medical detail, it exists here for the sole purpose of explicating emotion. Hence the reader's receptivity to its depiction of the etiology of brain tumors is much akin to the detail that Roth would expend on leatherworking in *American Pastoral* or the diamond trade in his late-life novel *Everyman.*

Patrimony tells of Herman Roth's death: he died in 1989 of a brain tumor. But the reason the book so succeeds—it received stunning reviews, won for Roth a National Book Critics Circle Award, and was beloved by many readers who had long avoided him—lies in how well it manages to lay out the simple if also breathtakingly astonishing reality of one's eventual oblivion. Having been told by a surgeon that an operation on Herman's brain would likely take from eight to ten hours (another physician would soon up this to thirteen), Roth writes, his prose here less propulsive than elsewhere but no less unforgettable:

> After the impoverished childhood and the limited education, after the failure of the shoe store and of the frozen-food business, after the struggle to gain a managerial role in the teeth of the Metropolitan's Jewish quotas, after the premature deaths of so many loved ones. . . . After all that he had weathered and survived without bitterness or brokenness or despair, wasn't eight to ten hours of brain surgery really asking too much? Isn't there a limit?[3]

Roth produced here a portrait as receptive to human frailty as *Deception*—the two books alike in their insistence on the need to face life's more unsettling facts. There is nothing, Roth knows, to be accomplished, for instance, at the grave of his mother, who died several years earlier, except to sit there. And as he haltingly comes to recognize, there is nothing he can do to rid his eighty-six-year-old father of his massive brain tumor than help him regain a bit of eyesight to better enjoy his last months of life.

Jewishness is pervasive in this story of an old Jew's end, but not religion. His father attends a traditional synagogue mostly to hear its Bulgarian-born gentile cantor sing ditties drawn from *Fiddler on the Roof* after services. Far more meaningful than this or, for that matter, his father's tefillin or phylacteries (which Herman dispenses of in a locker at the Y) is his grandfather's shaving mug with his name emblazoned on it that Herman passes on to Roth, moving him profoundly.

Among Herman Roth's most enduring capacities, as Roth sees it, was how intimately he managed to link himself to history, which for him meant family. Included in his immediate purview were his beloved brother Milton (hence Philip's middle name), a prodigy dead at nineteen, alongside the many other "illnesses, the operations, the fevers, the transfusions, the recoveries, the comas, the vigils, the deaths, the burials . . . a man at the edge of oblivion . . . to connect his brain tumor to a larger history, to place his suffering in a context where he was no longer someone alone."[4]

Roth admired this capacity to feel a deep family connection—something he finds himself unable to emulate—but still in so many other respects son and father are similar. "He understood," Roth says about his father, "like the rest of us, only what he understood, though that he understood fiercely."[5] Their aptitude for work, their obstinacy, their all-encompassing memories were qualities both shared. Yet what Roth failed to explore in a book built around the theme of family loyalty was his own meager capacity: Mother and father and brother he adored, though Herman and Sandy exasperated him for long stretches of his life. Rarely if ever beyond his fiction would he more than hint at exasperation with Bess.

Nearly all others he kept at a distance. The prospect of having children of his own seems to have terrified him until very late in life. Cousins with whom he shared so much of his childhood he would have little to do with. Sandy's sons Jonathan and Seth—mentioned frequently in *Patrimony*, yet altogether absent from his other books—would resent bitterly this indifference, the sense that they never measured up.[6] Here, in a book that explores with rare acuity the inner workings of family life, Roth devotes little attention to anyone beyond his most immediate relations.

The absence of an altogether different source of Jewish devotion unsettled one of the few sharply critical reviewers of the book—Neal Kozodoy, later editor of *Commentary*. Kozodoy reflects on the scene where Roth cleans up after Herman has befouled himself: his father begs him not to tell anyone, which the memoirist betrays. Here Kozodoy dwells less on the issue of betrayal than the nexus Roth draws between excrement and patrimony: "Now . . . the job was done. So that was the patrimony. And not because cleaning it up was symbolic of something else but because it wasn't, because it was nothing less or more than the lived reality that it was. . . . There was my patrimony: not the money, not the tefillin, not the shaving mug, but the shit."[7]

Kozodoy, who admits that he distrusts Roth's prose, which he describes as "preening," is certain that this as well as other moments in the memoir are fictionalized, like a psychopathic cab driver who seems to Kozodoy drawn straight out of Roth's ample repertoire of the semicrazed. (As it happens, a friend of Roth's confirmed with me the incident's accuracy.) Kozodoy's main criticism, however, not dissimilar from Irving Howe's plaint years earlier, was the thinness of Herman's—and particularly his son's—Jewishness. How, with everything else now gone, all that remains for Roth of this legacy is his father's shit. "Filially devoted to the last, . . . [he] stands forth with his patrimony in his hands, cleaning it up as he must, futilely protecting it with art."[8]

Unsurprisingly, Roth's sense of his book's achievement was altogether different. As he wrote to his novelist friend Don DeLillo soon after *Patrimony* appeared:

> You're right about the writing of it. It wasn't like writing. It was more like the work that my father and I were doing together. He didn't have a store to which I could go to help after school, and we rarely, in my memory, ever stood out in the driveway throwing a baseball back and forth. I remember him taking me to the doctor when I was ten or so and had to have a hernia operation—I remember that closeness, and this was something like that. But, no, it wasn't writing.[9]

Reactions to *Patrimony* were, with the rarest exceptions, still more wildly enthusiastic than to any of his other books. His friend Richard Stern recalled that Roth's mail was now "thick with letters from weeping and laughing admirers," with Herman himself emerging—this, no doubt, something of an exaggeration—as "an American character up there with Hester, Huck,

Holden and Herzog." When Stern sought to sketch out a roughly similar book-length portrait of his sister—it would be published two years after *Patrimony* under the title *A Sistermony*—Roth's memoir remained an inescapable reference point, which served to shape even Stern's choice of an awkward title.[10]

I first met Roth as he was preparing for the 1992 tour promoting *Patrimony*. Over the course of several weeks before the visit to Stanford, he would phone me at home to talk about his plans, speaking especially—and with some discomfort—about a meeting I proposed with Jewish Studies graduate students and faculty. He sought to avoid it, declaring he had nothing to say that would prove meaningful. Eventually, I suggested that he merely stick a pin into one of his books and read whatever passage it settled on, certain that it would rest onto something of interest. I can't recall whether he followed this advice, but the meeting occurred, and it was disastrous.

The evening before, he gave a public reading in one of Stanford's largest auditoriums. The talk—which was built largely around sections of *Patrimony*—was decorous and without incident. The next morning, after time spent with Stanford's Creative Writing Program, I joined Roth to accompany him to the Jewish Studies lunch. Standing beside him—surrounded also by a clutch of creative writing students—was a young, blond woman dressed unlike any I had seen before on campus, her silky blouse all but open at the bosom, laughing at every passing comment Roth made, and now prepared (at his invitation) to accompany him to his Jewish meeting. Here was Philip Roth, seeking to rile his own people with an awe-struck, seductive gentile at his side.

She sat giggling beside him at the table as he warded off nearly all questions asked of him with a quick word or two. Students fumed. And the discussion soon died down as Roth and his new friend flirted with each other for an hour or so before departing. I walked them back across campus, as Roth mused about his now close connection with Israel's Mossad (he was then at work on *Operation Shylock*, with its fictional description of his links to Israel's secret service). My graduate students—particularly the females—spoke bitingly for at least a month or two about the encounter, and I recall feeling I had witnessed an expertly executed instant theater.

Years later, now reacquainted after he contacted me about a book I wrote about the writer Isaac Rosenfeld, I mentioned the incident, asking him whether I remembered it accurately. He said that I did and walked over to a bookshelf at his 79th Street apartment, then handed me a copy of Cristina Nehring's *A Vindication of Love: Reclaiming Romance for the Twenty-First Century*. It featured on its flap a photo of the same blond he had brought along to lunch. "Take it," he told me, "I don't need it."

When I opened it upon arriving home, a note from its author fell out, dated Friday, June 27. In it she says that she is in New York—in one of its worst hotel rooms—and would much like to see him. She adds that she is now game, and her Holiday Inn room number is 1508.

Bloom had accompanied him on the book tour, the two now married. He would now declare to friends that theirs was a perfectly happy relationship. "My ordinary, everyday life with Claire, especially in the country, fills me with a satisfaction I've never known before," he writes DeLillo in January 1991: "It unnerves me a little that I can [be] made happy by the life I used to be impatient with. In the old days everything outside of writing bored the shit out of me. Now it's the writing that bores the shit out of me, and the walks, the eating, the swimming, the sleeping, the comradery that thrills me."[11]

Soon, all this shifted badly. Why marry amid this downturn (they would separate barely two years later) he would explain in various ways. His health was increasingly fragile—he wore a brace under his clothes during much of the tour for *Patrimony*—and stepping away from Bloom just now felt unwise. His agent Andrew Wylie tells the following version: Philip told Claire that he would marry her once Nelson Mandela was freed from jail, and then in February 1990 the unexpected occurred. "Oh fuck," Wylie recalls Roth saying to him on the phone on hearing the news.[12]

What is clear is that Roth was now, at the very least, intensely ambivalent. In response, Roth's lawyer drew up a document absolving him of nearly all financial obligation if the marriage failed. Avishai recalled being invited to the wedding held at the home of Roth's friend Barbara Epstein the night before a slapdash ceremony and Roth asking him to make a toast and where he was led to understand that he would serve as best man. He would describe Roth at the event looking ashen, incapable of uttering a word.

Still, he had the wherewithal at the ceremony to reassure Maletta Pfeiffer that the marriage wouldn't have an impact on their romance. She recalls that she wore "a suit with a white jacket and a black skirt," and once the ceremony ended, she noted happily how Philip walked by her "taking in my cleavage. It was his signal. He was still my American boyfriend."[13]

And Roth's romance with Maletta Pfeiffer was indeed rekindled. It had sputtered on and off for years, but now that she had confronted her alcoholism at a rehabilitation center, they were closer than ever—so close that at Bloom's sixty-second birthday, in 1993, Roth placed Pfeiffer's mother at his side. It was soon after this party that his marriage to Bloom all but ended. Stricken again that summer with excruciating pain—back pain coupled with mental anguish—he now told Pfeiffer, as she describes it in a self-published memoir, "I can't be alone with Claire in this house anymore. Please do not leave me."[14]

It was during this convulsive time that he wrote his most explosive book since *Portnoy's Complaint. Operation Shylock* would be celebrated by some as the best of all his works while seen by others, including John Updike (the reader he took more seriously than nearly anyone else), as incoherent.

It is, to be sure, a work openly at war with itself, a self-consciously conflicted meditation on Israel, Jewish identity, and the perpetrators of Nazism—but also Shakespeare, Jung ("Duality" was among the titles Roth considered), even the jailed spy Jonathan Pollard. As Roth summed it up, "All these were passing through the collective brain at the time, and I wanted to get inside the Jewish mind." The novel set out to interrogate, often breathlessly, all that Roth had done since the start of his literary career. Here, the most articulate, least untrustworthy figure is a Palestinian intellectual modeled—as acknowledged by Roth in his notes but strenuously denied in public—on Edward Said.

Richard Stern visited Roth while he was hard at work on *Operation Shylock.* Roth explained a technique he now used to free himself from all preoccupation with what it meant to write such a wildly presumptuous book at this stage of his life: "He tells himself, 'I'm free, I'm nineteen, I'm unpublished, I can write what I want. . . .' That Philip not only doesn't censor, but yields to and encourages . . . irrational blips in what is otherwise an exceptionally rational character once surprised me. Used to them now, I think it has to do with the terrific strain and discipline of his life."[15]

Operation Shylock is a novel packed with ideological speeches regarding Zionism's origins and trajectory, Palestinians, American Jewish identity, the prospect of exilic Jewish life—all this aired at extraordinary length by a novelist who had long expressed indifference to platforms or theories of any sort, insisting that his Jewishness was something instinctive, even uncerebral. A book built out of an admixture of boisterousness and ideological exposition with nearly every aspect of contemporary Jewish life—Leon Klinghoffer, Meir Kahane, Arik Sharon—thrown into its hopper. As Claudia Roth Pierpont says admiringly, "The whole thing is vastly implausible on anything but the deepest level, where it is often moving and profound," and then adds, "What is more implausible than Jewish history in the twentieth century?"[16]

Interpreters of Roth have long noted his reliance on Shakespeare—Lear is all but a character of this novel, surfacing soon afterward also in *Sabbath's Theater*—but despite these echoes of Lear, *Operation Shylock* may have been inspired, at least in part, by something far more mundane. Around the time of its writing, Roth likely learned that a little-known writer, Richard Elman, was attracting the attention of beautiful women, including famous screen actresses and fashion models, because he so closely resembled Roth.

Elman found that he would sleep with women who, the next morning, insisted on calling him Phil. "Oh come on," said one of his conquests, "I'd recognize you anywhere, Phil Roth. I loved every minute of *Portnoy*."[17]

Elman's published account came out shortly after his early death, in 1997, but the story of his escapades had circulated earlier. It was just such a blend of the mundane, even absurd, in *Operation Shylock*, a novel shaped by a medley of Shakespeare's Lear, Israel's Demjanjuk trial—where the defendant claimed he was misidentified as a pro-Nazi killer—and perhaps also the escapades of Richard Elman that provided the book's ribald buttressing. "It is both at odds with [what] life is thought to be about and, at the same time, precisely where life is where 'nothing adds up' and all is 'too coincidental' "—this is how Roth captures his intent in notes he took while writing *Operation Shylock*. "I can't perceive it. Know too little. This is life then." At the same time, the book is an extended meditation on figures as diverse as Henry Kissinger and Hitler, who seek to change the course of the world, which he now envisioned as little more than "a phantasmagoria of voices. Conflicting Jewish claims. Every Jewish thought. . . . The ghosts of the Jewish murdered."[18]

The book begins just as Roth is about to leave London for Israel to interview writer Aharon Appelfeld—a close friend and author of much-acclaimed fiction on the Holocaust—for the *New York Times.* From Appelfeld, and soon others too, he learns that an imposter calling himself Philip Roth is now in Jerusalem promoting diasporism, which calls on Jews to abandon Israel (slated for destruction) for Europe, especially Poland, where so many of their immediate ancestors hailed from and which will now, it is claimed, welcome them back enthusiastically. Roth confronts his double soon after leaving the Demjanjuk trial—where the accused insists that someone else, not him, was the notorious Nazi camp killer Ivan the Terrible. And now, shortly after his dreadful bout with Halcion, he is recruited into the service of the Mossad.

Operation Shylock is, as Roth recorded in his notes, intended as "a virtual autobiography"—much as he describes *The Facts, Deception*, and *Patrimony.* All these, he says, are the product of loathing for fictionalizing. Roth now dons the role of a man with a mission: to save Jews from themselves. The novel's protagonist—so different from passive, writerly Zuckerman—relishes action. "I have been hiding. Enough Art!" he writes in his notes. "So this is what it feels like to be a practical animal as opposed to an aesthetic animal. You dare to do it! ACT OUT!"[19]

The idea of diasporism Roth took from his friend, the artist Kitaj: "I have always been a Diasporic Jew, but as a young man I was not sure what a Jew was," Kitaj declares in *The First Diasporic Manifesto.* "I was unaware that such questions were debated within Jewry, even in the Knesset itself."[20] Never did Roth subscribe to the notion of America as the new Jerusalem—which he found fanciful or even silly, although it was sporadically implicit in nearly all his writing. Hence, assigning Roth (the character) as an exemplar of diasporism was by no means altogether inconceivable. *Operation Shylock*, though, designed as a pastiche of the inconceivable, proposes as arguably the most absurd of all its notions that a novelist can bring about a major change on the larger world. It is this that is meant as the greatest of all fictions.

Roth had considerable hopes for the book, seeing it as a breakaway novel. Subtitling it "A Confession," he insisted at first—for reasons that remain unclear and perhaps simply for fun—that it was a true story. In the interviews Roth gave to the *New York Times*, *San Francisco Chronicle*, and other media, he would state—often frustrating his interviewers, who felt he was playing with them—that its story was accurate and that he had worked for the Mossad.

Some loved it. Harold Bloom declared its protagonist Roth's most brilliant character, comparing its genius to that of Aristophanes, the greatest of all Greek comic writers. Painful to Roth—perhaps devastatingly so—was Updike's reaction. While bowing respectfully to the author's "precocity," feverish pacing, and his eagerness to test the boundaries of realism, Updike blasted it just where it hurt most: namely, that as a novel it becomes little more than "a dumping ground . . . for everything in Roth's copious file of Jewishness." Only readers with a particular interest in Roth himself, or the postmodern novel, or Israel—Updike wrote—could find it compelling. Inside every Jew, Roth says in the book, "is a mob of Jews," each with their own personalities, clamoring for self-expression. Updike clearly found the clamor unbearable.[21]

The book was certainly no less noisy than Updike said it was, but among the features that stand out is its promiscuous attachment to community. Years earlier, in Tony Tanner's study *City of Words: American Fiction, 1950–1970*, the author observed how, for both Saul Bellow and Roth, memories remain their sole link to anything beyond themselves, with such recollections representing their only point of contact "with 'externals,' that is the experience of ordinary life which . . . is all the reality they know."[22] Here, Roth upended such expectations, knowingly or not. *Op-*

eration Shylock—an oddity among Roth's works—is among his most communally alert, even loving of books. There is little battle here with abusive Jewish ghosts. Others—above all, Jew haters—weigh it down, but Jews here are either dear friends, like Appelfeld, or sagacious courtroom judges, or the Roth double whose plans are well-meaning, if also absurd.

15

Maletta

Philip would often ask:
"Why do all my women have terrible fathers?"

In a draft of her memoir, later revised and privately published, Maletta Pfeiffer describes her first sexual experience with Roth—this in the summer of 1976, after Roth's breakup with Barbara Sproul, and at a low point in his life. She had just finished her physiotherapy work on his neck and arm. The Connecticut house was dark, with a hospital bed in the living room: "It must have been before Claire. As I was about to leave, Philip put his hand on my elbow and guided me to a bedroom. He began to undress me. Philip surprised me. When he kissed me his thin-lipped mouth held no tenderness, no tongue. But his sexual force was irrepressible."[1]

Maletta and her husband, Werner, would become part of Roth's small cluster of close local friends. Pfeiffer's role, however, was incomparable: She was, as he would later acknowledge, the main reason why his longstanding liaison with Bloom was even conceivable. Their secret relationship (more or less—both C. H. Huvelle and Ross Miller and one or two others knew of it) grew closer and more intimate, if also more sexually explosive, with the passage of time.

A vividly attractive woman, she possessed, or so Roth believed, a sexual appetite comparable to his own. Still more crucial was her desire to do anything to please this man of genius. The intermittent relationship lasted more than a decade and a half, leaving an indelible mark also on his life as a writer. Rarely, or so he told Blake Bailey, did he produce a figure so manifestly drawn straight out of his own life as he did with the entrancing Drenka of *Sabbath's Theater*, whose character, if not her body, was modeled on Pfeiffer's. And he would say much the same about Drenka's adoring, hirsute, ungainly lover Mickey Sabbath: "The nearest I've come in all my fiction to drawing a realistic self-portrait."[2]

Pfeiffer was a woman of great vitality and efficiency: an attentive and loving mother, a gracious wife—and an alcoholic. Her father had committed suicide, and her mother abandoned her. Pfeiffer suffered from a welter of terrors she managed to sequester from view. Intelligent and inquisitive but not well read (Roth once gave her his list of favorite books, which she never managed to start), she proved to be a magnetic and, perhaps most important, singularly loving figure in the lives of those she cared about.[3]

Roth later speculated that they had sex—at his Connecticut home when Bloom was away, or outdoors in nearby grottos or forests—no fewer than a thousand times. "Addicted to sex" is how Pfeiffer would describe them both. Throughout the many years of their affair—which tapered off at times, then reignited—they managed to live outwardly respectable, sedate domestic lives.[4]

Roth and Bloom both described nearly all their Connecticut evenings spent reading by the fire or in bed. Yet meanwhile, Roth reveled with great frequency elsewhere in the tantalizing mystery of transgression with Pfeiffer. Sex in a hotel elevator,

Norman Manea recalled Roth claiming. And Roth described Pfeiffer's outrageous appetite to Bailey: "Four men in a single day," including her husband, Werner. Pfeiffer acknowledged that she shared with Roth details of trysts with others, but this, she insists, is untrue. Still, looking back at these tumultuous times, Pfeiffer says that her happiest moments with Roth were when she and her husband shared congenial dinners together with him and Bloom, the four of them casual, easygoing friends.[5]

It was just this interplay between the orderliness of their daily lives and these anarchic eruptions—sometimes drawing others into their coupling, too—that lent the relationship its irresistible quality and longevity. Together, they spoke, sometimes in copious detail, about their sex with others. And among the more significant reasons why their bond imploded was—as is captured at the start of *Sabbath's Theater*—that Pfeiffer suggested monogamy after Roth had left Bloom. "Either forswear fucking others or the affair is over" is *Sabbath's Theater*'s first sentence.[6]

Bloom was blind to the affair, and even when her memoir *Leaving a Doll's House* appeared in 1996, she knew nothing of its longevity. She had suspected Roth of infidelity, certainly after reading the draft of *Deception*, but apparently had put the concern out of her mind, especially once they married. The wedding was followed, as Roth described in letters to friends, by a surprisingly (if also quite brief) blissful period.

Bliss is far from how he would come to remember the marriage. It ended in the summer of 1993, soon after the appearance of *Operation Shylock*, with Roth suffering from debilitating back pains as well as severe mental anguish so overwhelming that he admitted himself as a psychiatric patient to Silver Hill Hospital. Roth discovered that Bloom—"fragile, volatile . . . whose pervasive sense of crisis he'd mistaken for a deep spirit," as captured in *Sabbath's Theater*—was incapable of caring for him, concerned mostly with herself, at times literally running away from him, terrified.[7]

"The breakdown was complete," Roth told his friend Benjamin Taylor of his stay at Silver Hill. "I was in physical and mental agony. It was the lowest point in my life. . . . I could find no grounds for going on."[8] When Claire visited him there, he declared he wanted a divorce.

Soon the details of their impending divorce became gossip-page fodder, with Roth eventually writing her off completely—indeed, coming to see Bloom as one of the worst of his foes with the publication of her memoir. It included a lengthy, overwhelmingly devastating description of him: "Under Roth's brilliant inventiveness, beneath his diamond-sharp observation, was a deep and irrepressible rage: anger at being trapped in marriage; fear of giving up autonomy; and a profound distrust of the sexual power of women."[9] Excerpts appeared in *New York* magazine—featuring Roth's face on its cover—as well as *Vanity Fair*. Bloom was interviewed on *Dateline NBC*. Little would haunt Roth more for the remainder of his life than Bloom's acidic portrait, which now persuaded him to search for a biographer who would set the record straight. He was also fearful that if he didn't have a hand in selecting the biographer, someone might well surface who would take Bloom at her word.

Bloom later admitted that she found herself unable to care for Roth at the time of his breakdown, fearful of her future, especially her precarious financial situation as an aging actress with few opportunities. Before the breakdown, by far the source of the greatest tension between them was the mutual dislike between Roth and Anna, Bloom's daughter. Roth came to see Anna as obsessively needy, if also frustratingly oblivious to his charm and stature, and describes in memos to biographers excruciating dinners together at which Anna took little notice of him. Eventually he set strict limits on the frequency with which Anna could visit her mother in Connecticut. Complicating all this was Roth's pursuit of one of Anna's closest friends, Rachel: "For many weeks," recalled Pfeiffer, "he would talk about how obsessed he was over her. Like Lolita. How he finally managed to seduce her into doing what he wanted . . . a beautiful auburn." Anna now sought to break off all ties with him.[10]

Roth would come to depict Bloom as weak, absurdly needy, incapable of thinking beyond her own childish desires, bludgeoned by her daughter, a snob, and (despite Jewish parentage) an antisemite. Pfeiffer recalls reminding him, while the couple was still married, of how taken he had been by Bloom's beauty, especially when they were first involved. "Little good it does me now," he would reply. Toward the end of their time together, he complained that Claire's snoring kept him awake and shunted the beauty queen off to sleep in a different bedroom.

There are several accounts of these same events, their differing details significant since more than anything since *Portnoy's Complaint*, Roth remained convinced that her book's account of their marriage did much to cost him the Nobel Prize.[11]

There is Bloom's own published account of their relationship. And there is Roth's unpublished version, initially slated to be the basis of a book, then consigned to several hundred pages of memos. There are three further versions, differing in texture and detail, written by Maletta Pfeiffer, one of which she sent to Blake Bailey, who shared it with Roth. There is also a self-published version of Pfeiffer's recollections, entitled *Overcoming*, completed after Roth's death; several chapters devoted to her time with Roth were, she told me, produced to explain her life to her children. And then, too, there is a diary-like account in the form of emails never sent, many of these furious, produced soon after Roth abruptly ended their relationship.

Pfeiffer's diary was typed in a feverish state, replete with uncorrected typos, produced in the dead of night and never seen by either Roth or Bailey. At the time of the split with Bloom in 1993, Roth and Maletta were all but living together, either at her own condo near Roth's home or at his guest house. When *Sabbath's Theater* was published in January 1995, some four months before the divorce, Roth declared it a veritable love poem: "Write a book as a love poem. You atre [*sic*] such a pervert," she would type deep into the night on April 20, 1995.[12]

She had long been his "sidekicker"—Roth, much like Mickey Sabbath, relished her offbeat English constructions—with Roth acknowledging to her experiences as well as urges that he was convinced few others could understand. He reveled in the belief that theirs were kindred sexual passions, with Roth convinced that hers were still more experimental and even wilder than his own. She was privy to secrets he felt certain would never be aired. Benjamin Taylor captured this trusting, even naive side of Roth: "That Philip was both an ardent lover and a sexual anarch was the inner dynamism of his life as well as his art. 'Monogamy would not have been in me had I lived in the era of Cotton Mather. As it was, I lived in the era of *Screw* magazine and Linda Lovelace.' "[13]

Nonetheless, Pfeiffer described their best moments together as quiet, calm companionship:

> There are times when I am with Philip in the evening. They play old jazz music on the radio. I am flirtatious. I am happy. I am in love. We laugh. We dance. We play. He tells me he loves me. In a warm entanglement, he gazes at me. He likes my Nordic looks, my high cheek bones. He likes my foreign accent. He likes my malapropisms, a word he taught me. He is my American boyfriend. We are lovers. We are best friends. I am hopefully mesmerized.[14]

And long after their break Roth, in a moment of happy recollection, spoke of a relationship better than any he had ever known before: "The passion never waned. It was extraordinary and so was she, this beautiful, hyperenergetic, hyperorgasmic woman who was totally without inhibition."[15]

During a visit of Pfeiffer's to London, he recorded the sex talk she engaged in with lovers. Often, he would ask her to interrupt her physiotherapy work to listen to him masturbate on the phone. Visiting her when she was briefly in the hospital in the spring of 1979, she watched him, just as he was leaving, "jerking off at the foot of my bed." She noted his capacity to "be your friend at one minute and your enemy the next. As long as his mercurial temper was not directed at me I choose [*sic*] to ignore it."[16]

And Pfeiffer cared meticulously for Roth during his breakdown. She left her marriage on the advice of Roth's friend Ross Miller, or so she recalled, assuming that this was what Roth wanted her to do (though he never said anything like it to her). Roth had beseeched her just before his time at Silver Hill never to leave him, and she planned to honor the pledge—looking forward to a life with Roth free from the escapades of their past.

Finally living together free from Bloom, Pfeiffer found Roth crabby, often impatient, more insistent than ever about having things his own way. She recollected that she now shuddered while turning the page of a book when in bed with him, fearing he would say she was making too much noise. She remained in love with him, as she would continue to be long after he broke up with her. Decades later, she would still relive that moment when he first reached for her breasts: "Feeling stirred, I thought, *Of all the women he could have, he wants me.*" Yet in retrospect, she insists that she would have found it impossible to remain with him and would have eventually left.[17]

Pfeiffer and Roth both agree that it was New Year's Day 1995 that the relationship ended. The incident was, as Roth describes it, Pfeiffer's sudden demand that she be allowed to inform her children of their plans to travel together to Sweden. Often, they had spoken about traveling there once Roth won the Nobel Prize—he seemed rather certain this would occur—and they would stay at the Grand Hotel, with Pfeiffer showing him her childhood haunts. That morning, she spotted a folder with the title "Sweden," which prompted her to raise the issue.

Roth may well have feared that she now hoped, on top of making their relationship public, that she anticipated eventually marrying him—the apprehension reinforced by her proposal they cease having sex with others.

Roth refused her request to inform the children, she balked, one or the other shouted (they differ on this detail), and after a long silence on Roth's part, he announced that plans had changed. He walked out of her condo and out of the relationship. Shortly thereafter Pfeiffer learned that Roth had already met a new love, a practicing psychiatrist named Julia Golier, whom he would come to declare brought him more happiness than anyone ever before.

In early April, once he cleared out all Pfeiffer's belongings from his house in Warren and sent them back to her, she exploded: "All the things you did to me," she wrote in a diary entry in April 1995: "You made me go and talk to whores. Sat in your studio in London. Looking at the Playboy girls. That never excited me. I just did it to please you. When you dressed in my bra and underwear and pretended to be a woman. Wanted me to be a man. I never liked it. All the things I did with you. I cannot even write about them. What you put in the book."[18]

The same morning, at 4:30 a.m., still awake and fuming: "Even when I saw you the last time and you went on with your long tirad [*sic*] why you admired me . . . because I lived like a man took men when I wanted them . . . used them as I like and always was in charge . . . I had the power . . . did I? That was my way of surviving the pain."[19]

Decades after the relationship ended, Pfeiffer remembered an evening when Roth sought to explain to her the rules of baseball. She recalled him standing up, showing her the body movements of a pitcher, when suddenly he said, apparently jokingly but perhaps not entirely: "Beware of knowing an author! He will steal from you!"[20]

* * *

Roth wrote *Sabbath's Theater* soon after his breakdown and the end of his marriage, the book finished before his relationship with Pfeiffer ended. From the novel's first sentence—"Either forswear fucking others or the affair is over"—Pfeiffer is a constant presence. But so too is Janet Hobhouse.[21]

Insanely funny and deliberately abrasive, amid its onslaught on life's pieties and obfuscations, it is, Claudia Roth Pierpont writes, the most powerful of explorations of the most outrageous of all of life's certainties: that no matter what, we all face extinction, probably preceded by excruciating pain and other dreadful humiliations. Sex can momentarily soften, even momentarily obscure the onslaught, but it can do no more than that—which, to be sure, is more than anything else can do.

Mickey Sabbath is a failed puppeteer, upended by arthritis and charges of sexual abuse. He is financially beholden to his wife, Roseanna, a schoolteacher and an alcoholic whose AA-inspired bromides (these drawing on Pfeiffer, too) only manage to deepen his loathing. Contemptuous of nearly everything in the present, he remains fixed on the wrenching losses of his past. Above all, his beloved brother's death—killed by the Japanese in the Second World War—and the resultant trauma to his mother, who never spoke again. These weigh constantly on him as he yearns to disappear, albeit without a coherent plan as to how this might be achieved. Always he sees the dead most clearly, with his mother rising in front of him, as he faces his most beloved of all spaces: the vagina of his love Drenka. The only source of happiness in his miserable life, Drenka, too, is confronted with imminent death and dies of cancer soon after the novel's start.

Sabbath haunts cemeteries, rifles through the drawers of the daughter of one of his few remaining friends (to masturbate into her underwear), and tries to seduce the friend's wife. Sex talk is replete in the novel: It includes the transcript of a phone sex episode running like a footnote across some twenty pages of the novel. But at its core, it is a study of one man's unseemly, if utterly comprehensible, protest of the most astonishing feature of life: our inevitable oblivion. Yet before its onset, there are those blessed moments that serve to obstruct the horrors to come. Here is Sabbath reveling amid the underwear of his friend's daughter: "Brimming! A treasure trove! Brilliant hues of silk of satin. Childish cotton underpants with red circus stripes. String bikinis with satin behinds. Stretch satin thong bikinis. Floss your teeth with those thongs. Garter belts in purple, black, and white. Renoir's palette! Rose. Pale pink. Navy. White. Purple. Gold. Red. Peach."[22]

All this, so that he might forget his beloved Drenka, who alone was able to help him dispense with the inanities of daily life, its humiliations and utter senselessness. His feelings toward her are suffused with a devotion comparable to what he continues to feel for his brother or mother. Pierpont writes:

> Yet the character of Drenka, in all her sunlight, is drawn from imagination as much as memory. The great gift that Roth bestows on her is not beauty but an absolute, good-natured freedom, which is based in strength and radiates joy. An intoxicating earth mother, Drenka is absolved of sentimentality by raunchy sex and weight around the hips. It is easy to enjoy her, and impossible not to weep along with Sabbath at her deathbed. Although she does not live the way most women live, or might want to live, she enlarges the sense of female possibility, and that's what heroines are for.[23]

What exists beyond the bliss experienced between Drenka's legs is gray and listless. Sabbath stays over at the tony apartment of a friend from his days as a puppeteer only to discover that his is a sexless marriage—one that keenly frustrates his restless wife, held together by a tissue of compromises that serve only to deaden them: "The house on Nantucket. The weekend at Brown as Debby's parents. Debby's grades would tailspin if they split up. Call Michelle a whore, throw her the hell out, and Debby would never make it to med school. And there's the *fun* besides: the skiing, the tennis, Europe, the small hotel they love in Paris, the Université. The repose when all is well."[24]

Or, alternatively, what life might offer up instead is the slow, grim deathlessness of pathetic, useless old age. This Sabbath encounters at Bradley Beach, to which he returns at the book's end, to discover his cousin Fish—a man with the face of Sabbath's father, with a look much like that of an entire generation of Jews—who carried with them, as Roth describes so beautifully, "the weight of life, the simplicity to bear it, the gratitude not to have been entirely crushed, the unwavering, innocent trust—none of that has left his face." One hundred, all but deaf, his clothes streaked with urine stains, and unable to do much more than walk up and down the stairs. All he can acknowledge about his longevity is that it's "better than being dead."[25]

Benjamin Taylor, a writer as close to Roth as anyone else in his last years, says that what most impressed him about the book was the scene in which Mickey Sabbath tells Drenka about swimming at the Jersey shore—a moment to which he would return repeatedly but never more strikingly: "Sand scratching your eyes, stuffing your ears, packing the crotch of your suit . . . and then, spurred by a sudden heroic impulse, spinning about onto your belly for the dive to the ocean floor. Sixteen, eighteen, twenty feet down. *Where's the bottom?* Then the lung-bursting battle up to the oxygen with a fistful of sand to show Morty."[26]

Few if any of Roth's books elicited quite the range of reactions: Michiko Kakutani at the *New York Times*, a frequent critic of Roth's, found it "distasteful and disingenuous." Sabbath's adventures, she wrote, add up to little more than a "black hole," with him learning nothing from Drenka's death except the need to reaffirm much the same narcissism that had informed the rest of his life. In the end, the book teaches little if anything, with

Sabbath pathetic throughout. "The immensity of your isolation is horrifying" is what his generous, expansive friend Norman says to him after he learns that Sabbath sought to sleep with his wife, and this, as Kakutani sees it, sums up the novel's useless, pitiful protagonist.[27]

In stark contrast, Frank Kermode—among the most influential and erudite literary specialists of his day—finds in the death and mourning that animate the novel a "great subject," best compared in its execution to Genesis or *Paradise Lost.* What Kakutani found tasteless, Kermode declared an exercise in brilliance, with Roth capable of eliciting in readers a rare outrage: the capacity to startle even the most hardened. He likens Sabbath's "id on the loose," with its threat to respectable society, to Robert Musil's *Man Without Qualities,* with the book's insight into the "captivity of civilized life," its capacity to reveal Sabbath's ability to love, alongside the immensity of his loathing, which is comparable, says Kermode, to that of Shakespeare's Lear:

> King Lear, with whom Sabbath advertises a certain affinity—each, in his own way, a foolish and a fond old man—rages not against his own faults but against Justice as it is conceived by its exponents, the corrupt judge and the beadle and the lash—all covert lechers, all enemies of life, of a sexual freedom they secretly envy. It is this justice that Sabbath rages against; and so, with all his characteristic ironies and reservations, does the author of this splendidly wicked book.[28]

Sabbath's Theater won Roth the National Book Award. He considered it the favorite of all his books. An "immaculate intertwining of filth and beauty, his hymn of praise to the sex drive out of season," as Taylor summed it up. It was a lengthy passage from *Sabbath's Theater* that Roth chose to read at the celebration of his eightieth birthday at the Newark Museum, declaring there that he loved it precisely because it revealed "the unmanageable man, the unexonerated man—better, the refractory man, refractory meaning 'capable of enduring high temperatures.' Refractory not as a pathology but as a human position. The refractory man being the one who will not join."[29]

Pierpont told me she brought the book along with her to Roth's funeral—her copy heavily scuffed—remaining behind when others left the gravesite for a reception. She then dropped it into the grave, doing so with the thought that Roth might well like to have it beside him for good reading in the beyond.

16

America

A LITTLE MORE than a year after *Sabbath's Theater* came *American Pastoral*, perhaps the shaggiest of all Roth's monsters, yet celebrated like few of his books since *The Ghost Writer* or *The Counterlife.* (Then again, loathed by some with an intensity comparable to the contempt heaped onto *The Breast.*) Roth had started it twenty years earlier, at just the time he had embarked on *The Breast*, tinkering with it since but choosing to set it aside until now. An odd, misshapen if also astonishing novel, as literary critic Ross Posnock writes: "Here Roth seems to yield to the kitsch temptation to attempt a 'great American novel.' . . . The kind of panoramic survey of the state of the union and the American soul that committees award Pulitzers to (which in fact *American Pastoral* won). The chronicle novel diagnoses a family as a microcosm of the nation and the era, a genre that the country doctor of Europe famously mined, to borrow Nabokov's teasing remark about Thomas Mann."[1]

The book's protagonist, Seymour Levov, nicknamed "the Swede" when a high school athletic phenomenon because of his Nordic looks, is all that Mickey Sabbath is not, which seems to have been much of the attraction. No cynicism, no dissimulation, the sparsest adultery, a happy man in love with his wife, daughter, and work—in love with life—with all this laid to waste by the senselessness of everyday existence. A gorgeous male beast devoid of "craving depths," he is the "embodiment of nothing."[2] Yet even he is scorched indelibly, as Nathan Zuckerman (revived for the first time since *The Facts*) discovers, much to his surprise, by all that can befall a human being.

The novel's first section, "Paradise Remembered," is devoted once again to bucolic, dizzyingly optimistic postwar Newark. ("Everything was in motion. The lid was off. Americans were to start over again, en masse, everyone in it together.")[3] If anything, Roth's exaltation of that past here is fuller, fiercer, more overpacked with nostalgia and yearning and regret than encountered elsewhere. He begins with a declaration of fealty to the Swede, who once, memorably, spoke to the young Zuckerman, calling him by his nickname Skip, because he had skipped two grades in school. This extraordinary athlete—one of a small phalanx of other male heroes, all objects of awe—is soon cut down to size much like the other heroes in Roth's much-acclaimed American Trilogy, Ira Ringold in *I Married a Communist* and Coleman Silk in *The Human Stain*.

Soon after the description of the Swede as seen through the eyes of a besotted, albeit only passable ballplayer (much like nearly all the Jews he knew), Roth imagines a speech never delivered, sketched deep into the night after a forty-fifth Weequahic High reunion. The women there at the reunion had aged more markedly than the men—a disproportionate number of the men felled or at least touched by prostate cancer—and yet the hours spent at the reunion leave him astonished, even in awe. No fewer than three times in the span of the final three sentences of his unspoken valedictory remarks does he employ the word "astonishing," Roth an exemplary wordsmith who wrestled, ceaselessly, with every published syllable.

What astonishes him above all is what he learns, almost in passing, from the brother of the Swede, a high school pal named Jerry, who had always been explosively aggressive and is now a highly successful knife-wielding surgeon, big-chested and bombastic with his small army of divorced nurse-wives. Zuckerman tells him his brother contacted him for dinner some years earlier to discuss, or so he said, writing an homage to his father, which never came up. It was a desultory, aimless conversation from which Zuckerman emerged with the impression of the Swede as a blandly uninteresting, still handsome, and clearly successful man whose life offers no surprises. "I was wrong. Never more mistaken about anyone in my life," he now learns.[4]

What Zuckerman now knows is little more than a few stray details of anguish, bafflement, and unceasing guilt that he turns into a complex novel: The Swede's daughter Meredith, or Merry, at the age of sixteen blew up the country store in their wealthy, bucolic suburb to protest the Vietnam War, killing a local physician who'd been picking up his morning mail, then fleeing. The Swede locates her years later; she's subsisting, just barely, on one of Newark's worst streets, by then the object of rape herself, and having killed three more for the sake of the cause. The Swede, still absurdly dutiful, seeks to make sense out of all this hopeless chaos.

Jerry, a rageful man altogether different from his brother, offers no credible explanation as to why the Swede's daughter became a murderer. What Zuckerman sets out to explore is whether there might have been alternatives to this fate or whether life is little more than an endless cycle of twists—mostly appalling. Jerry tells him that he attended the reunion only because he was already in town, having just come from his brother's funeral. Despite his robust appearance when he'd dined with Zuckerman, the Swede had already been stricken with prostate cancer.

Blake Bailey says that Roth's idea for the book originated in the 1970s with a story told to him by Alan Lelchuk about the child of a happy family who morphed into a terrorist. At the time, Roth had been friendly with the congenial, left-liberal parents of Kathy Boudin, part of the Weather Underground. What Roth comes to explore is whether any effort to act reasonably amid life's uncertainty is no more than a flight into fantasy, with the novel taking its epigraph from a Johnny Mercer song from the 1940s: "Dream when the day is thru,/Dream and they might come true . . . "

The book provides an array of beautifully crafted moments, all eventually interlinked, yet each impressive on its own terms. Roth draws on varied literary influences, some seemingly profoundly dated, including Theodore Dreiser and John Dos Passos, both giants of a much earlier age. Yet the book is curiously unobstructed by these literary antecedents.

The conversation about that aimless dinner with the Swede is followed by a description of the forty-fifth reunion, where Zuckerman finds himself dancing with a once-fetching classmate named Joy ("I should have let you undo my bra," she tells him. "Undo it now, if you'd like to"). And it is especially that moment in Joy's arms that prompts him to return to this past, to more fully imagine the Swede's fall from paradise. As Zuckerman now reconstructs it, the daughter, scrawny and stuttering—raised amid the splendor of her eighteenth-century home by a former beauty queen mother—descends into the grim routine of a lonely pre-teen and then a fierce opponent of the Vietnam War, eventually consorting with older New York activists in the city.

Her mother's reaction is one of utter desperation. In contrast, the Swede remains a model of reasonable, flexible liberalism: He throws himself into antiwar activity, he demonstrates empathy for his daughter's ever-escalating fury. And he urges her to consider all that might be done right there to fight the war in their own community, but once she blows up the country store, killing the local doctor, his advice becomes the source of unceasing guilt and anguish for him.

And the Swede also remains obsessed, flattened, by a moment years earlier, when Merry was eleven. The two of them, having spent the day together swimming, were sitting close to each other in the front seat of the car when Merry begged him to kiss her like he kissed her mother. And this he does, losing himself momentarily, but later convinced, in his darker moments, that it was this that turned his innocent, vulnerable daughter into a crazed murderer.

Is Roth drawing here on an episode from years ago, when he admitted to his lover Lucy Warner, a twenty-two-year-old University of Iowa student, that he was concerned that he might find himself sexually attracted to Maggie's daughter once she was a few years older and grew breasts? Holly, Maggie's daughter, like Merry, was known to have been consumed by a ferocious hatred of the war.[5]

In a newspaper interview Maggie's son David (the interviewer Robert Cohn at the *St. Louis Jewish Light* couldn't locate Holly) spoke warmly about his and his sister's past relationship with Roth without a hint of anything unseemly. David did recall that Holly so treasured her relationship with Roth that for years she kept a framed photograph of him on her desk. And Roth told his friend Charles McGrath of the *New York Times* that he had broken off contact with Holly because he feared she was becoming obsessed with him sexually.[6]

Here, as was often true for Roth, there was likely a tendency to confess whatever crossed his mind, however shameful and avoided by others—this being one of his more telling, and winning, characteristics. Of course, this trait coexisted with an equally pronounced inclination to dissimulate, to mask whatever he possibly could. Roth may well have drawn into these pages of *American Pastoral* a wellspring of shame—albeit hugely exaggerated and distant from reality—in his creation of a scenario that would drive the Swede to distraction until the end of his life.

The most fully executed sections of the book are its detailed, exacting descriptions of glove making: the source of the Levov family's wealth. It's a depiction of a charmed, multigenerational family whose prosperity is the byproduct of bloodstained, filthy labor. It is not the detail that Roth lavishes here on leatherwork—and elsewhere on the diamond trade—that sets his work apart, but, as Sidra DeKoven Ezrahi has observed, the emotion that accompanies these experiences.[7]

The family business was started by the Swede's father, Lou. The glove factory is humanely run and long maintained in Newark, despite the city's devastating July 1967 upheaval; eventually, though, it is relocated to Costa Rica. (Roth had considered the prospect of situating the factory in Prague.) Roth uses the factory—whose products are delicate and beautiful but whose industrial process is revoltingly rancid—in his exploration of the horror lurking just beyond life's most luscious moments. Everything about the work that goes into the pickling, the hair removal, the cutting, the lavish use of saliva to wet the leather is testimony to the chasm between what lies just beneath civility's exterior, its gruesome if inevitable cost.

"Anyway," as the Swede explains to a visitor, at first unrecognized as a coconspirator, perhaps lover, of his fugitive daughter:

> This skin . . . is called a cabretta in the industry's terminology. Small sheep. Little sheep. They only live twenty or thirty degrees north and south of the equator. They're sort of on a semiwild grazing basis—families in an African village will each own four or five sheep, and they'll all be flocked together and

> put out in the bush. What you were holding in your hand isn't raw anymore. We buy them in what's called the pickled stage. The hair's been removed.[8]

The family's complacency dissolves at a dinner party—on its surface congenial and civilized until an eruption of sudden violence at its very end. Here the Swede learns of his wife Dawn's affair with an old-line gentile neighbor, which will soon bring their marriage to an end. This despite an especially satisfying sexual relationship between the Swede and his wife, this the only instance in all his writing where Roth lays out the details of such union: "He was just overtaken by the desire to do something more, and so he lifted her buttocks in one hand and raised her body into his mouth. To stick his face there and just go."[9]

That night the Swede learns that not only has he lost his wife's love but that a casual lover of his—his one and only indiscretion, with Merry's speech therapist—has betrayed him, having hidden his daughter in her home after the terrorist attack. He watches as other dinner guests badger his uneducated, generous father, teasing him relentlessly regarding his distaste for the pornographic movie *Deep Throat*, which was at the time screening in conventional movie theaters. So irked by the father's persistent, annoying solicitude is the drunken wife of Dawn's lover that she pokes a fork right into his face.

> There was blood on Lou Levov's face. He was standing beside the kitchen table clutching his temple and unable to speak, the once-imposing father, the giant of the family of six-footers at five foot seven, speckled now with blood and, but for his potbelly, looking barely like himself. His face was vacant of everything except the struggle not to weep. He appeared helpless to prevent even that. . . . He never could, though only now did he look prepared to believe that manufacturing a superb ladies' dress glove in quarter sizes did not guarantee the making of a life that would fit to perfection everyone he loved.[10]

* * *

Literary success after success in these years. Many critics lauded *American Pastoral* as Roth's finest book: a crucial, multifaceted, and original intervention into the troubled history of the sixties. But nothing would assuage Roth's sense of betrayal over the wretched portrait of him in Bloom's *Leaving a Doll's House*, whose accuracy tended to be taken for granted. On top of this treachery, as he saw it, was Pfeiffer's as well, since she had agreed to be interviewed by Bloom for the book, acknowledging that they'd had only the briefest affair. Called Erda in Bloom's memoir, she was described as "a beautiful woman who had been a close friend to both of us for years," for whom Roth had abandoned Bloom.[11] Stunned, Roth now wrote Pfeiffer off; they never spoke again.

I Married a Communist, published two years after Bloom's book, in 1998, was his response to Bloom: a novel blisteringly vindictive in its portrayal of Eve Frame, depicting her here as an aging, spineless beauty queen, readily manipulated as her talent fades, and now distinguished by little more than her clever choice of hats. Still, the novel is impressive—less in its portrait of McCarthyism, which serves as the focal point for its portrait of betrayal, than in its close study of a young man's coming of age amid the left-wing politics of the 1950s. Roth's talent here, and elsewhere, is not historical fiction but his capacity to study how males especially confront life's staggeringly tangled choices, embracing, then rejecting, role models.

The book opens with Nathan Zuckerman in his mid-sixties. Now calmed, and a consummate listener, he encounters quite by accident the most impressive of all his high school teachers, Murray Ringold. Spending several evenings with him, Murray relates the tragic story of his brother Ira, long considered in Zuckerman's adolescence the truest and most courageous of life's guides.

Zuckerman describes his small universe of indispensable and

inspirational male high school teachers (female teachers were erased as next to useless at that particular juncture): Most of these men veterans, some wartime heroes ideally suited to teach boys about life both inside and beyond the classroom: "how to be rambunctious without being stupid, how not to be too well concealed or too well behaved, how to begin to release the masculine intensities from the institutional rectitude that intimidated the bright kids the most."[12]

Ira Ringold—modeled on the loud, high-spirited left-wing veteran who married Roth's cousin Florence—leaves a trail of misery in his wake because of his hopelessly rigid politics. He had been something of a celebrity, an Abraham Lincoln look-alike, starring in a popular radio program, but a fierce dispute with a McCarthyite senator made him a pariah.

Zuckerman recounts that Ira had embarked on the writing of dreadful radio plays, drenched in politics and full of disdain for Truman during the fateful 1948 presidential election. Soon Ira was blacklisted, even accused of being a Soviet spy; Murray, his left-leaning brother, lost his teaching job and was now compelled to make a living by selling vacuums. His wife Doris began to work full-time, then fell ill, with Murray—one of a long array of Roth's exemplary family men—stalwart, loyal, and hardworking.

When Zuckerman meets Ira, he is still a celebrity and married to Eve Frame. Nathan falls in love, overwhelmed less with the content of Ira's politics—straight-line communism, a textbook postwar Red—than with his heady, hard-hitting irreverence: "There was no invisible line of propriety observed and there were no conventional taboos. You could stir together anything and everything: sports, politics, history, literature, reckless opinionating, polemical quotation, idealistic sentiment, moral rectitude. . . . There was something marvelously bracing about it, a different and dangerous world, dangerous, straightforward, aggressive, freed from the need to please."[13]

In fact, Ira is a simpleton full of canned answers and, shockingly, also a murderer. Disenchanted with him, Zuckerman searches for other (always male) mentors, discovering while a student at the University of Chicago an effete, bookish teacher whom he eventually recognizes as nearly as objectionable. Yet he puts into this teacher's mouth some of Roth's most deeply held convictions regarding the chasm separating the fictional and political imagination. Much like in *The Counterlife*, Roth appreciates here the seductiveness of politics while seeing its pull as antithetical to fiction of any value:

> "Politics is the great generalizer," Leo told me, "and literature the great particularizer, and not only are they in an inverse relationship to each other—they are in an *antagonistic* relationship. To politics, literature is decadent, soft, irrelevant, boring, wrongheaded, dull, something that makes no sense and that really oughtn't to be. Why? Because the particularizing impulse *is* literature. How can you be an artist and renounce the nuance? But how can you be a politician and *allow* the nuance?"[14]

Less original is the book's tour of the various paraphernalia of 1950s communism: ubiquitous Paul Robeson, Red Army chorus songs, Henry Wallace rallies—all solid historical depictions but rarely engrossing here as fiction. Ira never really rises beyond his soapbox, with his brother Murray's voice the monotone of an undoubtedly decent man but without much evidence of the charismatic high school teacher depicted by the young, awe-struck Zuckerman.

The novel added to the pantheon that shaped Roth's imagination: Eleanor Roosevelt, perhaps also Henry Wallace, Truman's third-party opponent and erstwhile vice president, who found himself supported in his unsuccessful run for president by an enthusiastic slice of the left. These surface as influences on Roth no less salient, at least for a time, than Henry James or Flaubert. The book is a study of a rich medley of influences first potent, then found wanting, an exploration that encourages comparisons to *Goodbye, Columbus* in its intention to signal farewell to so much that had once claimed his fealty in the past, especially his movie star wife.

Roth claimed, for reasons hard to discern, that the novel was among his favorites. Where it soars is in its meticulous portrait of Zuckerman's coming of age, perhaps meant to be read as a precursor to the nervy, ambitious writerly young man at Lonoff's, watching eagerly for material, seeking validation, straining for a glimpse of his own glorious future.

Critics were ambivalent—many pleased by Roth's new emphasis on listening, others unimpressed, even bored by Ira's rote hectoring as well as Murray's lengthy, deadpan narrative. Some loved it: "Roth has seamlessly woven the political and the personal. . . . There are no minor characters in a novel this careful," wrote the *Christian Science Monitor* reviewer. "Even the briefest walk-ons seem endowed with all the complexity and depth of real life."[15]

At sixty-eight, Roth was lauded even by those who found him repetitive, his rage overbearing, the voices of his unnervingly loquacious characters sounding much like their creator as American fiction's towering figure. And now at the cusp of old age, the author, as some saw it, of the greatest of his books, *The Human Stain.* "The novel not only stares death . . . in the face, it stares the whole unruly parade of our lives in the face, and declares . . . that we are imperfect fabricators of our own destinies. And, by the way, that as a novelist Roth is in a league of his own."[16]

Still, as secure in the fictional world as any writer of his age, he would continue to exasperate leading critics with far more than mere quibbles, inspiring at times utter frustration with something so basic as differentiating between himself and his characters. James Wood's exasperation over *The Human Stain* was acute—its inexhaustible polemicizing and incessant reminders of life's chaos—which, he admits, provide undeniable clarity but all-too-sparse fictional buttressing.

And others concurred: A "shrieking, lyrical work" is how a *New York Times* reviewer summed it up. Yet the same reviewer acknowledged that Roth's novels remained unsurpassed in their importance: "In terms of sheer productivity, brilliance, distinctly American diction, philosophical rage, comic irritability, dramatic representations of solitude, uniqueness of voice and unwavering repugnance toward heterosexual convention, it is difficult to think of a contemporary artist with whom Roth might even be compared."[17]

Even Michiko Kakutani, whose lacerating criticism in the *New York Times* inspired Roth to caricature her in his fiction, spoke of the same book as "large and stirring," a novel of "uncommon insight and perception."[18]

The Human Stain appeared barely two years after *I Married a Communist*, with Roth now dubbing this the last of his American Trilogy, his effort to portray the country in which he came of age. Once again, it is a tale of Newark, with the city defining the essential character of postwar America.

Much like *American Pastoral*, the novel is an exacting illustration of the importance of biography for Roth, perhaps especially now that he had managed to persuade his close friend Ross Miller to write his life. Here the subject is Coleman Silk, and again, Roth places the task of telling the story in the hands of Nathan Zuckerman. And again, Zuckerman manages to tease out the vagaries of a life with only the barest hints to work with—as Roth feels certain, all that anyone ever has at their disposal to comprehend another life.

Biography—and the inconceivability of ever doing it with accuracy—is an overriding preoccupation of the book. And here, too, the touchstone for a successful work of fiction is, as Roth sees it, in its capacity to seek to rival the overflowing concreteness of life itself—a task never truly achieved, except in the rarest of masterpieces, like Joyce's portrait of Dublin.

Thus, packed into *The Human Stain* are moments from Roth's own life and those of others close to him. The basic details of Coleman Silk's fall from grace—he is a classics professor at a small college of some stature—are all but identical to those of Roth's friend Melvin Tumin. Tumin, a sociologist whose area of expertise was race relations, was investigated by Princeton for asking about the failure of two students who had never come to class (he had never met them and it turned out that both were Black), saying "Does anyone know these people? Do they exist or are they spooks?"[19]

Following his resignation, Silk begins a romance with a cleaning woman at his college, which draws on a sexual liaison of Roth's with a local woman. And his inability to finish a second book that he desperately wishes to complete, while living his life as a Jew hiding his African American identity, may well have been inspired by Ralph Ellison, the author of *Invisible Man.* Roth keenly admired Ellison, whom he met at the 1962 Yeshiva University event in a particularly vulnerable moment at the start of his own writing life.[20]

But perhaps the most crucial of all aspects in the novel drawing on Roth's own life—with its details shorn of all specificity, but as intimately personal as any feature of this remarkable book—is the story of Silk's betrayal of his family so that he might freely live his life. This theme is, of course, among the more persistent of Roth's but never explored by him before with comparable breadth or poignancy. Roth reveals here an unambiguous attachment to his characters with none of the sardonic distance that is such a marked feature of his work since *Goodbye, Columbus;* here there is a palpable rapport with their missteps and sympathy for the wretched, ever-unpredictable unkindness of fate.

The story the book tells has no fewer than three openings. In the first, Coleman Silk has his first glimpse of cleaning woman Faunia Farley, soon to be his lover. Then an excursus situating Silk's story of the summer of 1998 into the larger frame of twentieth-century American history with the use of a shrewd comparison to the Clinton-Lewinsky affair. Finally, the start of Zuckerman's biographical quest, his meeting Silk's sister Ernestine at his funeral, where Zuckerman learns Silk's meticulously kept secret.

But at its start is a brilliant journalistic description of the secrets that nearly brought down Clinton. Roth greatly admired first-rate journalism. I recall his praise for then–*New Yorker* writer Hendrik Hertzberg whose writing, Roth insisted, made a real difference (unlike fiction). And few have captured the hysteria surrounding the Clinton-Lewinsky affair more powerfully than does Roth in his prologue:

> It was the summer in America when the nausea returned, when the joking didn't stop, when the speculation and the theorizing and the hyperbole didn't stop, when the moral obligation to explain to one's children about adult life was abrogated in favor of maintaining in them every illusion about adult life, when the smallness of people was simply crushing, when some kind of demon had been unleashed in the nation and, on both sides, people wondered "Why are we so crazy?," when men and women alike, upon awakening in the morning, discovered that during the night, in a state of sleep that transported them beyond envy or loathing, they had dreamed of the brazenness of Bill Clinton. . . . It was the summer when a president's penis was on everyone's mind, and life, in all its shameless impurity, once again confounded America.[21]

The book then veers back to Coleman Silk and his abrupt resignation, the crisis effecting—or so he is convinced—not only the end of his career but also the death of his wife, suddenly felled by a stroke. Overwhelmed by rage, he bursts into the

Berkshire cottage of his neighbor Zuckerman, someone whom he barely knows, the writer an isolate and impotent in the wake of prostate surgery several years earlier. Silk does so with the hope that Zuckerman might take up his cause and write an accurate account of these misconstrued events (here, perhaps, an echo of Hertzberg's excellent chronicling of Clinton's saga). Thus Zuckerman, long estranged from life's everyday tumultuousness, finds himself thrust into the vortex of Silk's life, with the seventy-one-year-old classicist crazed by revenge.

Soon enough, Silk will be calmed by the unanticipated boon of exuberant late-life sex with the janitor and dairy worker, a woman singed by unspeakable tragedy, whose capacity for carnal pleasure is all but unmatched. Hounded by college authorities for this relationship too, both Coleman and his mistress are murdered by her ex-husband, a Vietnam veteran who suffers from dreadful wartime scars. Chaos is what engulfs all here—not the snug protection of a college career or even the exuberance of sex. Chaos is life's truest, most potent force.

If there is a fiend in the book, it isn't the Vietnam veteran but rather a young, Paris-born, Yale-educated feminist at Coleman's college, now a dean, who circulates word of Coleman's new—in her mind, dangerously inappropriate—sexual relationship. These scenes are among the book's sketchiest in contrast to its lengthy, superb portrait of Silk's coming of age and his anguished battle for independence.

Here again Zuckerman is a listener—also a biographer—eventually stumbling onto the greatest mystery of Coleman's life: that Silk is a light-skinned African American, not the Jew he claimed to be. Once again Roth draws into his narrative solid historical evidence that, for Silk, as for so many African Americans of his generation, Jews loomed large among the few non-Blacks with whom they had relationships—among them local merchants, landlords, record producers, civil rights activists, sometimes also spouses. For Silk, it is the Jews who competed with him in school for the best grades, and his training as a boxer came from a Jew as well—this at a time when Jews were ubiquitous in the ring.

The prospect of passing as a yellow-skinned Jew thus felt less a betrayal than if he sought to act as if he was white. Having passed as a Jew while fighting in the ring on the advice of his coach, he tasted what it felt like and now yearned for a life spent amid such freedom: "Growing up in East Orange, he was of course a Negro, very much of their small community of five thousand or so, but boxing, running, studying, at everything he did concentrating and succeeding, roaming around on his own all over the Oranges and . . . down across the Newark line, he was, without thinking about it, everything else as well. He was Coleman, the greatest of the great *pioneers* of the I."[22]

On the death of his father—an indomitable self-taught Shakespearean forced by bankruptcy to work as a train porter—Silk abandons his mother and siblings. His final act as a Black man is to bring home a white woman he deeply loves—indeed, the last woman he would ever love—to whom he had not revealed his background, with the meeting so unsettling that she breaks off the relationship. Eventually, he marries the woman with wild semitic hair, "an escapee fresh from two nutty anarchist parents in Passaic . . . armed already with her thicket of important hair, big-featured and voluptuous, already then a theatrical-looking high priestess in folkloric jewelry, the biblical high priestess from before the time of the synagogue."[23]

Unable to erase the disastrous impact of his decision on his mother, he remains convinced that this is the only way he can claim his individuality while also aware that his own racial background is itself a result of the complex "maze of history" with ancestors married to Swedes, mulatto brothers who wed Dutch sisters, and runaway slaves brought north by the Underground

Railroad, passing for white. He seeks to justify his decision by recalling his extended family's joyous reunions, where they themselves openly embraced the intricacy of their American genealogy.[24]

Never before had Roth described so fully the price of freedom. Silk's anguish is alleviated—at least fleetingly—by the astonishingly uninhibited Faunia Farley. Here, Roth draws directly on the life, and eventual death, of a lover of the late 1990s: Nicole Prevatt. Broken, she nonetheless possessed what Roth described as "a kind of animalist sensuality that was her knowledge and that prevailed body and soul."[25]

Quite possibly, too, there is the looming presence of Ralph Ellison, whose warm encounter with Roth at Yeshiva University left its indelible mark. Roth gives Silk the sort of academic career he himself might have enjoyed had he pursued the university life for which he was preparing at Chicago and that was enjoyed by Ellison himself at Bard, Yale, and elsewhere. Roth shared with Ellison a firm commitment to literary aesthetics, refusing to measure the value of ethnic literature in terms of its contribution to the well-being of his own group, which exasperated many of Ellison's readers. And it was perhaps just such pressures that contributed to Ellison's being unable to complete a second great book.

Roth, too, had once worried that the negative reactions to his work among Jews might have a comparable impact, this being the reason he spent several long years writing *When She Was Good.* And, indeed, a vehement critic of Ellison's dereliction as a writer of the Black experience was Roth's own nemesis Irving Howe, who insisted on the inescapably political role that Ellison—the leading Black writer of his time—must occupy if he was to justify his prominence.

Once again, Roth produced a book that would be read on so many different levels: as a gripping story, as an extended meditation on the challenges facing the ethnic writer, as a study of the insidiousness of unchecked moral rectitude. Perhaps, above all, the novel explores with incomparable subtlety the same dilemma haunting his work since *Portnoy's Complaint*, if not before: the terrible price extracted by freedom.

17

"Old Age Is a Massacre"

"Can you imagine old age?" asks Roth's narrator David Kepesh—to whom he returns for the first time since his transmutation into a breast nearly thirty years earlier—near the start of *The Dying Animal*, a brief, brutal novel more akin to an essay than a fiction, with its raw summary of some of Roth's perennial themes. "Of course you can't. I didn't. I couldn't. I had no idea what it was like. Not even a false image—no image. And nobody wants anything else."[1]

Kepesh lives a self-contained, meticulously controlled life. He hosts a weekly radio program, teaches one class a year at a university in New York, and lives alone in a handsome, book-filled apartment with a page of a Kafka manuscript—a prized possession particularly useful in the romancing of bookish females—framed on one of its walls. At the end of each semester, once all students are graded, he seduces a woman from his classes, carefully attentive to today's strict guidelines. The novel is built around the most memorable of such seductions. But it is a story replete with far more anguish than pleasure—not because he finds her unattractive (Consuela is blessed with the most beautiful breasts of anyone he has ever encountered) but because, at twenty-four, she will, he knows for certain, abandon him, a man of seventy-one. "And that's what it's like to be an old man," says Coleman Silk to his new friend Zuckerman in *The Human Stain*. "To be like that ugly girl. To be in the corner at a dance."[2]

Consuela he considers rather dull, intellectually mediocre, though eager for a taste of culture. He even finds their sex overly mechanical, too spirited and practiced, too deliberately intent on giving him pleasure. Conversation with her is tedious. She speaks at length about her loving, wealthy Cuban family, her predictably keen, if intellectually modest cultural pursuits—all of which he listens to with feigned interest, if only "because I want to fuck her. I don't need all this great interest in Kafka or Velazquez. Having this conversation with her, I am thinking, How much more am I going to have to go through? Three hours? Four? . . . Twenty minutes into the veiling and already I'm wondering, What does any of this have to do with her tits and her skin and how she carries herself?"[3]

Nowhere else in Roth's writings—certainly not in *Sabbath's Theater*, where Drenka's mispronunciations, her exuberance, and much else delight her lover no less than her splendidly rounded body—is there a woman in Roth's fiction so reduced to little more than a breathtakingly alluring breast. And who else to be mesmerized by such a female than Kepesh? Roth lavishes attention on her nipples, their shape and perfection: "The type with the nipple like a saucer. Not the nipple like an udder but the big pale rosy-brown nipple. . . . The second thing was that she has sleek pubic hair."[4]

Yet the book's focus is not her body but Kepesh's all-consuming jealousy. He finds himself consumed with jealousy even regarding the few boys that this well-bred, conservative girl slept with in the past, a small cluster of lovers who come to obsess him endlessly. He suffers when she doesn't call, tormented still more in the immediate wake of a night spent with her when she must leave.

Nothing calms him, not even the delectable relationship he has at the same time with a woman closer to his age but still decades younger: "very attractive, very strong," and with "a scrutinizing intelligence, reliable in every way . . . a sensual expert, and attentive lover."[5] He reminisces about the sexual abandon of the sixties that gripped him like so many others, prompting him to leave his marriage and thus estranging him from his son, now an adult, a self-lacerating adulterer himself who can't help blaming his father for his missteps. In a book replete with excursions often sketchily unexplained, the most moving is the description of Kepesh's friendship with George, a poet, his only true male friend because it is only with him that he is able to be entirely free about his sexual urges. It is the capacity to achieve rare common language about one's truest desires that constitutes the key, as Kepesh sees it, to a true if also uncommon friendship between men.

Kepesh ruins the romance with Consuela, failing to appear at a party marking the completion of her college degree. Still, he cannot erase ever-persistent images of her: "I played Beethoven and I masturbated. I played Mozart and I masturbated. I played Haydn, Schumann, Schubert, and masturbated with her image in mind." The way she came "by pushing out the vulva" and the draping of her breasts over his penis while fondling all were endlessly haunting. "A man who has consistently been a roué now finds himself in his old age enslaved to the passion that once gave him such liberty," writes Rachel Stroup in a particularly perceptive essay, where she admits she had long avoided reading Roth but found this book—seemingly among his most offensive from a feminist perspective—a singular joy to read.[6]

Years pass, new lovers come and go, Kepesh's close male

friend dies at fifty-five of a stroke. And then on New Year's Eve 1999, Consuela leaves a phone message that Kepesh considers ignoring because he knows her reentry into his life would be a cause of ceaseless unease. But of course he responds. She is sitting in her car just outside his building. Now several years older and no less beautiful, she is there to tell him that she has breast cancer. She has lost her hair from the chemotherapy, unsure whether it worked or not, but feels certain she will lose at least some of her breasts. She asks him to photograph her, as someone who enjoyed her body more than anyone she has ever known, and to join her in the hospital if she is told that the cancer has spread so rapidly that the breasts must be removed. He is inclined to join her, now cautioned not to do so by a voice never identified:

> This morning they told what is going to happen; now it's night, and she's all alone and the whole prospect of everything. . . . I have to go. She wants me there. She wants me to sleep in the bed with her there. She has not eaten all day. She has to eat. She has to be fed. You? Stay if you wish. If you want to stay, if you want to leave. . . . Look, there's no time, I must run!
>
> "Don't."
>
> What?
>
> "Don't go."
>
> But I must. Someone has to be with her.
>
> "She'll find someone."
>
> She's in terror. I'm going.
>
> "Think about it. Think. Because if you go, you're finished."[7]

"Not a great work" writes Keith Gessen in a review, a book didactic, he says, in the vein of the "antimarital rantings of 'The Kreutzer Sonata.' " But comparable to Tolstoy—more so than any American writer of his time—is the urgency of what he seeks to say and his unwillingness to apologize for convictions expressed here more transparently, even more powerfully, than anywhere else in his work. "Deliberately offensive" is how Gessen aptly characterizes the novel, informed as it is with a sense of "desperation, that pulses through the book."[8]

For Roth, Kepesh is, as Gessen puts it, "the dullest and most methodical" of his protagonists and, at the same time, little less than a historian of the sexual revolution of the sixties. *The Dying Animal* is meant as an account of how this revolution transpired and—much like most other revolutionary convulsions—was betrayed. Kepesh's confidence in the essential rightness of his own life's trajectory has by now disappeared, with even homosexuals seeking to marry, with sexual life now ever-more regimented, and someone like Kepesh resembling, as he puts it, "a comic figure on the order of the village atheist."[9]

It is only during sex that you are, as Kepesh insists, "most cleanly alive and most cleanly yourself. . . . Don't ever forget it. Yes, sex too is limited in its power. I know very well how limited. But tell me, what power is greater?" Gessen ends this remarkable essay with a paragraph comparable in its discomfiting pertinence to the best of Roth's: "You could answer (virtuous reader), as you have answered Roth so many times before, that art, and its promise of eternity, is greater; or politics, with its promise of justice, is greater; or religion, and its promise of spiritual peace, is more powerful. You could answer Roth thus, but one of you would have to be lying."[10]

It may well have been his Connecticut friend Ross Miller, or perhaps C. H. Huvelle—the local physician near his Warren home whose biography he hastily sketched and published privately some years earlier—who inspired his praise in *The Dying Animal* for the rare experience of true, candid male camaraderie: "George was the whole of my male community, perhaps because the class of men we belong to is small to begin with.

And a single comrade-in-arms is sufficient: one doesn't need the whole of society on one's side."[11]

Miller had been one of his closest friends for decades, the friendship sealed once Miller spent more than half a day analyzing page by page an early draft of *The Counterlife*. "I've never talked to anybody this long and intensely and didn't get laid," as Miller characterized the experience, the comment particularly revealing since so much of this friendship was lathered by talk of sex. More earthy, less guarded than Roth, certainly less consumed by ambition—with his ambitions perhaps eventually ignited by his long, intimate proximity to Roth—he was tapped soon after the appearance of Bloom's lacerating memoir to be the first of Roth's authorized biographers.

Roth's choice of Miller—hired as biographer, then dropped and subsequently rehired—was the result of some truly surprising factors for someone as famously well connected as Roth. "I'm an observer," he would say to Maletta Pfeiffer, impressed by the range of her friendships and her willingness to throw herself into a wide range of activities. Several of his good friends described to me his isolation, especially in the wake of disappointing reactions to *Operation Shylock* in 1993, his subsequent breakdown, and then a few years later the appearance of Bloom's book. It was a veritable assault for him, despite the celebratory hubbub surrounding his American Trilogy, especially *American Pastoral*.

Roth had tested the prospect of other biographers: Judith Thurman, who insists she never seriously considered the idea, and Hermione Lee, who agreed to write it once she completed her biography of British novelist Penelope Fitzgerald. (Lee's 1982 book-length study of Roth remains an indispensable guide to his early writings.) Roth also spoke with me, perhaps others too. But Miller was close at hand, a warm admirer who knew

Roth's secrets and understood, or so Roth believed, the need to exclude those that might embarrass. Over the years he proved himself to be an astute judge of the drafts of Roth's books and may well have played a significant role in prompting Roth to confront some of the more awkward moments in his autobiography *The Facts*.

Miller's first proposal was mostly a lavishly detailed description of Roth's sexual adventures with the young Maxine Groffsky. Roth was appalled, though years earlier in *My Life as a Man*, he had done much the same thing. His relationship with Miller nonetheless remained strong. The French journalist Marc Weitzmann—friendly with Roth at the time he was writing *The Plot Against America*, published in 2004, and still resolutely proud that one of that novel's fiercest rants can be credited directly to him—recalls that Miller was an all but constant companion at the time. Weitzmann, Miller, Roth, and others frequented the Russian Tea Room, a favorite haunt of Roth's. Here, side by side with Miller, Roth enjoyed talking about women and flirting with those seated in nearby booths.[12]

Other close male friends came and went during these years. Roth feuded with his University of Chicago fellow writer Richard Stern, and he was estranged from his once-close friend and erstwhile editor Aaron Asher. Both relationships were eventually repaired. For some two years, among his dearest friends was Susan Rogers, whom he had known since she was born, the daughter of his novelist friend Thomas Rogers and his wife, Jacqueline. Susan emerged as a stalwart, if often overburdened, helpmate—assisting him so much with *The Plot Against America* that he dedicated the book to her. Rogers was also his lover. Still, the most ubiquitous presence was Ross Miller, who was appointed once again authorized biographer in 2004 after a hiatus of several years.

During Roth's long writing stints in Connecticut, he spent a great deal of time with Miller, whose devotion, solid judgment, and sense of humor provided Roth with considerable reassurance (if also with something comparable to the devotion of a courtesan—Judith Thurman's phrase). Now that Roth was living almost entirely in Connecticut and, by and large, without a woman at his side, Miller provided him with convenient, uncomplaining companionship; he was someone who could be summoned at a moment's notice or could be dispensed with when the writer found himself too busy. So close were they that when in 2004 homosexual marriage was made legal in Massachusetts, Roth jokingly proposed they take the plunge.

Roth understood his friend's limitations, but he admired Miller's book on the Chicago fire and saw him trapped in an inadequate university and stuck for many years in a loveless marriage. He viewed Miller as a man with a wealth of ideas but without the opportunity to write them down. Later, once the friendship ended, Roth would see these same characteristics as mediocrity, but he seems earlier to have been convinced that if given the right chance, Miller had the capacity to produce something noteworthy. This was particularly crucial since the accusations leveled by Bloom cut so deep: "I am sensitive to nothing in all the world as I am to my moral reputation," he admitted to Benjamin Taylor.[13]

By the time Roth asked Miller to try his hand once again at a biography, *The Plot Against America* was completed and the American Trilogy was roundly celebrated as a literary masterpiece. These were rare achievements for a writer of any age, let alone someone of seventy. Few now denied his preeminence. Harvard and the University of Pennsylvania awarded him honorary doctorates in 2003. The American Academy of Arts and Sciences gave Roth its Gold Medal in Fiction. The Library of America announced its plan to publish all his major works in a series of eight volumes, eventually ten, with Roth one of only three living writers (the others were Eudora Welty and Saul Bellow) that had been bestowed the honor.

Yet accusations of misogyny continued to weigh heavily, consolidated by Claire Bloom's description and augmented by feminist critics of the sort he so enjoyed savaging in *The Human Stain*. He described them to friends as sitting in perpetual judgment: ever-testy, morally disapproving, subjecting all he wrote to strictures that had little pertinence to literature. He would liken their repressiveness to that of Soviet censors before the fall of communism. A solid biographical treatment of him and his achievements might quiet this drumbeat, or at least marginalize it, reminding readers of what he had achieved. Ideally such a biography would offer a glimpse of a free, unfettered, lavishly talented man who managed to rise above not only the hypocritical mores of the 1950s but also the priggishness of the feminist 1970s and '80s and beyond.

Almost from the moment that Miller was announced in 2004 by Roth's agent Andrew Wylie as his authorized biographer, the project felt doomed. In an interview soon after the news surfaced, Miller blurted out, much to Roth's chagrin, that there remained only one prize still to give him—with the Nobel "all but inevitable." Roth berated him for saying this aloud, though there is good reason to believe that this is just what Roth himself had long before concluded.[14]

Exactly what caused the friendship to implode—in little more than a year, they would cease speaking to each other—remains unclear despite the many hundreds of pages Roth wrote explaining what transpired. In Roth's view, Miller proved too lazy and incapable of doing what any credible biographer ought to do: interview quickly elderly relatives and friends; spend time with those who knew Roth best, like his brother Sandy; listen to his interviewees rather than dominate meetings with them; and, perhaps above all, feel a deep empathy for his subject. From his vantage point, Miller seems to have felt that he already knew more about Roth than most of those he was now asked to listen to and soon bucked against Roth's intrusions.

Above all, what came to infuriate Roth most was Miller's claim—aired to several of those whom he did interview—that Roth was "manic-depressive." Miller described Roth as intent on manipulating all close to him, including Miller, now calling all of Roth's recent books—including the much-praised *The Plot Against America*—"shit." Even Roth's much-repeated gratitude to him for having saved his life during a particularly bleak period Miller said was nonsense, since Roth would never have jumped. He made all this up because, as Miller saw it, he was hopelessly needy, uncertain of the love even of those nearest to him.

Roth remained convinced that what had finally soured Miller was his criticism of the biographer's awful annotation of the Library of America volumes, which he had agreed to handle. Entries were incomplete and mistakes abounded, with biographical data hopelessly mangled.

This may have contributed to the fallout. But it is more likely that Miller came to tire of his subordinate role, now augmented by his job as his friend's chronicler. He had stood by Roth's side for so long, through so many illnesses, dark moods, and slipshod relationships, that he was likely weary of it all, especially now that he was expected to produce an admiring biographical portrait. He seems to have buckled under the weight of it, skeptical of Roth's capacity to continue to produce excellent books while also recognizing that he was increasingly the focus of Roth's worsening moods: For some six months in 2003, Roth went so far as to demand a moratorium on their friendship—this for reasons not explained—asking that they have no contact at all. The moratorium came after more than two decades of often daily conversations.

Already by the time Miller agreed to a second try as Roth's biographer, he had likely tired of Roth, his incessant demands, and his clumsy descent—as Miller saw it—into literary mediocrity. Nor was Roth oblivious of this slippage. Starting in 2006 with *Everyman* and continuing until his retirement a few years (and four books) later, he would chronicle with a remarkable self-awareness the waning of his talent, his "divine curse" as he often referred to it.

Roth would wreak revenge for Miller's betrayal. His manuscript "Notes on a Scandal Monger"—several hundred pages of typewritten text—was an all-out attack on Miller's intelligence, failings as a writer, and disloyalty as a friend. Miller would brood over the relationship's end. Several friends who had been close to Miller now distanced themselves because of Roth's antipathy as well as Miller's now-overwhelming preoccupation with his loss. As one mutual friend put it: "All the same, if Ross acquitted himself badly, he surely has been hugely hurt, even ruined, by being dismissed as Philip's biographer."[15]

The biography was now an ever-pressing preoccupation for Roth and the source of acute discomfort. This was made amply clear with Roth's involvement in protecting Saul Bellow, now a close friend, from the intrusions of a biographical work by James Atlas, who had labored on his book for some eleven years after Roth himself had proposed that Atlas write it. Atlas's *Bellow: A Biography* would be published in 2000, with Roth doing all he could to discredit it.

Atlas was the author of an excellent study of the brilliant, troubled Delmore Schwartz—among the most impressive if also enigmatic of Jewish writers to come of age in postwar America. Casting about for a new topic, Atlas was intrigued by his Upper West Side neighbor Roth's suggestion of Bellow. A few years later, with Atlas hard at work, Roth's friendship with Bellow deepened into one of his most meaningful, stimulated by Bellow's wife, Janis, a literary scholar and admirer of Roth's work. Her appreciation of *Operation Shylock*, which she reviewed favorably in the Boston University magazine *Bostonia*, left a deep impression on Roth; she persuaded Bellow to read it, which he did with great enthusiasm. For years, Bellow and Roth had maintained a wary distance, with Roth's wickedly brilliant portrait of Felix Abravanel modeled on Bellow in *The Ghost Writer* perhaps doing its part in ensuring that they stay away from each other. This long-time breach was now finally repaired.

The new, suddenly warm friendship didn't falter even when Bellow offered sharp criticisms of *I Married a Communist.* Roth defended his work vigorously while insisting that the friendship was inviolate: "You've been in my bloodstream," Roth now admitted, "since I read *Augie March.*" Indeed, Roth's copy of Bellow's breakaway 1953 novel, a paperback edition republished in 1960 shortly after the hubbub over *Goodbye, Columbus,* is extensively annotated, with a scribbled index of favorite passages in Roth's hand appended onto one of its first pages. Throughout the book—so frequently reread that it is falling apart—are passages that most impressed Roth, all bracketed, underlined, or starred. Indeed, starred by Roth are those he felt were the most beautiful: "The sand swallows burst out of their scupper holes in the bluffs and out over the transparent drown of the water, back again to the white, to the brown, to the black, from moving to stock-still sand waves and water-worked woods and roots that hugged and twisted in the sun."[16]

In anticipation of the appearance of Atlas's book—by which time the biographer's relationship with Bellow, never close, had soured, with Bellow anticipating severe criticism of his temperament and especially his treatment of the women of his life—Roth now vigorously interjected himself. He conducted his own interviews with Bellow about his work and reached an agreement with the *New Yorker* to publish, just before the appearance of Atlas's biography, a book-by-book analysis of Bellow's writings starting in 1953 with *The Adventures of Augie March* until the last of his masterpieces, *Humboldt's Gift* in 1975. This was all an effort to underline how a true and honest literary biography ought to be written.[17]

Then Roth played an active part in identifying an alternate biographer for Bellow, resulting in the choice of Zachary Leader, whose massive two-volume *The Life of Saul Bellow* was published from 2015 to 2018. Curiously, this definitive, painstakingly detailed account differed little in its portrait of Bellow from that of Atlas, described there too as a writer of rare genius riddled with glaringly acute imperfections. Still, the overall experience provided more than ample reason for Roth to fear more than ever the impact of biography and its unavoidable intrusiveness, while remaining convinced that he greatly needed it.

18

Horror at Home

Roth's last major work of fiction, his first bestseller in many years, was *The Plot Against America*. It is a horror story infused with love. Told with the scholarly sobriety of an older man reminiscing about the worst moments of his life (with a "formality, sometimes even the hint of academic reserve" is how Paul Berman captured its tone in a shrewd review), it describes an attempted fascist takeover of the United States and overflows with tenderness for the narrator's mother, for Newark, for FDR, for America.[1]

It is, above all, once again the incontrovertible importance of family—still more so than the eruption of domestic totalitarianism—that is the book's cornerstone. The mother, Bess (here Roth dispenses with pseudonyms), is indispensable, the father, Herman, flawed—exasperated by his sudden powerlessness but celebrated too, if less fervently. The older brother, Sandy, finds himself seduced by Lindbergh's allure but is eventually won back.

But nothing proves more devastating, not even the onset of fascism, than loss of family: "Motherless and fatherless you are vulnerable to manipulation, to influences—you are rootless and you are vulnerable to everything."[2]

Love pervades the text despite its dark opening: "Fear presides over these memories, a perpetual fear."[3] The reader is immediately reminded of the novelist's implacable patriotism, faith in Roosevelt's sagacity, and above all his celebration of the mother as seen through the eyes of the eight-year-old protagonist Philip Roth. The book may well have been a late-life effort by Roth to offset the grim impression of Roth's mother in *Portnoy's Complaint*, to distinguish this book's heroine from the compulsively intrusive Sophie Portnoy.

Despite considerable emphasis elsewhere, it is in this book that Roth lavishes by far the greatest attention on the details of his Newark childhood neighborhood. Already on the book's second page is a list, captured in one of Roth's meticulously overpacked sentences (this one nearly half a page in length), of Weequahic's glories: its grand park, the homes of its doctors and lawyers with their finished basements, the proximity of the airport, its boating lake, golf course, harness racing track. And then "the Republicans nominated Lindbergh and everything changed."[4]

At first Roth gives a worshipful depiction of Lindbergh's heroism and, of course, the tragedy of his child's abduction—all this eventually darkened by his isolationist declamations. These uncluttered, prosaic declamations resembled, as many saw it at the time of publication, the speech patterns of George W. Bush. Unsurprisingly, more recently many have viewed the book as a still more eerily precise depiction of the rise of Donald Trump. Roth insisted that he hadn't been thinking of Bush and, once the book appeared, credited its inspiration to a passage in Arthur M. Schlesinger's memoirs, where he noted that there were some

Republicans who thought it a good idea to nominate Lindbergh, already a vocal opponent of the prospect of war, to run against Roosevelt in the presidential election of 1940.

Still, the novel retains an eerie prescience that reads today as a description of something far more devastating than the latter Bush era. The novel's leader is a thoroughgoing threat to the democratic order with his interplay of facile statements and warnings of apocalypse, and he garners widespread support for his authoritarian antisemitism, even among some Jews. When novelist J. M. Coetzee reviewed the book, which he much liked, it seemed to him that "by the standard of plausibility to which [Roth] subjects himself, this historical framework is more than a little rickety." Now such criticism feels like the product of a more innocent age.[5]

Roth's story begins just before the election of 1940, with Roosevelt adored by Jews, popular with the rest of the population, but faced with mounting anxiety about the prospect of America's being drawn into Europe's turmoil. Charles Lindbergh, one of the nation's greatest heroes, rendered compelling and sympathetic years before with the kidnapping of his baby, overturns a lackluster array of Republicans seeking to unseat the unbeatable Roosevelt. He is nominated as Republican presidential candidate, roundly defeats the president, and immediately negotiates neutrality with the Nazis. This is followed by a steady cascade of pronouncements about Jews, accompanied by policies (on the surface quite benign) aimed at their assimilation, with this spilling into the lives of the Roth family. "Because what's history?" his father asks at the dinner table. "History is everything that happens everywhere. Even here in Newark. Even here on Summit Avenue. Even what happens in his house to an ordinary man—that'll be history too someday."[6]

This is the most transparently Jewish of Roth's books. Its first sentence: "Fear presides over these memories, a perpetual fear. Of course no childhood is without its terrors, yet I wonder if I would have been a less frightened boy if Lindbergh hadn't been president or I hadn't been the offspring of Jews."[7]

No depiction of Jewish ritual or beliefs, but a full-throated Jewish identification with beloved America:

> These were Jews who needed no large terms of reference, no profession of faith or doctrinal creed, in order to be Jews, and they certainly needed no other language—they had one, their native tongue, whose vernacular expressiveness they wielded effortlessly and, whether at the card table or while making a sales pitch, with the easygoing command of the indigenous population. Neither was their being Jews a mishap or a misfortune or an achievement. . . . Their being Jews issued from their being themselves, as did their being American. It was, as it was in the nature of things, as fundamental as having arteries and veins.[8]

In contrast with nearly all of Roth's novels in the previous several years, this is a densely plotted work, packed full of vivid, believable characters—above all Alvin, the distressingly flawed nephew who because of the death of his parents lives with Roth's immediate family. Alvin joins the Canadian army, loses a leg, and turns into a high-class criminal. Eventually, things get so bad that he is beaten up by Roth's sorely disappointed father. Young Philip, too, is rendered as more complex—also more conniving—than elsewhere: a boy of eight or nine suddenly faced with the prospect of political horror. A rare source of hope for Jews comes from gossip columnist and Lindbergh hater Walter Winchell, one of the few stridently public voices of opposition: a flawed, hyperbolic, but decent presence in a darkening America.

Roth also offers up here the most gruesome of all the awful rabbis in his repertoire. Rabbi Lionel Bengelsdorf is an avid Lindbergh supporter, a shrewd opportunist though also perhaps the finest Jewish orator in Newark. A widower, rich and splendidly well connected, he inspires the devotion of the boy's Aunt Evelyn, still another of Roth's portraits of intensity gone berserk who implodes by the novel's end. There is the hapless neighbor Seldon, betrayed by Phil in a moment that still weighs heavily on him many years later. And, of course, the portrait of his brother Sandy—in love with an antisemitic American president throughout much of the book—at war with his family, whose ghetto mentality he comes to despise. The book is more straightforward than Roth's previous works; largely absent here are Roth's breathlessly packed sentences. It is a book narrated, it seems, by an older, rather bemused man seeking to capture the experience of a boy confounded as his world goes awry.

To the extent to which anything holds it all together, it is the mother's devotion. At its start is one of its very few colossal sentences, thirteen lines in length that begins and eventually concludes in this way: "The men worked fifty, sixty, even seventy or more hours a week; the women worked all the time, with little assistance from labor-saving devices, washing laundry, ironing shirts, mending socks, turning collars . . . while simultaneously attending to their children's health, clothing, cleanliness, schooling, nutrition, conduct, birthdays, discipline, and morale."[9]

There were, says the narrator, some intimations of anti-Jewish ghastliness before Lindbergh's election, but little reason to take these seriously. Union, a nearby town where Philip's father is offered a promotion if he agrees to move his insurance work there, is packed with German Americans including, it seems, a substantial number of antisemites, which dissuades Herman from accepting the offer. But once Lindbergh is elected such moments mount: exclusion from a hotel during the family's long-planned visit to Washington, DC, nasty comments directed at the family in a restaurant, Sandy's attraction to the new regime and his parroting increasingly widespread sentiments about the unhealthy, ghettolike rhythms of Jewish life.

This self-consciously counterintuitive novel was Roth's most realistic in years, with nearly everything seen through the prism of family. The narrator recalls that in the midst of the Lindbergh years, his father fell apart ("crying like both a baby abandoned and a man being tortured"), his mother was compelled to work outside the house to supplement their now meager income, and Sandy was all but lost for a time as a Lindbergh devotee. A reminder of what transpires when the world takes a sudden nasty turn, overwhelming everything that came before.

The book was so meticulously plotted that it readily lent itself, unlike nearly all of Roth's other books, to other media, with the HBO adaptation of it remaining true to Roth's story, both ending with an unsettling abruptness. Roth may have decided that he had said all he wished to say about Lindbergh—who suddenly disappears with FDR eagerly reelected. The declaration at the book's start that once the Republicans "nominated Lindbergh and everything changed" now falls flat: Seldon comes to live in Philip's bedroom, Sandy has already returned to the fold. Aunt Evelyn is—like so many of the rageful in Roth's writing—ruined.[10] Roth appends to the novel a postscript with documentary evidence covering the period, but this does little to complete this saga, the most straightforward, most concrete, most realistic novel he would ever write.

And the most Jewish. Certainly, its rabbi is a cad, religion offers no relief to rampant antisemitic suffering, and many Jews succumb to Lindbergh's charms. Nonetheless, as Coetzee writes—while acknowledging that when judged against *Sabbath's Theater* this is not one of Roth's major works—it provides a perspective on Jewish childhood unique among Roth's works:

> What the plot against America does to young Philip between the ages of seven and nine is terrible. It forces upon him—though less, it must it be noted, at first hand than through the medium of newsreels and radio programs and from eavesdropping on his parents' worried conversations—a vision of a world based on hatred and suspicion, a world of them and

> us. It turns him from a Jewish American into an American Jew, or in the eyes of his enemies just a Jew in America. In waking him up to "reality" too early, it strips him of his childhood.[11]

Susan Rogers and Roth reconnected as he was struggling with the start of *The Plot Against America*. Thin, athletic, and drawn to Roth since she was a teenager, she would act out scenes in the book to help Roth as he wrestled with it. He describes his first impressions of her in *The Humbling*, published in 2009: "a lithe, full-breasted woman of forty, though with something of a child still in her smile—a smile in which she automatically raised her upper lip to reveal her prominent front teeth—and a lot of the tomboy still in her rocking gait."[12] This a playful romance, with Roth lavishing gifts and Rogers keenly attentive to his writerly needs. Throughout, as she later recalled, he failed to show any interest at all in her own work on wilderness travel, kayaking, and the like, topics of no concern to him.

Roth said to her, once their sexual relationship ended, that he had truly loved her. But he was furious that she abandoned him to accept a research grant to study in Antarctica—so furious that he portrayed a woman modeled on Rogers in *The Humbling* as "nothing," little more than "a child-adult" and a "cunning naif." Rogers recalls that she felt sick to her stomach when she finished the book.[13]

By then, Roth had already embarked on a romance with Lisa Halliday, forty-three years younger, and he would also react angrily once she broke off their relationship to join a man she was in love with in Rome. Later there was thirty-three-year-old Kirby Woodson and then the beautiful Caro Llewellyn, an Australian-born author and cultural administrator until she, too, as he saw it, disappointed him.[14] "Eventually his needs and mine collapsed under their own weight" Llewellyn writes in a memoir, *Diving into Glass*, adding, "When we were in the country together we listened to Susan Kennedy's *Big Band Hall of Fame*. . . . He sang along with Frank Sinatra and the Andrews Sisters and quizzed me about the tracks. Sometimes we danced."[15]

These liaisons occurred during an extended period of excruciating physical ailments, but Roth showed himself attentive to his young lovers. He met Llewellyn just as she began to suffer from the disabilities of multiple sclerosis, and he watched over her with great care—though interspersed with stretches of dark moodiness. When attentive, he could be extraordinary. Llewellyn describes her summer with him in 2011:

> Philip looked after me. I didn't have to do anything when we were together. He planned where we'd eat and made the reservations, and when we were in the city, if he noticed I was tired, he ordered a car service to take me home. When my insurance no longer covered my physical therapy sessions, he sent me a cheque. . . . For once in my life I needed someone else to take charge and he did it graciously, without making me feel coddled, disempowered or that I owed him anything in return.[16]

But he had mounting concerns about his health: chest pains, mouth pains, discomfort often so severe that he found himself compelled to lie on his back during meals or make one of his frequent trips to the hospital emergency room. In 2012 he endured back surgery. He also worried about his waning capacity to remember all that must be recalled when writing a sustained work. Artist Judy Hudson, who spent much of the summer of 2010 in Connecticut with him (they had met at a cocktail party, after which Hudson sent him a note saying she'd "adore" having a drink with him), described to me a despondent Roth at breakfast after the completion of *Nemesis*, with Roth trying to start something new. His head on the table, he admitted in a voice suffused with fear and loss that he couldn't manage to write another novel.[17]

Instead, he issued an announcement—much like that, say,

of an insurance agent—of his retirement in 2012. He followed the retirement with an obsessive exercise in self-exculpation: two manuscripts—one devoted to attacking Claire Bloom for her depiction of him in her memoir, the other a full-fledged onslaught on the failings of Ross Miller. His friend Jack Miles and others close to him dissuaded him from publishing the attacks, making the case that they would do little but show him to be vindictive and unforgivably defensive. His mood was so dark at the time that Llewellyn feared he was planning to kill himself.[18]

Eventually, the women in his life rarely shared a bedroom with him. His sexual urges, it seems, never diminished even as his capacity may well have. He met Kirby Woodson to interview her about the Houston school from which she had graduated and which the lovely Jamie Logan attended in *Exit Ghost*. The two began a romantic relationship that lasted, on and off, for two years. (I recall Roth complaining to me about her overuse of the word "awesome.") Judy Hudson described to me her surprise at their sleeping in separate rooms during her summer's stay in Connecticut, and, once she pressed him on this score he revealed to her that his sexual potency had by now much diminished. When I repeated this to his close friends Norman and Cella Manea, they laughed, saying that Roth had simply lied to her: He found her—despite her beauty—unattractive because of her gray hair. Yet the blond, far younger Llewellyn speaks also of their sleeping in separate rooms, though often she climbed into his bed in the morning. She describes, for a while at least, a thoroughly congenial relationship but one devoid of the sexual energy Roth had brought to his romantic entanglements of the past.[19]

He loved having beautiful women close at hand, even in the absence of sexual activity. Hence the curious presence in his last years of his cook Catherine von Klitzing.

Thin, winsome, beguiling as a model, von Klitzing remained his cook, both in New York and in Connecticut, for years despite the fact—as observed by Benjamin Taylor, who spent more time with Roth in his final years than anyone else—that she had limited capacity to function in the kitchen. When Taylor would come for dinner, he would bring his own food to eat, rather than share the food she served Philip. And Roth too would, according to Taylor, rush to serve himself a bowl of cereal as soon as she left for the night. She was a professionally trained cook, but one who favored use of nuts, seeds, and grains—"bird food," Taylor pronounced it. Von Klitzing claimed in a conversation with me that she hid from Philip noisome aspects of her past, including that her Austrian father, old already at the time of her birth, had been a Nazi. She retained deep religious beliefs that she also hid from the stalwart atheist. A painfully shy, emotional woman, an alcoholic with questionable cooking capacity but an enchanting beauty, she remained crucially important to Roth long after she left his employ. Roth advised her about her choice of men, urging her to break with one of them because he didn't merit her affection. There at his bedside at the time of his death, nurses found her clutching his body until she was told that he had passed. In his will Roth left her a sizable inheritance. And in a conversation with her a few months after his death, she told me that he continued to communicate with her.[20]

These women all describe his infectious sense of humor, a joyful laugh little different from that of a young, ever-playful man. And a handsome man he remained almost to the end: The photograph of him on the cover of the *New York Times* style section taken in late 2014 shows his vibrant, alert face resting on his right hand, dapper in a fresh white shirt and dark jacket. ("Old Books, New Thoughts" was what prompted this cover story, which announced an auction of first editions of *Portnoy's Complaint* and the work of six other well-known writers to support the writers organization PEN American Center.) Meeting with him in the last years of his life, I found him faster on his feet,

Catherine von Klitzing was Roth's favored cook, and a fixture of his last years, a source of devotion and youthful beauty. (Photo reproduced with permission of Catherine von Klitzing)

and sharper, and certainly more bitingly funny than nearly anyone I had ever met. In a conversation shortly before his death in 2018 about the biography of Bernard Malamud by critic Philip Davis, a friend of mine, it became clear that I liked the book more than Roth, though I added that Davis's account stumbled at times because he seemed to have permitted himself to like Malamud more than he should as a biographer. Philip looked at me sharply, also amusedly, saying in response: "I'll have nothing to worry about on that score from you, will I?"

Charming, expansive, and attentive as he was, he could also behave cunningly, or worse. With Halliday, he tried a bribe to dissuade her from marrying and moving away from him. Llewellyn he dropped because of von Klitzing's jealousy, though

Roth blamed Llewellyn for the debacle.[21] And, of course, Rogers he savaged in a novel.

Still, all retained a deep attachment to him. Rogers, alongside many of the other women in his life, was at his bedside when he died, crashing at his 79th Street apartment so as to remain close to him in the hospital. Poet and memoirist Mary Karr, a good friend in his final years, told me, "No one knew to listen more attentively." They enjoyed long, rambunctious conversations on many topics, including the virtues of feminism.[22]

The prospect of friendship—for several, also intimacy—with a living legend, a writer whose work would most likely continue to live and breathe long after his death, was sufficient reason for some to stay close by. So was the joy of his rapid-fire comedic talk—interspersed, to be sure, more and more with gray, despondent moods. Roth understood all this and would explore the inner workings of these relationships in the last of his books. He would readily admit that he found otherwise alluringly attractive women like Mary Karr or Judith Hudson too old—though only in their forties or fifties at the time they met—gravitating instead to women in their twenties, whom he then feared would abandon him, as eventually they did.

By far the most painful of these episodes was with Catherine Steindler, twenty-nine at the time they met; he was seventy-one. Once he fell for her, some months after their first meeting at David Plante's Columbia classroom, he fell hard. He would depict her physical presence joyfully—her temperament rather more equivocally—in *Exit Ghost*, written a couple years after their turbulent end: "She was a tall, slender young woman. . . . Her long, narrow face was curtained by straight, fine black hair that fell to her shoulders and a little below, the cut seemingly designed to conceal some disfiguring blemish, though by no means one that was physical—she had an impeccable, creamily soft surface, whatever else she might be hiding."[23]

Right after seeing her at the Russian Tea Room a few months

after their first encounter at Columbia, he declared that he was in love. The two danced to show tunes in Connecticut, went on a clothes shopping spree in Soho, and attended a *New Yorker* party. She did striptease for him and sang a loving rendition of "Mr. Hard On." There were plans for her to move into the 79th Street apartment, and he went so far as to consult a doctor about the prospect of siring a baby at this stage in life.

Marc Weitzmann recalled Roth's immense joy during this time. Curiously, he was now at work on one of the grayest of all his last books, *Everyman*. Weitzmann remembers plotting together with him and others at the Russian Tea Room about how Roth might best keep Steindler; the consensus was that he should impregnate her. Roth acknowledged feeling an immense love for her. And once it ended, Weitzmann observed, "he suddenly was an old man."[24]

It was the incomparable excitement of this time—no doubt accentuated by the fear that it could all come crashing down at any moment—that he captured in *Everyman*, where the old but fit and sexually hungry protagonist strikes up a conversation with a shapely jogger he spots as he sits on a bench. He stops her, asks her whether she might be "game," to which she shows no shock but "took it with an agreeable little catlike smile that could easily have been accompanied by a purr." And while engaging in this banter, suddenly he started "feeling himself growing hard in his pants unbelievably, magically quickly, as though he were fifteen. And feeling, too, that sharp sense of individualization, of sublime singularity, that marks a fresh sexual encounter or love affair."[25]

It was just such moments he now sought, even at the height of the relationship with Steindler, concerned that this might well eventually slip out of his grasp. And then in fall 2005 it did. Roth was convinced that Steindler backed away because of a bribe from her father, who offered to buy her a condo in Brooklyn Heights if she left Roth. (The apartment has been described to me as lavish with exceptionally high ceilings, Steindler having managed to buy the floor above as well.) More likely, Steindler may well have found herself in over her head, as Judith Thurman put it.

The decision to end the affair shocked him terribly. He argued with her about it for hours and would come to despise her afterward. Seeing her later walking near his 79th Street apartment, he spat in her direction. "Nuts" is how Steindler would now describe him. Her sudden departure left him in such a fragile state that he took refuge at Joel Conarroe's cramped West Village apartment.[26]

Still, years later Roth would reminisce about "my beautiful Catherine," who—as he described it—arrived at a party flying in from Oregon without proper clothes, prompting a Soho shopping spree together: a green blouse—a "knockout"—purchased along with matching dress and shoes.

While the implosion of his relationship with Steindler did nothing to end his pursuit of much younger women, none of these liaisons would measure up in their importance to him. Lisa Halliday, whose affair with Roth predated his meeting Steindler, captures these patterns well in *Asymmetry*—a fiction, to be sure, but with transparent similarity to the details of their romance. Here her lover, the famous novelist who turns heads wherever he goes, interviews Alice at his Upper West Side apartment soon after she assures him that she is "game." She sits first in his living room, where the "seat of his reading chair was black leather and low to the ground, like a Porsche" and then he gestures her to his bed, where she discovers:

> From his stomach all the way up to his sternum ran a pink, zipperlike scar. Another scar bisected his leg from groin to ankle. Two more made a faint circumflex above his hip. And that was just the front.
>
> "Who did this to you?"
>
> "Norman Mailer."[27]

In her early twenties, Halliday's Alice is still directionless but with at least vague literary aspirations. She's in love with baseball and astonished that she knows, and is now intimate with, one of the world's smartest men, fitting herself (not always joyfully) into his strict writing schedule, rarely if ever spending the night. Once when ill, he invites her to remain with him and spends a restless night, admitting that this was a mistake. He gives her gifts, asks for her to run errands for him, and is in constant fear that a young man will take her from him: "He ran a hand over his eyes, fingers trembling. 'I'm afraid some man is going to come along and fuck you up.'" He declares love at moments of tenderness or gratitude, never quite meaning it, and jokes in ways only Roth might: "I just killed the biggest wasp," she tells him. "I thought George Plimpton was the biggest wasp."[28]

She will buckle at the chores, but never does he lose his wit, his distinctive voice explaining to her while on his hospital bed:

> "Well, if you say you're Catholic and it looks like you're getting close to the end, they send a priest around. If you're Jewish, they send a rabbi around."
>
> "And if you're an atheist?"
>
> "They send Christopher Hitchens around."[29]

19

Everyman

And now, book after book depicting the onset of old age—its indignities, its diminishments, literary as well as sexual. "It's the commonness that's most wrenching," as he puts it in *Everyman*, "the fact of death that overwhelms everything."[1] Rare amid this outpouring of slim volumes published between 2006 and 2010—*Everyman*, *Exit Ghost*, *Indignation*, *The Humbling*, *Nemesis*—were those exuberant sentences that had set his work apart almost since its start. Indeed, with only one exception—unsurprisingly built around luscious recollections of childhood on Bradley Beach—in *Everyman*, by far the most laconic of this final cycle. Here a return to the incomparable joys of swimming far beyond where you ought to go, where you can feel "the waves from way out" hitting your body. Here a single sentence of sixteen lines recalls the pleasure of those risky youthful swims far beyond the rope, if also his waning capacity to compose breathless, sweeping prose:

> Or was the best of old age just that—the longing for the best of boyhood, for the tubular sprout that was then his body and that rode the waves from way out where they began to build, rode them with his arms pointed like an arrowhead and the skinny rest of him following behind like the arrow's shaft, rode them all the way in to where his rib cage scraped against the tiny sharp pebbles and jagged clamshells and pulverized sea-shells at the edge of the shore and he hustled to his feet and hurriedly turned and went lurching through the low surf until it was knee high and deep enough for him to plunge in and begin swimming madly out to the rising breakers—into the advancing, green Atlantic, rolling unstoppably toward him like the obstinate fact of the future—and, if he was lucky, make it there in time to catch the next big wave and then the next and the next and the next until from the low slant of inland sunlight glittering across the water he knew it was time to go.[2]

"Time to go" is this book's—indeed, all his subsequent books'—essential theme. *Everyman* tells of an unnamed protagonist with his several marriages, two adopted children, a successful career in advertising, and retirement spent painting. In its bare bones, it is a story resembling the life of his brother Sandy. With its title inspired by a fifteenth-century morality play and a cadence as close to Chekhov's as anything Roth would write, it was in its earlier drafts—as Weitzmann recalls—far sparser. Even in its final version, its characters are among his most sketchily drawn: the astonishingly generous brother Howie, the ever-generous daughter from his second marriage and her mother, Phoebe, both modeled it seems on an idealized Ann Mudge, with whom Roth had now reconnected. The fullest of all characterizations in the book are those of sons from his first marriage, now middle-aged but still consumed by bitterness toward their father, this portrait modeled largely on the behavior (which he found deplorable) of Saul Bellow's sons at his funeral a few years earlier:

"men in their late forties and looking, with their glossy black hair and their eloquent dark eyes and the sensual fullness of their wide, identical mouths, just like their father . . . at their age. Handsome men beginning to grow beefy and seemingly as closely linked with each other as they'd been irreconcilably alienated from the dead father."[3]

Fear of death, says the narrator, had pursued him since childhood, with even his memories of young love infused already with such fears: "The profusion of stars told him unambiguously that he was doomed to die." Now an old man, he undergoes a seven-hour surgery and soon afterward moves to a bucolic retirement community on the New Jersey shore, which eventually bores him. He tries without success, of course, to pick up a young woman, tires of his painting and everything else except for his even-tempered daughter. And then, once again, surgery punctuated by cardiac arrest and immediate death. The novel's last words: "He was no more, freed from being, entering into nowhere without even knowing it. Just as he'd feared from the start."[4]

"Late Roth," writes James Wood "is simpler, more urgent, more vocal."[5] If anything, the mood of his next book, appearing soon afterward in 2008, was still grimmer, with the protagonist of *Indignation* already dead while narrating the story. This, too, among the darkest of Roth's books, was written against the backdrop of a cascade of stunning honors: a PEN/Faulkner Award for *Everyman* (the third time he won the prize), the first winner of the PEN/Saul Bellow Award for Achievement in American Fiction, a conference in his honor at Columbia, another at Queens College, and shortly afterward named a Commander of the Legion of Honour by the French government. A few months before his death, in 2018, the decision was announced to release his complete works in French in the prestigious Pléiade series of Gallimard.

But few if any of these celebrations appeared to touch him

as deeply as did the honorary degree conferred by the Jewish Theological Seminary at its 2014 graduation ceremony. The decision to confer the award was, as it happens, altogether uncontroversial. As Arnold Eisen, the seminary's former chancellor, recalls, the idea to honor Roth was first proposed by a member of the board of trustees, a decision that seemed self-evident. To Roth, however, it felt like nothing less than a milestone: "The first time I've been applauded by Jews since my bar mitzvah," he said in his acceptance speech. Eisen remembers having been informed by Julia Golier that Roth was unlikely to remain for the entire lengthy ceremony, which involved conferring degrees on all graduates including the rabbinic class, but there he remained—chatting with grateful readers at the reception following the formalities, enjoying this warm embrace, surprising, it seems, to no one except Roth himself.[6]

Indignation, published two years after *Everyman*, has the feel of something akin to a transcript. Indeed, its lengthy section on what it felt like to grow up in a butcher shop drew on interviews with Roth's close childhood friend Stuart Lehman, who was raised by his grandparents after the death of his own parents and whose grandfather was a butcher. Here, too, Roth revisits a theme he made his own years before—the Korean War—and the terror of the wartime draft during the bloodiest juncture of its battles in 1951.

Although old age haunts *Everyman*, it is the prospect of early death on the battlefield that is the source of terror in *Indignation*, a fear so pervasive that it wreaks havoc on the previously harmonious relationship between the narrator, Marcus Messner, and his father.

Praised by some as his best since *The Counterlife*, *Indignation* is a book drenched in blood: carnage in Korea and the gory routines of the kosher butcher, particularly the evisceration of chickens, related in copious, dreadful detail.[7] To escape his father's agonizing worries, Messner chooses, hastily, to study at a

Baptist institution modeled on Roth's Bucknell and located in Winesburg, Ohio, the terrain of his beloved Sherwood Anderson. There Messner rehearses his atheist convictions to an exasperated, pious dean (the text torn straight out of Bertrand Russell's "Why I Am Not a Christian") and undergoes a series of unfortunate dorm assignments that appear to show his unwillingness to compromise with roommates. This stubbornness haunts him almost from the moment he arrives.

And soon Messner falls for the wrong girl. Roth's description of male desire here fixated on the smallest of movements by the beautiful—if also, as he soon learns, troubled—Olivia Hutton is extraordinary. Here he is watching her intently, patiently as she sits in the library:

> She was at one of the long tables on the reading room floor, diligently taking notes out of a reference book. Two things captivated me. One was the part in her exquisite hair. Never before had I been so vulnerable to the part in someone's hair. The other was her left leg, which was crossed over her right leg and rhythmically swaying up and down. Her skirt fell midway down her calf, as was the style, but still, from where I was seated I could see beneath the table the unceasing movement of that leg. She must have remained there like that for two hours, steadily taking notes without a break, and all I did during that time was to look at the way that hair was parted in an even line and the way she never stopped moving her leg up and down. Not for the first time, I wondered what moving a leg like that felt like for a girl.[8]

They date, and she unsettles him by revealing her own desire and her intention to please him by engaging in oral sex, without even the hint of struggle. What most unnerves him is the absence of any hesitancy. It is now revealed that he's narrating the story though dead, struck down in Korea at the age of nineteen. "Is that what eternity is for, to muck over a lifetime's minutiae?"[9] His father's prediction that the smallest of mishaps could lead to disaster he now knows carries a good deal of truth. Dead, he can't stop from puzzling over Olivia's actions, which he tends to attribute to her parents' divorce, though when pressed by him she explains that she did it simply because she liked his looks, his seriousness, his intensity.

Messner's argument with another roommate about Olivia prompts another move, now followed by the dean's interrogation. He admits in this encounter that as an "ardent atheist" he loathes the school's obligatory chapel attendance, where he sings the Chinese national anthem under his breath, relishing especially the line, "Indignation fills the hearts of all of our countrymen." No fewer than fifty times he would recite the song during the weekly sermon, "every time giving special emphasis to each of the four syllables that melded together form the noun 'indignation.'"[10]

The vagaries of fate haunt him most now: the father who couldn't cease obtrusively interfering in the life of his son, compelling him to escape home for a wholly inappropriate school. Messner himself can't ever compromise, with a rigidity that subverts not only his chance to excel in college but eventually leads to his death, with an unanticipated blow job by a troubled, beautiful, and devoted girlfriend—this, too, the cause of endless discomfort. He is rigid, and principled, and relentlessly focused, with these very same qualities contributing to his eventual downfall. "I wanted to do everything right," Messner recalls, this impossible, even destructive.[11] Instead, he is the only member of his class killed in Korea. From start to finish, it is a dour, crabbed tale.

No lessons felt more indisputable or pressing at this juncture in Roth's life—haunted by the proximity of death, the grim aftermath of Claire Bloom's accusations in her 1996 memoir, the fear that feminist disapproval would forever shadow his reputation—than these, the novel's final words: "one's most banal, incidental, even comical choices achieve the most disproportionate result."[12]

Notes in search of a book is how Brooklyn College historian and columnist Eric Alterman has characterized to me *Exit Ghost.* Perhaps so, but the notes themselves are sufficient to make this the richest of all Roth's late-life books: a study of life's ghosts (Amy Bellette, George Plimpton, Nathan Zuckerman himself) and the inevitable tension between young and old. At the same time, it is Roth's fullest exploration of the urgency—brutal if also oddly justifiable—of biography.

On the surface, the novel is an unambiguous attack on the biographical impulse, scored as nothing more than the gouging of life's stories all in an effort to "transform them, garble them, distort them, misinterpret and misunderstand them."[13] Nathan Zuckerman resurfaces here—for the last time, and no less isolated amid Hawthorne's forests than Lonoff had once been—to discover Bellette, now seventy-five, dying of cancer, a shell of her prior luscious self but in her more lucid moments the most compelling figure in the book. Zuckerman learns that she had run away with Lonoff, who found himself unable to enjoy their love and spent the short remainder of his life miserable, incapable of finishing his next book, and wracked with shame over the betrayal of his abandoned wife.

On the one hand biography here is sheer desecration, prurience gone amok. Yet Zuckerman reveals himself, as in *The Ghost Writer,* obsessed by the interplay between imagination and the rest of life: this the core of any literary biographical quest. Learning from Bellette that Lonoff had left his wife for her, Zuckerman ponders this revelation:

> What *was* the story of those five years? Once something did happen to that sedate, reclusive writer who—assisted by the

> forlorn irony that pervaded his view of the world—had bravely resigned himself to nothing's ever happening to him, what then ensued? . . . Why should so ordinary a renovation—the middle-age life change, commonly thought to be replenishing, of taking a new mate and setting up house in a new locale—cripple a man with the forbearance of a Lonoff?[14]

Zuckerman arrives in New York, having been away for eleven years. Returning at the cusp of George W. Bush's reelection, Zuckerman is unsettled by the changes all around him, especially the ubiquity of cell phones. He decides rashly to stay, now enamored with a beautiful, married young woman, though he is impotent (this a byproduct of prostate cancer surgery). It is at the hospital, while exploring the prospect of a cure for impotence as well as his incontinence, that he discovers Bellette, who is embroiled—much like Roth in his battle with Bellow's biographer James Atlas—in thwarting a prospective biography about Lonoff, whose would-be author is young, impetuous, and ferociously ambitious.

Zuckerman recognizes the resemblance, of course, between his own younger self and the dreaded upstart. Kliman is his name (likely a play on the Yiddish *kleyn* meaning "small one"), and the biographer is convinced that the reason Lonoff was unable to finish another book was his humiliation for having engaged in incest with his sister in adolescence, something Kliman feels obligated to reveal but is paralyzed to do so. Roth draws here on the revelations of the famed novelist Henry Roth, who only late in life published—with the help of Liveright publisher Robert Weil—the story of his own incest, which as he then acknowledged had obstructed him for more than half a century from following up on his masterwork of the 1930s, *Call It Sleep.* Philip Roth sat for hours with Robert Weil, as he described his conversations with Henry Roth about his anguished silence.

Bellette is a wreck but also a paragon of devotion. She continues to protect Lonoff, seeing herself as a sentinel, guarding nothing less than cultural integrity and not only his now-scant literary reputation. In a brilliant passage, Zuckerman sets out to persuade her—maybe also to persuade himself—that Lonoff's dark secret wasn't real but a literary invention. It was no more than the product of Lonoff's fascination with the life of Nathaniel Hawthorne, said to have shielded a dark secret of his own, which some biographers have speculated was incest. This, proposes Zuckerman to Bellette, is the source of Lonoff's deeply original understanding of the unrepresentative nature of great fiction, though Zuckerman immediately undermines the credibility of his case:

> For this wholly unautobiographical writer, blessed with his genius for complete transformation, the choice was almost inevitable. It's what opened his predicament out for him and enabled him to leave the personal behind. Fiction for him was never representation. It was rumination in narrative form. He thought, "I'll make this my reality." While, in fact, I was thinking in much the same vein: I'll make this reality mine, Amy's, Kliman's, everyone's. And for the next hour I proceed to, effulgently, arguing its logic until I had come to believe it myself.[15]

"Effulgently" offers the clue, if one is needed, that Zuckerman is feeding himself a pack of convenient, if intriguingly erudite nonsense. And the novel itself is an extended exploration of the nonsense we're capable of telling ourselves to the point where we might, at least momentarily, believe it: The impotent Zuckerman dreams of taking the beautiful Jamie Logan away from her husband, though he recognizes its impossibility. He dreams of abandoning his seclusion for life on the Upper West Side—this, he appreciates well, "the most thoughtless snap decision I'd ever made." He recalls vividly his dream of marrying Bellette, whom he had many years before transmuted into Anne Frank, which then "seemed to an untried boy the answer to everything."[16]

Roth's interrogation here of the interplay between art and life is done with visitations from some of his favored writers: Conrad and Chekhov, Hawthorne, Henry James, and, of course, Anne Frank. This would be the last of Zuckerman's appearances, and—jagged as the book is, and while it is made of pieces never altogether glued together—it is also haunting and sad and masterful.

"Time," suggests Claudia Roth Pierpont, "is the real subject of the book."[17] How best to live life—like the reclusive Lonoff or, as Roth then interjects in a sudden aside that occupies several pages of the novel, like George Plimpton: the tantalizingly effusive founder of the *Paris Review* whose death stunned Zuckerman and who had provided the young Roth, as he relates, with his first glimpse of the gift of privilege, of a charmed life without guilt, or shame, or ceaseless struggle. Hence Zuckerman's decision to follow the overpowering example of Plimpton: to stay in New York, embrace all it offers, see distraction as opportunity, and shed all the inhibitions bred deep into him by his past. As Kliman says to him, "you haven't drifted. Your life has been an arrow. You've worked."[18] This Zuckerman at first chooses to do, and then soon enough flees once his cure for impotence proves ineffective, his pursuit of Logan no more than a fantasy, his desire to shed his semitic angst for Plimpton's genteel ease inconceivable.

It was the First Avenue apartment of Julia Golier, Roth's lover of the mid-1990s, that inspired the depiction of Bellette's grim flat: "The bedroom looked out on an air shaft and down to a tiny back alley where the restaurant's garbage cans were stored. A toilet, I discovered, was in a closet-sized room on the other side of a door beside the kitchen sink. A smallish bathtub raised on claw feet rested on the kitchen floor, fitted with barely inches to spare between the refrigerator and the stove."[19]

At the time Roth met Golier, she was a psychiatric research fellow at the Veteran's branch of Mount Sinai Hospital; later she was a resident psychiatrist and faculty member. Roth came to rely on her calm and sound advice for the remainder of his life. She persuaded him not to sell the Connecticut house, which he had planned to do because of all its dark memories. Golier distrusted Ross Miller, carefully walking Roth through their painful split. She showed herself to be sensible and caring without being commanding, loving him deeply, with the two deciding to separate only because she wanted children. And despite Roth's longstanding indifference to children, his relationship with her twins, born in 2003, would become one of the great joys of his last years.

Julia Golier provided him with the sense of constancy, of steady love, of loyalty and good cheer. Hers was a wry, puckish sense of humor wedded to a fierce protectiveness that persuaded him to name her his health proxy and an executor of his estate. And, while she balanced a demanding career and a suddenly large family, Roth's welfare remained among Golier's top priorities, as he gratefully recognized. A sign, perhaps, of her salutary impact on his life was his decision to write, soon after their meeting, a portrait of the gentlest of all his protagonists: Seymour Levov, the Swede.

20

Ghost Writer

He had no children, he had no wife, he had no family:
the only thing left was these pages.

By far, the most detailed description of Roth's last decade—when he finished his last book *Nemesis*, announced his intention to stop writing, aided his authorized biographer Blake Bailey with research for his nearly nine hundred–page book (longer still in its initial draft), wrestled repeatedly with ill health, and produced many hundreds of pages (never published) of attacks on Claire Bloom and Ross Miller—is found in Bailey's *Philip Roth: The Biography*. Here Bailey, whose book would be pulped by his publisher Norton within weeks of its publication in 2021 because of claims of sexual impropriety and worse, offers a sympathetic but by no means altogether uncritical portrait.

Still, the most perceptive portrait of his final years is the brief, deeply knowing book by Benjamin Taylor—*Here We Are: My Friendship with Philip Roth*, published in 2020. A talented, prolific writer of fiction and biography, Taylor grew close to Roth in the late 1990s. A homosexual without family obligations, living near Roth's New York City apartment, Taylor was grateful to be close to his most admired writer. A tolerant and patient man, he readily forgave the friendship's drawbacks, such as Roth's loathing for the theater as well as orchestras (he did love chamber music) and his dislike of planetariums (the Hayden Planetarium, a favorite of Taylor's, was just down the street from Roth's apartment). Taylor took notes on their meetings—Roth seems to have been aware that he was doing this—later distilling the notes into a remarkable book.

Especially noteworthy is Taylor's exploration of Roth's inability to acknowledge—this in stark contrast to the deep, nuanced empathy displayed in so much of his fiction—that he was at all at fault with regard to the failure of his marriages. "His own angle of vision was complete and unfailing," with this blind spot particularly striking when seen against the rare fluency and skill employed in his fiction in airing viewpoints at odds with his own. And Taylor describes the heavy toll on Roth from rejection after rejection every October by the Nobel committee, eventually referring to the prize as the "Anybody-But-Roth Prize."[1]

Roth reminisced with Taylor about his books, his parents, his loves; they would watch Roth's favorite Kurosawa films (Taylor much preferred *Now, Voyager*, which Roth disparaged), and Roth would bring him along on his visits to the city's grimmer, out of the way Hungarian restaurants, these among his favorites. Taylor watched over him as he wrestled with debilitating pain and—only slightly less harrowing—the numbing of painkillers. One night in Connecticut, Roth utterly flattened by a fentanyl patch he was wearing, came to the guest bedroom at three in the morning "and said, in tears, 'Ben, can you find out for me if I'm awake or asleep?' "[2] Starting in 2004, Roth was obliged to wear a defibrillator, placed under the skin of his chest, which was the size of a pack of cigarettes. There were numerous efforts, starting about five years before his death, to fix him with angioplasties and stents.

Taylor ends the book hauntingly with this handshake of a virtual brother:

> "You have been the joy of my life." "And you of mine," he replied. . . . Some months later I dream I've forgotten how to tie my tie. Over and under? Under and around? Under and over and back again? None of these work. Then he looms up behind me in the mirror, reaches over my shoulders, knots a perfect half-Windsor. I wake to no pall on that day. For I am here and it is now, and what I would not part with I have kept.[3]

Surrounding Roth in these last years was a family of sorts—above all, Julia Golier, who brought Roth squarely into her own family; he a doting relative to her twins. He deepened his friendship with his Connecticut neighbor Mia Farrow, and he was protected by remarkably generous, intuitive women like Judith Thurman and Barbara Sproul. Besides Benjamin Taylor, there were others—Nicole Krauss, Bernard Avishai, historian Sean Wilentz, David Rieff, Joel Conarroe, Andrew Wiley, the *New Yorker*'s David Remnick—who provided vibrant intellectual company when needed. And, indeed, it was the inescapable centrality of family, a topic never distant from him, that he situated at the core of the last of his books, *Nemesis*. On its surface *Nemesis*, published in 2009, was the story of a polio epidemic in Newark in the mid-1940s, but in truth the real source of terror was what it meant to face the epidemic without the ineluctable safeguard of mother or father.

> I knew only two boys in our neighborhood whose families were fatherless, and thought of them as no less blighted than the blind girl who attended our school for a while and had to be read to and shepherded everywhere. The fatherless boys seemed almost equally marked and set apart; in the aftermath of their fathers' deaths, they too struck me as scary and a little taboo. Though one was a model of obedience and the other a troublemaker, everything either of them did or said seemed determined by his being a boy with a dead father and, however innocently I arrived at this notion, I was probably right.[4]

The "embodiment of immovability" is how Roth characterizes the book's protagonist Bucky Cantor, this by no means intended as a compliment.[5] Orphaned (hence, in Roth's view, luckless) and ever well-meaning—if also, at best, moderately intelligent—Cantor, a gym teacher, is the figure at the center of this deceptively simple saga of epidemic in wartime Newark. Due to Bucky's poor eyesight and short, though muscled, stature, he is unable to join his friends to fight in the war. He is pictured as isolated (his friends now in Korea), while loved by grandparents who have raised him, and adored by a sweet girlfriend as well as her sisters and parents. All are overwhelmingly kind to him but never manage to appreciate the source of his anguish, about which he too seems unaware. For a time, he is the toast of Weequahic, having protected the children under his wing at the playground (his summer job is playground director) from a clutch of Italian American toughs, who tried to intimidate the neighborhood's Jews, threatening to infect them with polio by spitting on their sidewalks.

This is, arguably, the most communally preoccupied portrait Roth ever produced: a study of a man so loyal to those around him that he cannot bear to abandon them, even when offered a lifeguard's job that his girlfriend has arranged at a rustic camp outside Newark, where she awaits him and where they will finally be able to spend the night together.[6] Forever the lifeguard, he wrestles ardently, if also rather ploddingly, with the mysteries of God's intentions as he watches polio spread in Jewish Weequahic and as the children he coaches fall ill, one after the other. Rumors abound, with his neighborhood now the epicenter of Newark's polio scare. Soon Cantor's Weequahic is all but cut off from the rest of the city—with calls to build a barrier separating it from the rest of Newark—likely meant as an allusion to what Europe's Jews were then undergoing in the grip of Nazism.

All, even his girlfriend Marcia's father, a well-heeled doctor, are oblivious to the impending disaster, minimizing its severity. Bucky hungers for Marcia's girlish body and dreams of living a life spent in a commodious home like that of her parents. God's role in the world haunts him too, but he hasn't the words to express these concerns that gnaw at him incoherently: Sitting with Marcia's father on the veranda, "He thought to ask: Doesn't God have a conscience? Where's His responsibility? Or does He know no limits? But instead, he asked, 'Should the playground be shut down?' "[7]

With "Goodbye, Columbus" intended as Roth's gesture of farewell, a sign of estrangement from the homey parochialism of his immediate past, *Nemesis* offers a glimpse of just the opposite: solid reasons for loyalty to a wholesome neighborhood, a place whose children were until recently fearless and where "summertime was still a carefree adventure."[8]

Bucky abandons his job at the playground, escaping to the summer camp where Marcia works, but finds himself at odds with her, unable to settle down, and haunted by the weight of responsibility to his playground back home. And soon enough he discovers, or so he fears, that he himself is a carrier of the disease, having brought it to the camp, where many now fall ill, including Marcia's sisters. The camp is shut down with Bucky certain that he is responsible for having spread the illness.

Polio might well be the book's most obvious enemy, but a far greater source of misery for Bucky is precisely the same as his most commendable qualities: his devotion to community and the children under his wing. He is a man defeated by his own unyielding sense of rectitude: "That original face was now interred in another, fleshier face, a concealment people often see when looking with resignation at their aging selves in the mirror. No trace of the compact muscleman remained, the muscles having melted away while the compactness had burgeoned. Now he was simply stout."[9]

Certainly, it is among the tenderest of all Roth's books: It "stands out for its warmth" wrote novelist Leah Hager Cohen in her *New York Times* review. "'Nemesis' is surprisingly dense with happiness—a happiness that's ever-tenuous, and the sweeter for it. The word 'happy' crops up immoderately throughout."[10] But such happiness is not merely tenuous but illusionary, a state impossible for Bucky to enjoy because of his most outwardly praiseworthy qualities: a devotion to others that serves in the end to devastate. On the surface, it is a celebration of a good man, but it is a dark tale, among Roth's darkest—a study not only of life's daunting contingencies but of the terrible price paid for decency.

In the end—and here is where the book concludes—there is as Roth sees it only oneself, stretching every muscle at one's disposal to achieve whatever can be done in a life short and overwhelmingly brutish. It's unlikely that Roth knew at the time he wrote the book's final paragraph that this would be his last book, but its conclusion reads much like a snapshot of what both he and Bucky resembled at the height of his power: a master who manages to exceed even the greatest of what's expected of him, stretching oneself beyond endurance to achieve something more than merely extraordinary. It is difficult not to believe that in this final paragraph Roth does not seek to conflate himself with this—the last and most agreeable if also the most hapless of his protagonists. Here at the book's end, a vision of how Bucky ought to have spent his life:

> He threw the javelin repeatedly that afternoon, each throw smooth and powerful, each throw accompanied by that resounding mingling of a shout and a grunt, and each, to our delight, landing several yards farther down the field than the last. Running with the javelin aloft, stretching his throwing arm back behind his body, bringing the throwing arm through to release the javelin high over his shoulder—and releasing it then like an explosion—he seemed to us invincible.[11]

Hence the chasm left by the absence of family once again Roth's central theme. Still in these last years, Roth could discard people with suddenness, even apparent indifference. A case in point was his Iowa girlfriend Lucy Warner, her married name Kuemmerle, who reentered his life after Blake Bailey contacted her for an interview. She lived near Columbia, a quick subway ride away, and for some five or six years before Roth's death, they reestablished a convivial, warm friendship—one important to Kuemmerle and apparently to Roth as well.[12] He was at the time intent on reconnecting with former girlfriends, with nearly all having agreed except Maxine Groffsky, who maintained her distance. That Roth did this for the sake of forgiveness seems unlikely. Rather, those important in the past—men as well as women—remained much on his mind. David Rieff once pointedly asked me: How many of us have maintained close friendships of the sort that Roth enjoyed until the end of his life—with those we knew in high school or, for that matter, elementary school?

The renewed—platonic—relationship with Kuemmerle had them reading together all of *Moby-Dick*, no more than ten pages at a time. Once she did more than the ten and was rebuked by rule-stickler Roth. They would eventually complete their reading of it. There were frequent email exchanges, and often she accompanied him to medical appointments as well as procedures and surgeries. She met some of his close friends and once again was a part of his everyday life.

Describing this "lovely old-age relationship," she spoke of how they would meet "sometimes at [the restaurant] Nice Matin over lunch . . . walks in his neighborhood, sitting at benches at the Natural History Museum, but most often in his apartment talking, looking at books, catching parts of the Yankee games, telling stories, talking about age or history or Obama or Trump or parents or death."

Long ago they had enjoyed their brief, intense romance at the University of Iowa Writers' Workshop. She was then twenty-two, already married and divorced, having just returned to school. Their explosive relationship is described by Roth in *My Life as a Man*, where he calls her Lucy Oakes: "only twenty minutes after having fallen to my knees in your room to play the supplicant beneath your belly . . . ; cunnilingus aside, I don't think *teaching* has ever been so exciting, before or since, or that I've ever felt so tender or devoted to any class as I did to our English 312."[13]

Beautiful, wounded, and awed by Roth, whose explosive marriage to Maggie was now experiencing its excruciating death throes, she eventually left him, admitting, "I can't save you, Philip, I'm only twenty-two." A talented writer, as Roth discovered in class, a few years later she published a collection of her short stories with Knopf, described in the *New York Review of Books* as impressive descriptions of "disorder and early sorrow; fathers and mothers, divorced; dreams dissolving; siblings; brief encounters; homing instincts; cities; summer islands." The reviewer Denis Donoghue added that she was particularly good "at leaving the rest unsaid, knowing that everything is there in the cadence of feeling, given or implied. She never goes too far, never loses her head, never trips."[14]

Now re-meeting Roth, she was pleased to regain a friendship with someone she had once loved and whose talent she greatly admired, with every reason to believe this would persist. Then suddenly the emails all but ceased. This occurred as Roth experienced new and debilitating heart problems and had asked Lisa Halliday—living in Rome and writing *Asymmetry*—to return and assist him. Frightened by the sudden turn of events, Roth, it seems, turned to Halliday, whose presence had long energized him; when Kuemmerle visited him at the hospital, it was clear that their friendship had all but disappeared as rapidly as it had resurfaced.

When Kuemmerle was invited to Roth's funeral, she couldn't bring herself to go. Instead, she stood across the street from the bus leaving for Bard College where he was to be buried—watching, puzzled by his uncommon capacity for warmth and no less so by his ability to leave those who cared for him behind.[15]

Until the end, Roth remained acutely preoccupied with his posthumous standing, actively involved in the shaping of Bailey's biography, scripting the various commemorative plaques celebrating his achievements, including the one attached to his Weequahic home and on the apartment building at 79th Street where he lived his last years. He altered repeatedly the phalanx of speakers slated to appear at a posthumous memorial celebration and the names of his executors. He designed plans for his funeral, insisting on no recitation of the Kaddish, the traditional Jewish mourner's prayer, and demanding that all comments be limited to his books.

When first admitted to the hospital in late April 2018, his heart was found to be working at no more than 40 percent capacity. Initially doctors were optimistic that they could send him home, but soon they learned the coronary heart disease had progressed too far. If released, he was told, he would have no more than a few months to live with the help of powerful drugs and limited mobility. Roth decided that it was now time to stop resisting the inevitable.

Once it was clear that Roth was dying, Julia's mother, a Catholic, suggested that he might want to be baptized. As Julia described in her eulogy at Roth's memorial service at New York Public Library, her mother told her: "You should baptize him. All you need is water, and this way you will be sure he goes straight to Heaven." Julia ran the idea by him and said momentarily he considered it, then declined saying: "I don't think that all the real fun people will be in Heaven. And besides, I think the people in charge of these things will get me to go where I need to go."[16]

A veritable harem, in Judith Thurman's words, now surfaced, with women of all ages—older ones like Ann Mudge, Barbara Jakobson, and Barbara Sproul (who set about to manage the flow as best as possible), a younger group including Susan Rogers, Lisa Halliday, and Catherine von Klitzing, who had long before left his employ but now was unwilling to leave his bedside. Newer friends like Mary Karr stayed close by, she so new to his life that she mistakenly identified the writer Claudia Roth Pierpont as Claire Bloom, warning that the loathed ex-wife had suddenly surfaced. Nearly constantly there was Julia Golier.

Thurman described these moments vividly in a ceremony in honor of Roth at Stockholm: "There were more than a dozen remarkable women grieving at his deathbed, ranging in age from twenty-six to eighty-seven, half of them former lovers, the eldest going back more than a half century with him, and each of them, her own subject. Because we were so real to him, we were realer to ourselves."[17]

Eventually, most were encouraged to leave. Golier, his medical proxy, remained, of course, with Sproul, Thurman, Avishai, and Taylor close at hand. Catherine von Klitzing refused to go and would be found still in his bed even after he drew his last breath. When Roth awakened at one point asking, in a state of confusion, "What do they call this?" it was Thurman who took his hand, answering: "They call it dying." Several were certain that theirs was the final conversation with him. "I could have been a contender," Marty Garbus recalled Roth telling him.[18]

In the end, Andrew Wiley, Benjamin Taylor, and Julia were in the hospital room with him to hear his last words, an affirmation of family written down by Julia: "I love your kiddos. They were the joy of my life."[19] He died a few hours later.

Conclusion

No writer at the time of his death in the English-speaking world commanded comparable attention. Even the denial of the Nobel Prize—widely viewed as an intentional slight even by those who didn't greatly appreciate him—served to highlight this standing. Charles McGrath's front-page *New York Times* obituary started with the words: "Philip Roth, the prolific, protean, and often blackly comic novelist who was a pre-eminent figure in 20th-century literature . . . "[1]

Writing shortly before the appearance of Roth's last book, David Gates observed in *Newsweek* that Roth's "admirers include both the baldheaded and the shaven-headed. He remains a storyteller so addictive that you finish one book and reach for another. Who else has his range and depth in matters sexual, intellectual, psychological, emotional and political? And who else could play them all for laughs and *still* touch the heart? . . .

Don DeLillo, Thomas Pynchon and Cormac McCarthy have their partisans. But at this point, Roth is everybody's daddy."[2]

Perhaps not everyone's. With the appearance of HBO's *The Plot Against America* widely viewed as an eerily prescient foretelling of Trump, the acclaim of the American Trilogy that introduced him to a wide range of readers only dimly aware of *Portnoy's Complaint*, and his late-life and mostly tender, brief, and surprisingly accessible books—including his story of a terrible polio epidemic strangely presaging the Covid epidemic soon after his death—Roth's stature felt all but unassailable.

To be sure, none of the criticisms raised years earlier had disappeared regarding the misogynism said to have been baked into his books, with dark portraits of him a part of the larger cultural milieu. Woody Allen has an undeniably Roth-like writer brush up against his certain future in Hell in his 1997 film *Deconstructing Harry*. (Roth was known to have helped Mia Farrow write her memoir *What Falls Away*, with its accusation of Allen's child molestation.) In the film Roth's stand-in betrays all those close to him—including, of course, all the women with whom he has enjoyed sex. The film has the Rothian character reveling in sex in the presence of a blind relative and bringing a prostitute along to a ceremony honoring him at the college that had kicked him out.

In the 2008 movie *Definitely, Maybe*, Kevin Kline plays a cynical if also charming and funny writer named Hampton Roth, the author of the book *The Decline of Almost Everything*. He pursues much younger women, urges one to betray her well-intentioned boyfriend, and dies alone. Asked early in the film whether he was now involved with a sophomore, he responds that he is enjoying sex with two freshmen and the two may be said to add up to one whole sophomore. His cynicism is relentless, and shameless.

Roth's sullied reputation is not only found in the guise of rapacious males in film. When in 2011 Roth won the prestigious

Man Booker International Prize—awarded annually for the best work of fiction in the English language—one of the three judges, Carmen Callil, dropped off the panel because, as she put it, reading Roth leaves one with the unmistakable feeling of claustrophobia, of someone "sitting on your face" so that "you can't breathe." She added that she also objected to celebrating a writer from the American or European orbit with so many of the most talented literary voices today in Africa, Asia, or the Middle East—their achievements grossly underappreciated. But mostly she resented the prize going to Roth.

Yet by then Claire Bloom's charges seemed largely forgotten. Soon enough, however, they resurfaced with the rise and almost immediate fall of Blake Bailey's biography. On its appearance in spring 2021, *Philip Roth: The Biography* soared onto the *New York Times* bestseller list and, with some demurrals, was greeted with enthusiasm. The *New York Times Book Review* ran a veritable love letter by the formidable Cynthia Ozick, and the paper's Sunday magazine included a multipage fulsome celebration of the biographer. There journalist Mark Oppenheimer not only celebrated the book itself (adding some minor equivocations) but expressed his admiration of the look of Bailey's handsome study and the "historic" neighborhood in Virginia where he resided.[3]

And then, in a dizzying about-face unlike any in recent American literary life, little more than two weeks later the book was withdrawn by its publisher, Norton. This was in the wake of claims leveled against Bailey, first on a rather obscure literary blog and then by several major newspapers. Bailey was described as targeting high school girls at the school where he once taught and cultivating them until the age of seventeen or eighteen for sex—allegedly forcible sex, in at least one instance. Soon an unconnected accusation of rape surfaced as well.[4]

For some, Bailey's portrait of a sexually avaricious Roth would immediately be conflated with Bailey's behavior: "Of course," wrote Constance Grady in *Vox*, "the guy who defended one of American literature's most infamous misogynists has been accused of violence against women." A scant two or three years earlier, Lisa Halliday's widely praised novel *Asymmetry*—with its portrait of a romance with an aging novelist clearly modeled on Roth ("She got me," Roth admitted to an interviewer, asked about the striking similarity)—inspired very few charges regarding Roth's sexual predilections.[5] But now, in the wake of the Bailey debacle, these accusations were aired widely, and Roth was as often as not conflated—or at least situated in a comparably offensive predatory category—with that of the now-disgraced biographer. Bailey's book would soon be republished by Skyhorse, known for its willingness to pick up titles deemed unacceptable elsewhere, but the biography had been relegated to the shadows.

This transpired at much the same time, of course, that nearly all the white male literary giants of Roth's generation or somewhat earlier—Bellow, Styron, Mailer, Cheever, Updike—slipped from their once-unassailable perches, with the rise of new, often nonwhite voices, as often as not women. These changes occurred in the wake of rising ethnic and gender-related tumult, riots in America's cities over police violence, the ascent of Donald Trump. Certainly, Roth was not the only one of these authors to be sidelined in these years, though the crisis enveloping Bailey added a darkly distinctive mark beside Roth's now widely disparaged standing. Never a mainstay of high school reading lists, his books now appeared less and less frequently in bookstores and then rarely any others than *The Plot Against America* or his very first, *Goodbye, Columbus*.

Yet surprisingly enough, Roth seems to have weathered these cultural transmutations rather better than contemporaries like Updike or Mailer or Tom Wolfe, and though often critical of Roth's portrayals of women a new generation of writers, novelists as well as scriptwriters, have found themselves clearly enraptured by the many risks he took time and again on the page. Above all, Roth's willingness to insinuate himself deep, often uneasily, into the fabric of his own fiction invited imitation. Roth had expressed the fear many years earlier—this before *Portnoy's Complaint*—that he might well emerge as a "writer's writer," which seemed unlikely after his bestseller, followed as it was with book after book for the next half-century. Still, that status may now most indelibly define his literary standing.

For years, to be sure, leading, younger novelists and short story writers—Zadie Smith, Nicole Krauss, Nathan Englander, Joshua Cohen, Ben Lerner, Jonathan Lethem, Michael Chabon, Ayad Akhtar, Taffy Brodesser-Akner—have acknowledged their indebtedness. The same is true for lesser known, often quite young, authors of fiction in Germany, France, England, Israel, and elsewhere. But even well beyond these circles, his imprint as inspirational voice remains a resilient feature in contemporary culture.

It is his confessional voice, his willingness to insert himself or a character strikingly like him into his fiction, that has captured the attention of a still younger generation of writers and filmmakers whose admiration—albeit often tinged with a no less transparent uncertainty—is a marked feature of their work. For example, in what filmmaker Alex Ross Perry characterized as an act of homage to Roth, the feature film *Listen Up Philip* is built around two staggeringly unhappy, aggressively ambitious Roth-like writers—one young, the other old. Here the thirty-something narcissist Philip Friedman, played by Jason Schwartzman, who has just released a second novel, is inattentive to his girlfriend, sorely disappointed by his publisher, indifferent, even hostile to his readers. Philip is befriended by a now neglected but once lavishly celebrated older novelist (his dust jackets are designed like Roth's), who is still more self-absorbed than Philip. Both end up all but friendless, sorely disappointed, and animated only when attacked, preferably viciously. In one scene, Friedman is standing with his mentor at a book party for his new novel, grim and unhappy because all that he encounters is praise. "Wish someone would say something mean," he says, just before a woman walks over asking casually, "Is there trash here?" Gratefully the young novelist's response is "Yes, right here."[6]

Particularly astute in its wrestling with Roth's legacy is a 2017 episode of Lena Dunham's long-running series *Girls* entitled "American Bitch," where she explores the interplay—all extravagantly narcissistic—between the self-centered young woman played by Dunham and a Roth-like writer ever set on seduction. Prettying herself at the elevator mirror of his luxurious apartment building, it appears that Dunham's character too anticipates something similar, visiting him on his invitation to discuss a blog-based attack on him that she recently wrote. There in his apartment with its many framed awards—including PEN/Faulkner prizes, photos of him beside the likes of Toni Morrison, his bookshelves laden with signed copies of his many novels and copies of Roth's—he skillfully courts, gently cajoles, and manages to win her sympathy. He explains that he had invited her to speak with him about her essay where she attacked him after hearing he had recently enjoyed blow jobs with college girls during a book tour. As she wrote: "If one more male writer I love reveals himself to be a heinous sleazebag, I'm going to do a bunch of murders, create a new Isle of Lesbos, and never look back!"[7]

He compliments her on her humor, tells her that she writes well, that she has a pretty face, winning her over sufficiently so that when he walks her into his bedroom, she agrees to lie beside him on his bed. There he quickly pulls out his penis and maneuvers it onto her thigh and she obligingly touches him. Just before, he gives her his signed copy of Roth's *When She Was Good*, which Dunham admits she greatly admires, having heard the rumor that it was initially entitled "American Bitch," a title she loves. (Its Bantam paperback edition released in 1968 describes it on its cover as "A stunning portrait of an all-American bitch.")

Much the same sense of ambiguous indebtedness is made clear in the portrait of the "louche Philip Roth-like writer" (a *Kirkus Reviews* description) Leopold Lens in a 2023 novel by Julius Taranto, *How I Won a Nobel Prize.* Its title is meant to evoke, of course, the saga of the elusive Nobel. The book's narrator is a woman who is a brilliant scientist working with a Nobel-winning mentor and invited to join him on the faculty of a new, insurgent, rich university located on an island just beyond New Haven. The school is peopled with faculty who have run afoul of newly astringent guidelines, sexual and otherwise, with students indifferent to such behavior, past or present. "Rape Island" is how its critics refer to it. And there she finds, as described by Taranto,

> The great rabbi of my dad's religion. . . . He was a novelist, a satirist, an iconoclast. He had used his liberty, famously, with hundreds of women. Lens was a scholar of cultural ambivalence. He was allergic to ideology, to purity. He was, my dad emphasized, an unremittingly independent thinker, and it was only through this independence, this refusal to be pinned in any one place, that one could be both an American and as Jewish as my dad wished to be. . . . For years my Dad had been mailing me Lens excerpts. A typical Subject line: "More magic from the Maestro."[8]

And he looks just like Roth at his, albeit aging, prime: "His gaze lingered, or at least I thought it did. It was probing, not lascivious. He had this vaguely Roman nose, bold brows, and a blizzard of gray hair. His hair was vital and incongruous, as enticing as a beauty mark on a model's cheek."[9]

He meets her, flirts with her mildly, and admits that his decision to move to the university was easy if only because "I did not have much ivory tower approval left to lose." Despite herself, she is drawn to him, his striking looks, his palpable intelligence, his deep artistic devotion. She lingers beside him at a cocktail party and admits to herself that

> I wanted to hear about Saul Bellow, who had once been Lens's champion, and about Kathleen Turner, whom he had almost married. In the crevices of Lens's face I glimpsed ruins of a lost culture, a life of analog Romanticism, and glamour and solitude so outdated that no one I knew would tolerate it. . . . Lens had been such a merciless artist—a danger to himself and others. He had betrayed his family with the book that made him famous, and after that had managed to betray everyone else whose betrayal might bring literary profit. He had lived as if true virtue meant to never be co-opted, to be understood only on one's own terms. It was impossible not to envy this.[10]

Impossible not to envy this: Lens's undeniable devotion to his craft, his coming of age at a moment when the novel was all but unrivaled as a source of authority, when even Sartre and Camus wrote novels alongside their works of philosophy. This illustrious generation just a bit older than Lens—or Roth—still today the mainstay of American high school classroom reading lists, like Steinbeck's *Of Mice and Men*, or Salinger's *Catcher in the Rye*, or William Golding's *Lord of the Flies*.

Roth—his raucousness so often lavishly uncontained, his contentious likes and dislikes mostly undisguised—his books have tended to surface mostly as after-school reading, the sort you read at night alone, astonished at the audacity of someone publishing tales of middle-aged Jewish businessmen afflicted with gonorrhea or the rigors of adolescent masturbation yet printed, even at the start of his career, on the august pages of the *Partisan Review* alongside the earnestness of Susan Sontag or Lionel Trilling.

That is where I first read Roth: in the summer 1967 issue of *Partisan Review*, "Whacking Off" the lead piece on the magazine's ever-sedate cover, beginning with its now-famous and hilarious and terror-ridden discharge:

> Then came adolescence—half my waking life spent locked behind the bathroom door, firing my wad down the toilet bowl, or into the spoiled clothes in the laundry hamper, or splat, up against the medicine-chest mirror, before which I stood in my dropped drawers so I could see how it looked coming out. Or else I was doubled over my flying fist, eyes pressed closed but mouth wide open, to take that sticky sauce of buttermilk and Clorox on my own tongue and teeth—though not infrequently, in my blindness and ecstasy, I got it all in the pompadour, like a blast of Wildroot Cream Oil. Through a world of matted handkerchiefs and crumpled Kleenex and stained pajamas, I moved my raw and swollen penis, perpetually in dread that my loathsomeness would be discovered by someone stealing upon me just as I was in the frenzy of dropping my load.[11]

I absorbed all this headed soon for rabbinical school in Chicago—not in search of a pastoral career but hoping to locate answers to the dreaded questions prompted by my scattered readings of atheist Bertrand Russell or Marx, Spinoza, Sontag, Baldwin, Camus, or Eugene O'Neill, every one of whose plays I read over the course of one desultory summer. I was an Orthodox Jewish teenager eager not to abandon the only way of life I knew but wrecked by reading the likes of Roth, whose confessional voice, explosive intelligence, and impatience with dishonesty to oneself all had the feel of a barrage of urgent letters addressed just to me.

Most of all, what I took away from Roth's incendiary text was a terrible, crucial lesson: The world beyond religious devotion for which I was now desperately grasping provided no thoroughgoing solace, no more definitive answer than the cloistered corner that was now mine. And, indeed, for all his freedom, his apparent success in life as well as sex—the two in my adolescent mind inextricably linked—Alexander Portnoy remained a hopeless neurotic. Already here in this early work of Roth's—I had no idea then, of course, that he would write another two or three dozen books—was a vexing argument challenging life's overriding coherence, a case unrelenting in its starkness and honesty. Nowhere, Roth announced, was there a true and full escape from life's onslaught. The most essential challenge to the prospect of everlasting peace was carried right there in one's own body, in the perplexing urgency of one's own sexuality, and in the frailty, the impermanence of life itself.

Never was Roth easy. Not in raucous books like *Zuckerman Unbound* or *The Anatomy Lesson*, which both frustrated me greatly coming so soon after the lyrical and, on its surface at least, sedate *Ghost Writer.* But nothing he would write would so excite and exasperate and preoccupy me as his odd, brilliant, self-consciously misshapen masterwork *The Counterlife.*

Its start intentionally off-putting: coronary surgery followed by impotence followed by hopefully corrective surgery followed by death, funeral, family. Soon, a scrambling of it all with an altogether different death, different mistress, an indecisive trip to Israel's West Bank, time spent with one of its fanatics, and finally an outwardly bucolic London Christmas.

Never is the storyline itself what is most critical. Here as elsewhere, Roth's narratives are fully fleshed out in a detail reminiscent of the fiction of a bygone epoch of the 1930s or '40s. But under the surface all remains in flux, with everything one touches (throughout his is an intensely tactile fiction) ready to melt in the air. He hectors, but never dogmatically, and rarely is there anything akin to neatness in any of his narratives: Here Nathan Zuckerman dies in one chapter, travels to Israel in the next, marries his love Maria, and then watches as she chooses to abandon the novel altogether. The prose is forever luscious—the relationship to art, the recognition that text can never truly replicate life is among the many insights that make reading him endlessly, if often exasperatingly, pleasurable. And deep, if also often annoyingly unforgettable knowledge—more direct and more candid than handled by anyone else, it seems to me—about the stunningly complex, wondrous, and exasperating workings of the world.

At *The Counterlife*'s closing:

> The pastoral stops here and it stops with circumcision. That delicate surgery should be performed upon the penis of a brand-new boy seems to you the very cornerstone of human irrationality, and maybe it is. . . . But why not look at it another way? . . . Maybe that's what the Jews had in mind and what makes the act seem quintessentially Jewish and the mark of their reality. Circumcision makes it clear as can be that you are here and not there, that you are out and not in—also that you're mine and not theirs. There is no way around it: you enter history through my history and me. Circumcision is everything that the pastoral is not and . . . reinforces what the world is about, which isn't strifeless unity.[12]

NOTES

Abbreviations

Individuals

AL	Alan Lelchuk
BA	Bernard Avishai
BJ	Barbara Jakobson
BS	Barbara Sproul
BT	Benjamin Taylor
DP	David Plante
MG	Martin Garbus
MGr	Maxine Groffsky
MP	Maletta Pfeiffer
PR	Philip Roth
TS	Ted Solotaroff

Archives

ADL	Anti-Defamation League Archive. New York.
AJC	American Jewish Committee Archives and Research Center. New York.
AJHS	American Jewish Historical Society, Center for Jewish History. New York.
Alison Lurie Papers	Alison Lurie Papers. Division of Rare and Manuscript Collections, Cornell University. Ithaca, NY.
Berg Collection	David Plante and Alfred Kazin Papers. Henry W. and Albert A. Berg Collection of English and American Literature. New York Public Library.
BT Collection	Benjamin Taylor Collection of Philip Roth Materials. Department of Rare Books and Special Collections, Princeton University.
Butler	Special Collections, Rare Books, and University Archives. Butler Library, Columbia University.
CB Collection	Claire Bloom Collection. Howard Gottlieb Archival Research Center, Boston University.
HM	Houghton Mifflin Company Records. Houghton Library, Harvard University.
Klau Library	Klau Library. Hebrew Union College-Jewish Institute of Religion. Cincinnati.
L of C	Philip Roth Papers. Library of Congress.
Motion Picture Collections	Special Collections, Academy of Motion Picture Arts and Sciences. Los Angeles.
MW Papers	Mike Wallace Papers. Syracuse University.
PR, Newark Library	Philip Roth Personal Library. Newark Public Library.
TS Papers	Ted Solotaroff Papers. Manuscripts and Archive Division, New York Public Library.
YIVO	YIVO Institute for Jewish Research. New York.

YU — Archives and Special Collections, Yeshiva University. New York.

Private Collections

Betty Lehman Papers
Barbara Sproul Papers
Joel Conarroe Papers
Maletta Pfeiffer Papers
Robert Heyman Papers

References to the published writings of Philip Roth are, with few exceptions, drawn from the Library of America edition of his work published 2006–2017:

LOA1 *Novels and Stories, 1959–1962*
LOA2 *Novels, 1967–1972*
LOA3 *Novels, 1973–1977*
LOA4 *Zuckerman Bound: A Trilogy and Epilogue, 1979–1985*
LOA5 *Novels and Other Narratives, 1986–1991*
LOA6 *Novels, 1993–1995*
LOA7 *The American Trilogy, 1997–2000*
LOA8 *Novels, 2001–2007*
LOA9 *Nemeses*
LOA10 *Why Write? Collected Nonfiction, 1960–2014*

Introduction

1. Interview with MG, November 5, 2019; American Jewish Congress, "Second Dialogue in Israel," *Congress Bi-Weekly*, September 16, 1963.

2. Ayten Tartici, "Fiction in Review," *Yale Review* 106, no. 4 (2018): 154–62.

3. Joseph O'Neill, "Roth v. Roth v. Roth," *Atlantic*, February 27, 2012, https://www.theatlantic.com/magazine/archive/2012/04/roth-v-roth-v-roth/308911/.

4. PR, *The Ghost Writer*, LOA4: 12.

5. Interview with MGr, April 26, 2021; PR, *Exit Ghost*, LOA8: 530.

6. PR, interview with *The Paris Review*, in *Why Write?* LOA10: 146.

7. PR, *The Human Stain*, LOA7: 745.

8. J. M. Coetzee, *Inner Workings: Literary Essays, 2000–2005* (London: Harvill Secker, 2007), 235; BA, *Promiscuous: "Portnoy's Complaint" and Our Doomed Pursuit of Happiness* (New Haven: Yale University Press, 2012), 8.

9. BT Collection, box B-001208, folder 3.

10. Aimee L. Pozorski, ed., *Roth and Celebrity* (Lanham, MD: Lexington, 2012), 2; Michael Gorra, "Philip's Theater," *New York Review of Books*, April 8, 2021, https://www.nybooks.com/articles/2021/04/08/philip-roth-biography-theater/?srsltid=AfmBOoq8UUsktIcT_lvt2skCP--2lQLw9neWY7aDmOxGp-4cxvwe4GoP.

11. James Wood, "My Hero: Philip Roth," *Guardian*, March 22, 2013.

12. PR, *The Ghost Writer*, 12.

13. Quoted in Hermione Lee, *Biography: A Very Short Introduction* (Oxford: Oxford University Press, 2009), 90.

14. PR, *American Pastoral*, LOA7: 37.

15. PR, "Writing About Jews," in *Why Write?* 52.

16. PR, *The Counterlife*, LOA5: 8.

17. PR, "Imagining Jews," in *Why Write?* 83–84.

18. TS Papers, October 22, 2018; DP diary, April 2–June 24, 1982, Berg Collection.

19. PR, *The Counterlife*, 136–37.

20. PR, *The Plot Against America*, LOA8: 97.

21. Asher Z. Milbauer and Donald G. Watson, "An Interview with Philip Roth," in *Conversations with Philip Roth*, ed. George J. Searles (Jackson: University Press of Mississippi), 244.

22. Janet Hobhouse, *The Furies* (New York: New York Review Books, 2004), 195, 197–98.

23. Blake Bailey, *Philip Roth: The Biography* (New York: Skyhorse, 2021), 539.

24. Ibid., 323; PR letter to AL, L of C, July 2 [1969?].

Chapter 1. Father, Mother, Family

1. Claudia Roth Pierpont, *Roth Unbound: A Writer and His Books* (New York: Farrar, Straus and Giroux, 2013), 209.

2. BT Collection, box B-00267, folder B.

3. Philip Roth, "Recollections from Beyond the Last Rope," *Harper's*, July 1959, 42.

4. Ibid., 43.

5. Ibid., 48.

6. PR, *Operation Shylock*, LOA6: 198.

7. Alfred Kazin papers, October 31, 1989, Berg Collection.

8. PR, *My Life as a Man*, LOA3: 449.

9. Ira B. Nadel, *Critical Companion to Philip Roth: A Literary Reference to His Life and Work* (New York: Facts on File, 2011), 159; PR, *Patrimony*, LOA5: 631.

10. *History of the Flaschner Family: Victory Edition*, privately printed in Boston, 1951; *The Most Distinguished Surname Flaschner*, privately printed, n.d. Thanks to David Cohen for forwarding copies of these volumes.

11. *History of the Flaschner Family*, 11.

12. Ibid.

13. Ibid., 10.

14. PR, "'I Always Wanted You to Admire My Fasting'; or, Looking at Kafka," in *Why Write?* LOA10: 16–17.

15. *History of the Flaschner Family*, 12.

16. PR, *The Facts*, LOA5: 317.

17. PR, *The Human Stain*, LOA7: 833.

Chapter 2. Genesis

Epigraph: PR, *The Ghost Writer*, LOA4: 3.

1. PR, *The Plot Against America*, LOA8: 99; PR, *The Anatomy Lesson*, LOA4: 288.

2. Ross Posnock, *Philip Roth's Rude Truth: The Art of Immaturity* (Princeton: Princeton University Press, 2006), 102; Mark Shechner, "Newark: The Shtetl," in *Roth After Eighty: Philip Roth and the American Literary Imagination*, ed. David Gooblar and Aimee Pozorski

(Lanham, MD: Lexington, 2016), 173. For a thoughtful analysis of Roth's reliance on Newark in his fiction see Michael Kimmage, *In History's Grip: Philip Roth's Newark Trilogy* (Stanford: Stanford University Press, 2012).

3. PR, *American Pastoral*, LOA7: 27.

4. John Cotton Dana, foreword to Walter Prichard Eaton, *Newark: A Series of Engravings on Wood by Rudolph Ruzicka* (Newark: Carteret Book Club, 1917).

5. Federal Writers' Project of the Works Progress Administration for the State of New Jersey, *New Jersey: A Guide to Its Present and Past* (New York: Viking, 1939), 313.

6. Joachim Prinz, *Joachim Prinz, Rebellious Rabbi: An Autobiography—the German and Early American Years* (Bloomington: Indiana University Press, 2007), 294.

7. Robert Curvin, *Inside Newark: Decline, Rebellion, and the Search for Transformation* (New Brunswick, NJ: Rutgers University Press), 40–44.

8. Robert Rockaway, "Gangsters Versus Nazis: How the Jewish Mob Fought American Admirers of the Third Reich," *Tablet*, July 2, 2018.

9. PR, *I Married a Communist*, LOA7: 462.

10. Shechner, "Newark: The Shtetl," 173.

11. AL and PR Tapes, PR, Newark Library, II, part 1, 1968-10-06 (audio).

12. Edward Rothstein, "To Newark," in *Conversations with Philip Roth*, ed. George J. Searles (Jackson: University Press of Mississippi), 274; George Orwell, *Decline of the English Murder and Other Essays* (Middlesex, UK: Penguin, 1995), 93; PR, *The Facts*, LOA5: 440.

13. John Wesley Johnson, Jr., "Mount Zion Which Cannot Be Removed: A Study of Weequahic, the Genealogy of Community, and the Limits of Liberalism in Newark, New Jersey," Ph.D. diss., State University of New Jersey at Rutgers, 2014, 78.

14. PR, *The Anatomy Lesson*, 326.

15. PR, *American Pastoral*, 43.

16. Johnson, "Mount Zion Which Cannot Be Removed," 108–9.

17. PR, *The Facts*, 330.

18. PR, *The Counterlife*, LOA5: 101.

19. PR, *Patrimony*, LOA5: 595.

20. PR, *I Married a Communist*, 459.

21. PR, *The Facts*, 320–21.

22. BT, *Here We Are: My Friendship with Philip Roth* (New York: Penguin, 2020), 67–68.

23. Blake Bailey, *Philip Roth: The Biography* (New York: Skyhorse, 2021), 57.

24. PR, *The Facts*, 317.

25. Ibid., 320.

26. BT, *Here We Are*, 26; Bailey, *Philip Roth*, 255.

27. BT, *Here We Are*, 27.

28. PR, "His Mistress's Voice," *Partisan Review* 56 (1986): 157.

29. PR, *Portnoy's Complaint*, LOA2: 288.

30. PR, *The Facts*, 315; interview with Doreen Marcus, June 24, 2020; interviews with BS, June 29, 2020, and September 12, 2022.

31. Interview with MGr, April 26, 2021; interview with Jonathan Roth, April 26, 2021.

32. Interview with Jonathan Roth, May 26, 2020.

33. TS Papers, November 14, 1961.

34. Interview with Sally Priesand, May 6, 2020.

35. BT Collection, C1609_BxB001209__f9 (8).pdf, 4–5.

36. Bailey, *Philip Roth*, 22.

37. PR, *The Facts*, 329.

38. PR, interview with *Le Nouvel Observateur*, in *Why Write?* LOA10: 131.

39. PR, *The Facts*, 331; BS email, October 15, 2019.

40. Robert Leonard Berkowitz, "The Long Damn Summer of '42: An Untold Story of Stolen Dreams," *Medium*, November 17, 2017.

41. Deborah Dash Moore, *At Home in America: Second Generation New York Jews* (New York: Columbia University Press, 1981).

42. Interview with Seymour Feldman, October 16, 2020; interview with Betty Lehman, November 9, 2020; Arnold H. Lubasch, "Weequahic Overtones and French Fries," *San Francisco Sunday Examiner* and *Chronicle*, March 9, 1969.

43. Robert McCrum, "Interview: The Story of My Lives: Philip Roth on Why His Next Book Will Be His Last," *Guardian*, September 20, 2008.

44. PR and AL Tapes, PR, Newark Library, II, 1968-10.8 (audio).

45. Interview with David Cohen, October 15, 2020.

46. Albert Goldman, "*Portnoy's Complaint* by Philip Roth Looms as a Wild Blue Shocker and the American Novel of the Sixties," in Searles, *Conversations with Philip Roth*, 30–31.

Chapter 3. Indignation

1. PR, *I Married a Communist*, LOA7: 421.

2. Arnold H. Lubasch, "Weequahic Overtones and French Fries," *San Francisco Sunday Examiner* and *Chronicle*, March 9, 1969.

3. A glimpse of Sgt. Irving Cohen, then stationed in Iran, may be seen in a letter to the editor of *Yank, The Army Weekly*, December 1, 1944.

4. Obituary for Sandy Roth, *Chicago Tribune*, May 12, 2000; interview with Inez Saunders, July 9, 2022; interview with Jonathan Roth, April 26, 2021.

5. Jesse Tisch, "Responsible Mischief: Roth as Reader," *Philip Roth Studies* 20, no. 1 (2024): 15.

6. AL and PR Tapes, PR, Newark Library, I, 1968-10-04 (audio).

7. Claudia Roth Pierpont, *Roth Unbound: A Writer and His Books* (New York: Farrar, Straus and Giroux, 2013), 27.

8. PR, *Et Cetera*, Spring 1953.

9. Charlotte Maurer to PR, October 17 [1972]. L of C.

10. PR, *My Life as a Man*, LOA3: 397.

11. PR, *The Facts*, LOA5: 351–53.

12. Interview with Charlo Maurer (Charlotte's daughter), September 6, 2022; Charlotte Maurer to PR, April 26, 1990, and March 19, 1994, L of C.

13. Bob Maurer to PR, June 7, 1966, L of C.

14. PR and AL Tapes, PR, Newark Library, IV, 1968-10-8 (audio).

15. PR, "The Final Delivery of Mr. Thorn," *Et Cetera*, Spring 1954, p. 26.

16. Ibid., 28.

17. Interview with Harold Itzkowitz, June 9, 2021.

18. Ibid.

19. Interview with Betty Lehman, November 9, 2020.

20. Interview with MGr, April 6, 2024.

21. PR, "Goodbye, Columbus," LOA1: 7.

Chapter 4. Goodbye

Epigraph: PR, *Sabbath's Theater*, LOA6: 386.

1. PR to Stuart Lehman, January 23, 1955, Betty Lehman Papers.

2. PR, *My Life as a Man*, LOA3: 405.

3. Robert Heyman Papers, October 22, 1955.

4. PR, "Novotny's Pain," in *A Philip Roth Reader* (New York: Farrar, Straus and Giroux, 1980), 266.

5. Interview with MG, November 5, 2019.

6. Ibid.

7. TS, *New American Review*, no. 3, April 1968.

8. PR to TS, March 7, 1962, L of C.

9. TS, *First Loves: A Memoir* (New York: Seven Stories, 2014), 197.

10. Robert Kelly, "Are You Now or Have You Ever Been . . ." *New York Times*, October 11, 1998.

11. PR, Interview with *The London Sunday Times*, in *Why Write?* LOA10: 138; interview with Arthur Geffen, October 27, 2021.

12. PR, preface to 30th anniversary edition, *Goodbye, Columbus and Five Short Stories* (Boston: Houghton Mifflin, 1989), xi.

13. TS, *First Loves*, 219.

14. Louis Menand, *The Free World: Art and Thought in the Cold War* (New York: Farrar, Straus and Giroux, 2021), 402; American Jewish Congress, "Second Dialogue in Israel," *Congress Bi-Weekly*, September 16, 1963, p. 71.

15. Irving Howe, *Selected Writings, 1950–1990* (San Diego: Harcourt Brace Jovanovich, 1990), 330.

16. HM, March 4, 1958.

17. Martin Greenberg to PR, January 25, 1958, L of C. I thank Jesse Tisch for a copy.

18. Interviews with BJ, October 20, 2023, and May 27, 2024; interviews with MGr, October 13, 2020, and October 12, 2021.

19. Interview with MGr, October 12, 2021.

20. PR and AL Tapes, PR, Newark Library, IV, 1968-10-8 (audio).

21. Interviews with MGr, October 12, 2021, and March 31, 2021.

22. PR, "Goodbye, Columbus," LOA1: 7.

23. Ibid., 13–14.

24. Ibid., 21.

25. Ibid., 57.

26. Ibid., 7.

27. Ross Posnock, *Philip Roth's Rude Truth: The Art of Immaturity* (Princeton: Princeton University Press, 2006), 102.

28. Michael Gorra, "Philip's Theater," *New York Review of Books*, April 8, 2021, p. 6; PR, *The Ghost Writer*, LOA4: 77.

29. James Wood, *The Broken Estate: Essays on Literature and Belief* (New York: Random House, 1999), 234.

30. American Jewish Congress, "Second Dialogue in Israel," *Congress Bi-Weekly*, September 16, 1963, p. 70.

Chapter 5. Apprenticeship

Epigraph: PR, *The Ghost Writer*, LOA4: 33.

1. HM, May 23, 1958.

2. Ibid., July 25, 1958; TS Papers, March 14, 1961.

3. PR, "Writing About Jews," in *Why Write?* LOA10: 54.

4. PR, *Portnoy's Complaint*, LOA2: 364.

5. PR, "Defender of the Faith," in *Goodbye, Columbus and Five Short Stories*, LOA1: 154; Kazin cited in Blake Bailey, *Philip Roth: The Biography* (New York: Skyhorse, 2021), 170.

6. For an example of a rave review by an often jaundiced essayist, see Leslie Fiedler, "The Image of Newark and the Indignities of Love: Notes on Philip Roth," in *Critical Essays on Philip Roth*, ed. Sanford Pinsker (Boston: G. K. Hall, 1982), 25; Heather Clark, *Red Comet: The Short Life and Blazing Art of Sylvia Plath* (New York: Knopf, 2010), 560.

7. MW Papers, box 9, "Roth, Philip" folder.

8. Timothy L. Parrish, "Ralph Ellison: The Invisible Man in Philip Roth's 'The Human Stain,'" *Contemporary Literature* 45, no. 3 (2004), 429.

9. PR, *The Facts*, LOA5: 409.

10. PR and AL Tapes, Newark Library, IV, part I, 1968-10-8 (audio); PR, interview with *The Paris Review*, in *Why Write?* 147.

11. PR, *The Facts*, 407.

12. PR, "The Crisis of Conscience in Minority Writers of Fiction," YU (audio).

13. PR, "Writing About Jews," 59.

14. Ibid., 64.

15. PR, Writings File, 1944–2001, box 101, L of C.

16. BT, *Here We Are: My Friendship with Philip Roth* (New York: Penguin, 2020), 46; Eugene B. Borowitz, "Believing Jews and Jewish Writers: Is Dialogue Possible?" *Judaism* 14, no. 2 (1965); Joseph C. Landis, "The Sadness of Philip Roth: An Interim Report," in Pinsker, *Critical Essays on Philip Roth*, 171; Oscar Cohen letter to PR, Oscar Cohen Papers, the Jacob Marcus Center of the American Jewish Archives, MS-294, January 23, 1964.

17. PR, *The Facts*, 409.

18. Ibid., 448; TS Papers, March 7, 1962.

19. PR, "Crisis."

20. Ibid.

21. Ibid.

22. PR, *The Facts*, 51–52.

23. American Jewish Congress, "Second Dialogue in Israel," *Congress Bi-Weekly*, September 16, p. 196. Rabbi Saul I. Teplitz, "From Rabbi to Rabbi," *To Our Colleagues*, 4 (1964); Harold U. Ribalow, "*Letting Go*," *Chicago Jewish Forum* 21 (1963), 327.

24. American Jewish Congress "Second Dialogue," 70.

25. TS Papers, December 1, 1959.

Chapter 6. Marjorie Morningsickness

1. Jerre Mangione, "Philip Roth," in *Conversations with Philip Roth*, ed. George J. Searles (Jackson: University Press of Mississippi), 13.

2. PR, *The Facts*, LOA5: 372–73; on Maggie, see BT Collection, box B-001210, folder 1.

3. Interview with Herbert Gold, July 2, 2020.

4. TS Papers, July 31, 1959.

5. Ibid., October 23, 1958; HM, March 29, 1958; interview with William Frosch, May 20, 2019.

6. Janna Malamud Smith, *My Father Is a Book: A Memoir of Bernard Malamud* (Boston: Houghton Mifflin, 2006), 196; Stanley Edgar Hyman, "A Novelist of Great Promise," in *Critical Essays on Philip Roth*, ed. Sanford Pinsker (Boston: G. K. Hall, 1982), 39.

7. J. F. Knowles, "Philip Roth and the Struggle of Modern Fiction," Ph.D. diss., University of British Columbia, 2020, 64.

8. Interview with Susan Rogers, July 19, 2019; interview with Gene Lichtenstein, November 10, 2020.

9. BT Collection, C1609_001208_f11_small.pdf, 183.

10. TS Papers, July 16, 1959.

11. PR, *The Facts*, 381.

12. Ibid., 394; PR, *My Life as a Man*, LOA3: 411.

13. TS Papers, March 11, 1959.

14. BT, *Here We Are: My Friendship with Philip Roth* (New York: Penguin, 2020), 58.

15. BT Collection, box B-001208, folder 3, pdf; interview with Susan Braudy, August 20, 2021.

16. PR, *The Facts*, 447.

17. Blake Bailey, *Philip Roth: The Biography* (New York: Skyhorse, 2021), 253.

18. HM, December 4, 1959.

19. PR, *Letting Go*, LOA1: 566.

20. Interview with Gene Lichtenstein, November 20, 2020.

21. HM, March 24, 1959, and March 26, 1960.

22. HM, November 9, 1960.

23. PR, *Exit Ghost*, LOA8: 494.

24. Alice Denham, *Sleeping with Bad Boys: A Juicy Tell-All of Literary New York in the 1950s and 1960s* (n.p.: n.p., 2006), 203.

25. PR, "Writing American Fiction," in *Why Write?* LOA10: 27.

26. Peter Mark Richman, *I Saw a Molten White Light . . . : An Autobiography of My Artistic and Spiritual Journey* (Albany, GA: BearManor, 2018), 201.

27. PR, "Talks to Teens: They Won't Make You Normal," *Seventeen*, April 1963, 208.

28. Bailey, *Philip Roth*, 273.

29. Real People Draft no. 1, Alison Lurie Papers.

30. PR and AL Tapes, PR, Newark Library, I, part I, 1968-10-04 (audio).

31. Alison Lurie Papers, January 26, 1965.

32. Albert Goldman, "*Portnoy's Complaint* by Philip Roth Looms as a Wild Blue Shocker and the American Novel of the Sixties," in Searles, *Conversations with Philip Roth*, 32.

Chapter 7. *Hocker*

1. Blake Bailey, *Philip Roth: The Biography* (New York: Skyhorse, 2021), 235.

2. *New Republic*, January 1963; Stanley Hyman, *New Leader*, June 1962; AL to PR, December 20, 1986, L of C.

3. PR, Newark Library, box 5, folder 28 (text).

4. DP diary, January 1–March 18, 1983, Berg Collection.

5. Interview with MP, August 18, 2023; interview with BT, July 28, 2022.

6. Interviews with BT, July 28 and September 12, 2022; Albert Goldman, "*Portnoy's Complaint* by Philip Roth Looms as a Wild Blue Shocker and the American Novel of the Sixties," in *Conversations with Philip Roth*, ed. George J. Searles (Jackson: University Press of Mississippi), 30–31.

7. Susan Braudy, *Between Marriage and Divorce: A Woman's*

Diary (New York: Morrow, 1975), 103; interview with Susan Braudy, August 20, 2021.

8. American Jewish Congress, "Second Dialogue in Israel," *Congress Bi-Weekly*, September 16, 1963, p. 61.

9. Ibid., 75.

10. Ibid., 73.

11. Josh Lambert email, July 25, 2021: "Roth crosses out with his black Sharpie the original title 'A Homosexual Begins His Analysis.' "

12. Hillel Halkin, "How to Read Philip Roth," *Commentary*, February 1994, https://www.commentary.org/articles/hillel-halkin/how-to-read-philip-roth/.

13. Alison Lurie Papers, November 4, 1964.

14. PR, *When She Was Good*, LOA2: 136.

15. Wilfrid Sheed, "Pity the Poor Wasps," *New York Times*, June 11, 1967; Robert Alter, "When He Is Bad," *Commentary*, November 1967; PR and AL Tapes, Newark Library, V, 19.56 (audio).

16. Sandra Hochman, "Portnoy's Complaint," *Village Voice*, April 27, 1969.

Chapter 8. Portnoy

Epigraph: Yosef Hayim Yerushalmi, *Zakhor: Jewish History and Jewish Memory* (Seattle: University of Washington Press, 2011), 99.

1. Albert Goldman, "*Portnoy's Complaint* by Philip Roth Looms as a Wild Blue Shocker and the American Novel of the Sixties," *Life*, February 7, 1969, 58B; Albert Goldman, "*Portnoy's Complaint* by Philip Roth Looms as a Wild Blue Shocker and the American Novel of the Sixties," in *Conversations with Philip Roth*, ed. George J. Searles (Jackson: University Press of Mississippi), 23.

2. Steven J. Zipperstein, *Rosenfeld's Lives: Fame, Oblivion, and the Furies of Writing* (New Haven: Yale University Press, 2011), 171–77.

3. Jonathan Brent, "What Facts? A Talk with Roth," in Searles, *Conversations with Philip Roth*, 235; Scott Saul, "Rough: A Journey into the Drafts of *Portnoy's Complaint*," *Post45*, April 12, 2019.

4. PR, preface to 30th anniversary edition, *Goodbye, Columbus and Five Short Stories* (Boston: Houghton Mifflin, 1989), xi–xii.

5. Adam Gopnik, "Man Goes to See a Doctor," *New Yorker*, August 24 and 31, 1998, p. 114; Blake Bailey, *Philip Roth: The Biography* (New York: Skyhorse, 2021), 607.

6. Hans J. Kleinschmidt, "The Angry Act: The Role of Aggression in Creativity," *American Imago* 24 (1967): 98–128.

7. Ibid.

8. Gopnik, "Man Goes to See a Doctor," 117.

9. Patrick Hayes, *Philip Roth: Fiction and Power* (Oxford: Oxford University Press, 2014), 93.

10. Interview with David Rieff, May 27, 2021.

11. Albert Goldman, "Laughtermakers," in *Jewish Wry: Essays on Jewish Humor*, ed. Sarah Blacher Cohen (Detroit: Wayne State University Press, 1990), 83.

12. AL Tapes, IV, 5, 25.08 (audio); Zadie Smith, *Feel Free: Essays* (New York: Penguin, 2018), 338.

13. Hayden Carruth, "Is It a Masterpiece of Fiction or Just a Pornographic Joke?" *Philadelphia Inquirer*, February 16, 1969.

14. PR, *Portnoy's Complaint*, LOA2: 300–301.

15. Ibid., 304.

16. Ibid., 224.

17. Ibid., 448.

18. PR and AL Tapes, PR, Newark Library, IV, part II, 1968-10-8 (audio).

19. Goldman, "*Portnoy's Complaint*," in Searles, *Conversations with Philip Roth*, 25.

20. Interview with James Wolcott, July 3, 2020.

21. See Greil Marcus, *Dead Elvis: A Chronicle of a Cultural Obsession* (New York: Doubleday, 1992).

22. Albert Goldman Papers, 1927–1994, box 78, folder 11, 10/20/70-6, "Rothlog," Butler.

23. BS email, October 25, 2020.

24. Goldman, "*Portnoy's Complaint*," in Searles, *Conversations with Philip Roth*.

25. Albert Goldman Papers, 10/20/70-6, Butler.

26. Ibid.

Chapter 9. Grand Old Man of Letters

1. Adam Kirsch, "Philip Roth's Afterlife," *Tablet*, April 1, 2021, https://www.tabletmag.com/sections/arts-letters/articles/philip-roth-blake-bailey-adam-kirsch.

2. Motion Picture Collections, *Goodbye, Columbus*, 1969.

3. *Mad*, December 1969, p. 48; Ira Nadel, *Philip Roth: A Counterlife* (Oxford: Oxford University Press, 2021), 217.

4. AL Tapes, IV, 4, 27.53 (audio).

5. Janet Malcolm, PR Papers, L of C, circa 1996.

6. Albert Goldman Papers, July 22, 1969, Butler; interview with Hermione Lee, September 25, 2019.

7. Hillel Halkin, "How to Read Philip Roth," *Commentary*, February 1994, pp. 43–48.

8. TS Papers, March 18, 1969.

9. Ibid.

10. PR, *Reading Myself and Others* (New York: Farrar, Straus and Giroux, 1985), 37–50, 56–64.

11. Ibid., 232; Robert Towers, "Nervous Breakdowns: Shrinking," *New York Times*, May 21, 1978; L. E. Sissman, "Books, Most Distressful Nations," *New Yorker*, April 7, 1973, p. 150.

12. PR, *The Professor of Desire*, LOA3: 782.

13. TS Papers, December 10, 1979, and August 26, 1982.

14. AL, *Ziff: A Life?* (New York: Carroll and Graf, 2003).

15. BT Collection, B-001210, folder 4, pdf.

16. MW Papers, box 9.

17. Albert Goldman Papers, 10/20/70-6, Butler.

18. Interview with BS, June 29, 2020.

19. PR to BS, October 20, 2020, private collection.

20. Ibid., March 10, 1969.

21. PR to AL, July 2, 1968, L of C.

22. BS Papers, private collection.

23. PR to BS, April 2, 1969, private collection.

24. Joel Conarroe on Roth, September 13, 1977, private collection.

25. BS Papers, private collection.

26. PR, *Reading Myself and Others*, 64.

27. John Gardner, "The Breast, by Philip Roth," *New York Times*, September 17, 1972; Jonathan Yardley, "About Books," *Queensboro Daily News*, September 17, 1972.

28. Webster Schott, "Speak, Mammary," *Life*, September 22, 1972, p. 12.

29. PR, *The Anatomy Lesson*, LOA4: 313.

Chapter 10. "Thinness of Culture"

1. On Podhoretz's relationship with Roth see Blake Bailey, *Philip Roth: The Biography* (New York: Skyhorse, 2021), 369–71.

2. Howe's review of *Goodbye, Columbus* was published in *Commentary*, June 15, 1959; his subsequent attack on Roth, "Philip Roth Reconsidered," can be found in *Critical Essays on Philip Roth*, ed. Sanford Pinsker (Boston: G. K. Hall, 1982), 229–44.

3. Howe, "Philip Roth Reconsidered," 229.

4. Interview with BA, November 7, 2019.

5. Howe, "Philip Roth Reconsidered," 237.

6. The essay by Howe referred to by Roth in the novel was an extended rumination on Isaac Rosenfeld's novel *Passage from Home*. See Zipperstein, *Rosenfeld's Lives*, 86–89.

7. William Styron to PR, January 16, 1973, L of C.

8. TS Papers, December 1, 1973.

9. See the superb discussions of East Central European literary influences on Roth in Ira Nadel, *Philip Roth: A Counterlife* (Oxford: Oxford University Press, 2021), 268–85, and Brian K. Goodman, *The Nonconformists: American and Czech Writers Across the Iron Curtain* (Cambridge: Harvard University Press, 2023).

10. Claudia Roth Pierpont, *Roth Unbound: A Writer and His Books* (New York: Farrar, Straus and Giroux, 2013), 88.

11. James Wood, *The Broken Estate: Essays on Literature and Belief* (New York: Random House, 1999), 225.

12. PR, preface to 30th anniversary edition, *Goodbye, Columbus and Five Short Stories* (New York: Modern Library, 1995), x.

13. PR, *Reading Myself and Others* (New York: Farrar, Straus and Giroux, 1985), 97.

14. PR, *My Life as a Man*, LOA3: 586–87.

15. Ibid., 597.

16. Ibid., 541.

17. CB Collection, December 4, 1975.

18. PR, interview with *The Paris Review*, in *Why Write?* LOA10: 157.

19. Vivian Gornick, *The Men in My Life* (Cambridge: MIT Press, 2008), 125.

20. PR, *My Life as a Man*, 604.

21. Interview with BS, September 12, 2022.

22. AL to PR, Saturday no date, 1974, L of C.

23. BS to PR, Thursday night no date, private collection.

24. BS, private collection.

25. Letter to Ross Miller in Jack Miles Papers, MS-F045, Special Collections, University of California Irvine Libraries. Again, thanks to Jesse Tisch for sharing this document.

26. Daphne Merkin, introduction to Janet Hobhouse, *The Furies* (New York: New York Review Books, 2004), x.

27. Hobhouse, *The Furies*, 198, 203–4.

28. Ibid., 197.

29. Ibid., 201.

30. Interview with MP, January 6, 2023.

Chapter 11. Lonoff

Epigraph: PR, *Deception*, LOA5: 518.

1. PR, "'I Always Wanted You to Admire My Fasting'; or, Looking at Kafka," in *Why Write?* LOA10: 5.

2. Ibid., 11.

3. Ibid., 12–13.

4. Ibid., 14.

5. Ibid., 23–24.

6. Claudia Roth Pierpont, *Roth Unbound: A Writer and His*

Books (New York: Farrar, Straus and Giroux, 2013), 88; PR, *The Ghost Writer*, LOA4: 68.

7. PR, *The Prague Orgy*, LOA4: 490–91.

8. Interview with Norman Manea, November 5, 2019.

9. TS Papers, [circa 1972].

10. Interview with BA, November 7, 2018.

11. DP, *Worlds Apart: A Memoir* (London: Bloomsbury, 2015), 64.

12. CB Collection, June 9, 1976.

13. Ibid., June 25, [1976].

14. MP, "1st draft: memories of my relationship with Philip Roth," 12, MP Private Collection.

15. PR to Joel Conarroe, October 29, 1978, private collection; CB Collection, July 2, 1976.

16. PR, *The Ghost Writer*, LOA3: 38.

17. CB, *Leaving a Doll's House: A Memoir* (Boston: Little Brown, 1996), 168.

18. PR, *The Ghost Writer*, 12.

19. PR, *My Life as a Man*, LOA3: 385; PR, *The Professor of Desire*, LOA3: 681.

20. PR, *The Ghost Writer*, 3.

21. Ibid., 116.

22. Martin Green, introduction to *A Philip Roth Reader* (New York: Farrar, Straus and Giroux, 1980), ix.

23. Ibid., xv.

24. AL Tapes, IV, 4, part 1, 36.45 (audio).

25. PR, *The Ghost Writer*, 10.

26. Ibid., 17.

27. Ibid., 4.

28. Ibid., 27.

29. TS Papers, July 22, mid-1970s.

30. Patrick Hayes, *Philip Roth: Fiction and Power* (Oxford: Oxford University Press, 2014), 158–82. Roth's copy of the book, now located in the Philip Roth Room at Newark Library, is heavily annotated.

31. PR, *The Ghost Writer*, 78.

32. Ibid., 102.

33. Hayes, *Philip Roth*, xi, 165; TS Papers, July 28, 1973; PR, *The Ghost Writer*, 81.

34. PR, *The Ghost Writer*, 93.

35. Ibid., 33.

36. BT, *Here We Are: My Friendship with Philip Roth* (New York: Penguin, 2020), 146–47; PR, *Exit Ghost*, LOA8: 661.

Chapter 12. "Fuck the Middle Ground"

Epigraph: PR, *The Anatomy Lesson*, LOA4: 280.

1. Henry James, *The Figure in the Carpet and Other Stories* (New York: Penguin, 1986), 365.

2. TS Papers, October 1, 1983.

3. Ibid., undated 1981.

4. Edward Rothstein, "The Revenge of the Vrai," *New York Review of Books*, June 25, 1981.

5. Ibid.

6. Ibid.

7. Ibid.

8. Ross Miller letter to PR, July 21, 1985, L of C.

9. John Lahr, *Arthur Miller: American Witness* (New Haven: Yale University Press, 2022), 66.

10. PR to Conarroe, September 16, 1985, Joel Conarroe Private Collection.

11. Ross Miller letter to PR, June 12, 1984, L of C.

12. PR to John Updike, March 1984, L of C; John Updike, *Odd Jobs: Essays and Criticism* (New York: Knopf, 1991), 372.

13. PR, *The Anatomy Lesson*, 288.

14. DP diary, November 25–December 16, 1984, Berg Collection.

15. PR to Mildred Martin, November 26, 1986, L of C.

16. DP diary, November 25–December 16, 1984, Berg Collection; Hermione Lee, "'Life Is and': Philip Roth in 1990," in *Conversations with Philip Roth*, ed. George J. Searles (Jackson: University Press of Mississippi), 261.

17. DP diary, January 23–March 18, 1983, Berg Collection.

18. PR, *The Counterlife*, LOA5: 266.

19. MP, "1st draft: memoir of my relationship with Philip Roth," 16, MP Private Collection.

20. DP diary, May 1982, Berg Collection.

21. CB Collection, June 13, 1976.

22. PR letter to R. B. Kitaj, March 19, 1989, L of C.

23. Ira Nadel, *Philip Roth: A Counterlife* (Oxford: Oxford University Press, 2021), 297.

24. PR, *The Counterlife*, 203.

25. Ibid., 204.

26. PR to TS, July 13, 1963, L of C; PR, *The Counterlife*, 36.

27. PR, *The Counterlife*, 129.

28. Interviews with David Rieff, May 27, 2020, December 9, 2022.

29. Interviews with Clinton Bailey, May 27, 2020, April 20, 2024, and May 16, 2024.

30. DP, *Worlds Apart*, 103.

31. Interview with David Rieff, May 27, 2020; PR, *The Counterlife*, 71.

32. PR, *The Counterlife*, 111.

33. Ibid., 122–23.

34. Ibid., 111–12.

35. Ibid., 109–10.

36. Ibid., 303.

37. Janet Malcolm to PR, January 3, 1987, L of C.

38. PR to TS, January 28, 1987, L of C.

39. PR, *The Counterlife*, 130.

Chapter 13. Facts

1. PR, *The Counterlife*, LOA5: 170; PR, *My Life as a Man*, LOA3: 478; interview with BJ, September 12, 2022.

2. PR, *Sabbath's Theater*, LOA6: 375.

3. PR, Conversation in Turin with Primo Levi, in *Why Write?* LOA10: 189; Ian Thomson, *Primo Levi: A Life* (London: Hutchinson, 2002), 46.

4. PR, Conversation in Turin with Primo Levi, 190.

5. Ibid., 196.

6. PR, *American Pastoral*, LOA7: 35.

7. Interview with BA, November 7, 2019.

8. Ibid.

9. PR, *The Facts*, LOA5: 311.

10. Ibid., 311–12.

11. John Sutherland, "Facts Schmacts," *London Review of Books*, February 16, 1989.

12. Laura Cumming, "Do We Really Need to Know? *The Facts:* A Novelist's Autobiography," *Literary Review*, November 1988.

13. PR, *The Facts*, 437, 439.

14. Ibid., 448, 434.

15. John Updike, *Odd Jobs: Essays and Criticism* (New York: Knopf, 1991), 390; interview with Paula Fass, October 15, 2020.

16. PR, *The Facts*, 313.

17. BT Collection, box B-001208, folder 3.

18. Fay Weldon, "Talk Before Sex and Talk After Sex," *New York Times*, March 11, 1990.

19. Blake Bailey, *Philip Roth: The Biography* (New York: Skyhorse, 2021), 527.

20. Brian D. Johnson, "Intimate Affairs," in *Conversations with Philip Roth*, ed. George J. Searles (Jackson: University Press of Mississippi), 256.

21. PR, *Deception*, LOA5: 578.

22. Johnson, "Intimate Affairs," 257.

23. Sean Hooks "The Inceptions of Deception: Reconsidering Philip Roth's Most Underrated Book," *Athenaeum Review*, December 31, 2020, https://athenaeumreview.org/essay/the-inceptions-of-deception/.

Chapter 14. "He Understood . . . Only What He Understood"

1. PR, *Deception*, LOA5: 576–77.

2. Ibid., 505.

3. PR, *Patrimony*, LOA5: 651.

4. Ibid., 622.

5. Ibid., 640.

6. Interviews with Jonathan Roth, May 26, 2020, and April 26, 2021.

7. PR, *Patrimony*, 689.

8. Neal Kozodoy, "Patrimony, by Philip Roth," *Commentary*, May 1991, https://www.commentary.org/articles/neal-kozodoy/patrimony-by-philip-roth/.

9. PR to Don DeLillo, January 1991, L of C.

10. Richard Stern, *A Sistermony* (New York: Donald I. Fine, 1995), 12.

11. PR to Don DeLillo, January 1991, L of C.

12. Quoted in Ira Nadel, *Philip Roth: A Counterlife* (Oxford: Oxford University Press, 2021), 445.

13. MP, "1st draft: memories of my relationship with Philip Roth," 26, MP Private Collection.

14. Blake Bailey, *Philip Roth: The Biography* (New York: Skyhorse, 2021), 542; MP, *Overcoming* (n.p.: self-published, n.d.), 114.

15. Stern, *A Sistermony*, 45.

16. Claudia Roth Pierpont, *Roth Unbound: A Writer and His Books* (New York: Farrar, Straus and Giroux, 2013), 177–78.

17. Richard M. Elman, *Namedropping: Mostly Literary Memoirs* (Albany: State University of New York Press, 1998), 272.

18. BT Collection, C1609_BxB-001209_f9(8).pdf.

19. Ibid.

20. R. B. Kitaj, *First Diasporic Manifesto* (London: Thames and Hudson, 1989).

21. Justin Kaplan, "Play It Again, Nathan," *New York Times*, September 25, 1988; Harold Bloom, "Operation Roth," *New York Review of Books*, April 22, 1993; John Updike, "Recruiting Raw Nerves," *New Yorker*, March 15, 1993.

22. Tony Tanner, *City of Words: American Fiction, 1950–1970* (New York: Harper and Row, 1971), 299.

Chapter 15. Maletta

Epigraph: Email from MP to Blake Bailey, September 2014.

1. MP, *Overcoming* (n.p.: self-published, n.d.), 10–11.

2. Blake Bailey, *Philip Roth: The Biography* (New York: Skyhorse, 2021), 565.

3. Interview with MP, April 1, 2023.

4. Ibid., September 8, 2023.

5. Interview with Norman Manea, November 5, 2019; interview with MP, January 6, 2023.

6. PR, *Sabbath's Theater*, LOA6: 373.

7. Ibid., 389.

8. BT, *Here We Are: My Friendship with Philip Roth* (New York: Penguin, 2020), 156.

9. CB, *Leaving a Doll's House: A Memoir* (Boston: Little Brown, 1996), 145–46.

10. MP, "1st draft: memories of my relationship with Philip Roth," 21, MP Private Collection.

11. Bailey, *Philip Roth*, 754.

12. MP, private collection.

13. BT, *Here We Are*, 48.

14. MP, "1st draft," 13; BT Collection, C1609_BxB1_small.pdf.

15. BT Collection, C1609_BxB001209_f11-small.pdf, 16, 25.

16. MP, "1st draft," 18, 23.

17. MP, *Overcoming*, 110.

18. MP, "Diary," April 20, 1995, private collection.

19. Ibid.

20. MP, "1st draft," 15.

21. Interview with MP, April 1, 2023.

22. PR, *Sabbath's Theater*, 515.

23. Claudia Roth Pierpont, *Roth Unbound: A Writer and His Books* (New York: Farrar, Straus and Giroux, 2013), 195.

24. PR, *Sabbath's Theater*, 688.

25. Ibid., 720–21, 735.

26. BT, *Here We Are*, 97.

27. Michiko Kakutani, "Mickey Sabbath, You're No Portnoy," *New York Times*, August 22, 1995.

28. Frank Kermode, "Howl," *New York Review of Books*, November 16, 1995, https://www.nybooks.com/articles/1995/11/16

/owl/?srsltid=AfmBOoq9oTTj80oa2vaRA8uYIvLqWZE_qnWb4uKEDoKVV3AmVDyjNXgg.

29. PR, "Forty-Five Years On," in *Why Write?* LOA10: 398.

Chapter 16. America

1. Ross Posnock, *Philip Roth's Rude Truth: The Art of Immaturity* (Princeton: Princeton University Press, 2006), 110.

2. PR, *American Pastoral*, LOA7: 40.

3. Ibid., 41.

4. Ibid., 40.

5. Interview with Lucy Warner Kuemmerle, June 2, 2024.

6. Robert A. Cohn, "Papa Portnoy: Philip Roth as Stepfather," *St. Louis Jewish Light*, September 3, 1975.

7. Interview with Sidra DeKoven Ezrahi, November 1, 2019.

8. PR, *American Pastoral*, 114.

9. Ibid., 299.

10. Ibid., 393.

11. CB, *Leaving a Doll's House: A Memoir* (Boston: Little Brown, 1996), 233; Roth's—incomplete—list of the women in his life may be found in BT Collection, C1609_BxB001209_f11_small.pdf.

12. PR, *I Married a Communist*, LOA7: 401.

13. Ibid., 422.

14. Ibid., 606.

15. Ron Charles, "McCarthyism Still Generates Great Stories," *Christian Science Monitor*, October 1, 1998.

16. Nicholas Lezard, "Death and Dumb," *Guardian*, March 16, 2001, https://www.theguardian.com/books/2001/mar/17/fiction.philiproth.

17. Lorrie Moore, "The Wrath of Athena," *New York Times*, May 7, 2000.

18. Quoted ibid.

19. PR, *The Human Stain*, LOA7: 710.

20. See Timothy Parrish's suggestive essay "Ralph Ellison: The Invisible Man in Philip Roth's 'The Human Stain,'" *Contemporary Literature* 45, no. 3 (2004): 421–59.

21. PR, *The Human Stain*, 707.

22. Ibid., 804.

23. Ibid., 716.

24. Ibid., 839.

25. BT Collection, C1609_BXB001209_f 11_small.pdf; Blake Bailey, *Philip Roth: The Biography* (New York: Skyhorse, 2021), 666.

Chapter 17. "Old Age Is a Massacre"

1. PR, *The Dying Animal*, LOA8: 23.

2. PR, *The Human Stain*, LOA7: 735.

3. PR, *The Dying Animal*, 13.

4. Ibid., 19.

5. Ibid., 30.

6. Ibid., 61; Rachel Stroup, "A Feminist Reads Philip Roth," *PopMatters*, July 21, 2017.

7. PR, *The Dying Animal*, 91.

8. Keith Gessen, "The Professor of Desire," *Nation*, May 25, 2001, https://www.thenation.com/article/archive/professor-desire/.

9. Ibid.

10. Ibid.

11. PR, *The Dying Animal*, 68.

12. Interview with Marc Weitzmann, May 2, 2024.

13. BT, *Here We Are: My Friendship with Philip Roth* (New York: Penguin, 2020), 49.

14. Blake Bailey, *Philip Roth: The Biography* (New York: Skyhorse, 2021), 698.

15. Jack Miles email, February 8, 2019.

16. Zachary Leader, *The Life of Saul Bellow*, vol. 2, *Love and Strife, 1965–2005* (New York: Knopf, 2018), 609.

17. PR, "Rereading Saul Bellow," in *Shop Talk: A Writer and His Colleagues and Their Work* (Boston: Houghton Mifflin, 2001), 139–60.

Chapter 18. Horror at Home

1. Paul Berman, "'The Plot Against America': What if It Happened Here?" *New York Times*, October 3, 2004.

2. PR, *The Plot Against America*, LOA8: 426–27.

3. Ibid., 97.

4. Ibid., 100.

5. J. M. Coetzee, *Inner Workings: Literary Essays, 2000–2005* (London: Harvill Secker, 2007), 242.

6. PR, *The Plot Against America*, 263.

7. Ibid., 97.

8. Ibid., 299–300.

9. Ibid., 99.

10. Ibid., 100.

11. Coetzee, *Inner Workings*, 230.

12. PR, *The Humbling*, LOA9: 252.

13. Interview with Susan Rogers, July 29, 2019.

14. Roth to Llewellyn: BT Collection, box B-001210, folder 8, Caro, December 23–26, 2013.

15. Caro Llewellyn, *Diving into Glass* (Melbourne: Penguin, 2019), 292.

16. Ibid., 276.

17. Interview with Judith Hudson, January 10, 2024.

18. Llewellyn, *Diving into Glass*, 280; BT Collection, box B-001210, folder 8, Caro, December 23–26, 2013.

19. Interview with Norman and Cella Manea, January 12, 2024; Llewellyn, *Diving into Glass*, 278.

20. Interview with Catherine von Klitzing, October 18, 2018.

21. BT Collection, box B-001210, folder 8, Caro, December 23–26, 2013.

22. Interview with Mary Karr, May 31, 2024.

23. PR, *Exit Ghost*, LOA8: 483–84.

24. Interview with Marc Weitzmann, May 5, 2024.

25. PR, *Everyman*, LOA9: 73.

26. Interview with Norman Manea, November 5, 2019.

27. Lisa Halliday, *Asymmetry* (New York: Simon and Schuster, 2018), 9.

28. Ibid., 41, 73.

29. Ibid., 122.

Chapter 19. Everyman

1. PR, *Everyman*, LOA9: 11.
2. Ibid., 69.
3. Ibid., 11.
4. Ibid., 19; 98.
5. James Wood, "Parade's End," *New Yorker*, October 15, 2007, p. 94.
6. Interview with Arnold Eisen, July 19, 2024.
7. John Banville, "Indignation by Philip Roth," *Financial Times*, September 19, 2008.
8. PR, *Indignation*, LOA9: 126.
9. Ibid., 130.
10. Ibid., 145.
11. Ibid., 120.
12. Ibid., 222.
13. PR, *Exit Ghost*, LOA8: 594.
14. Ibid., 476–77.
15. Ibid., 598.
16. Ibid., 491, 564.
17. Claudia Roth Pierpont, *Roth Unbound: A Writer and His Books* (New York: Farrar, Straus and Giroux, 2013), 293.
18. PR, *Exit Ghost*, 579.
19. Ibid., 575.

Chapter 20. Ghost Writer

Epigraph: PR, *The Counterlife*, LOA5: 229.

1. BT, *Here We Are: My Friendship with Philip Roth* (New York: Penguin, 2020), 50, 64.
2. Ibid., 164.
3. Ibid., 171.
4. PR, *The Facts*, LOA5: 317.
5. PR, *Nemesis*, LOA9: 310.
6. See Timothy L. Parrish, "Philip Roth's Deathmatch with Judaism," *Philip Roth Studies* 18, no. 1 (2022): 103–18.
7. PR, *Nemesis*, 316.

8. Ibid., 351.

9. Ibid., 428.

10. Leah Hager Cohen, "Summer of '44," *New York Times Book Review*, October 8, 2010, p. 1.

11. PR, *Nemesis*, 446.

12. Interview with Lucy Warner Kuemmerle, June 22, 2024.

13. PR, *My Life as a Man*, LOA3: 586.

14. Denis Donoghue, "Couples," *New York Review of Books*, July 10, 1969.

15. Interview with Lucy Warner Kuemmerle, June 22, 2024.

16. Julia Golier. "Remarks for Philip Roth Memorial Service." I thank Golier for a copy of the text.

17. Judith Thurman email, July 2, 2024.

18. Ibid.; interview with MG, November 5, 2019.

19. Julia Golier email, October 18, 2024.

Conclusion

1. Charles McGrath, "Philip Roth, American Literary Giant, Dies at 85," *New York Times*, May 22, 2018.

2. David Gates, "The Rake's Progress Giving Up the Ghost," *Newsweek*, October 1, 2007, 79.

3. Mark Oppenheimer, "The Ghost Writer," *New York Times Magazine*, April 4, 2021, 42.

4. Alexandra Alter and Rachel Abrams, "Allegations Against Biographer Halt Shipping of His Roth Book," *New York Times*, April 22, 2021.

5. Constance Grady, "The Rape Allegations Against Philip Roth's Biographer Are a Damning Condemnation of Publishing," *Vox*, April 28, 2021, https://www.vox.com/culture/22398138/blake-bailey-philip-roth-biography-rape-sexual-assault-accusations-allegations-grooming.

6. Jeff Baker, "'Listen Up Philip' Review: Philip Roth Didn't Win the Nobel Prize, but He Did Get This Nasty Little Movie," *Oregon Live*, October 31, 2014, https://www.oregonlive.com/movies/2014/10/listen_up_philip_review_philip.html.

7. Lena Dunham, Jason Kim, et al., *Girls*, season 6, episode 3, "American Bitch."

8. Julius Taranto, *How I Won a Nobel Prize* (New York: Little, Brown, 2023), 52.

9. Ibid., 54.

10. Ibid., 63.

11. PR, "Whacking Off," *Partisan Review* 34, no. 3 (Summer 1967): 385.

12. PR, *The Counterlife*, LOA5: 303.

ACKNOWLEDGMENTS

I HAVE many debts to acknowledge for a book whose research started in earnest shortly before Philip Roth's death in May 2018.

First, thanks to Philip. From the start I found our conversations vibrant, taxing, consistently memorable. I'm so grateful for his trust and willingness to put me in touch with many of those closest to him. He encouraged several of them to share with me their impressions as well as the letters and other documents in their possession.

Barbara Sproul opened her home to me, piling onto her dining room table a treasure trove of papers. She has also been willing to field endless questions that she, close to Philip since the late sixties, was in the best position to answer. Joel Conarroe did much the same. Judith Thurman took me into her life and confidence in ways I'll always treasure. Both Barbara Sproul and Judith Thurman read an early draft of this book, and I benefited greatly from their comments. Benjamin Taylor and Jack Miles have also been consistently helpful with advice and access to otherwise unattainable material.

Interviewed were more than a hundred of Roth's friends, critics, relatives, and acquaintances; these are acknowledged in the endnotes. Certainly, among the most memorable are Maletta Pfeiffer and Maxine Groffsky. Both spent many hours with me—Maletta at her home in Stockholm—sharing memories, as well as a diary and other papers previously shown to no one else. Maxine, too, despite initial hesitation, offered considerable insight and encouragement laced with usefully astringent strictures.

Readers of drafts include Edward Rothstein, Judith Thurman, Jesse Tisch, Michael Gorra, Eric Alterman, and Bernard Avishai. I entered as something of an interloper into what is a lively community of Philip Roth scholars who proved astonishingly eager to help, share their insights, and correct errors. I owe particular thanks to biographer Ira Nadel—a man of rare sweetness and erudition—as well as Jesse Tisch, an independent scholar of astonishing range. I've learned much from conversations with Claudia Roth Pierpont, Ross Posnock, and Timothy Parrish. Thanks also to the Philip Roth Society's exuberant President Aimee L. Pozorski; Samuel Graham-Felsen, Curator of the Philip Roth Personal Library; and the institution's tireless maestro Rosemary Steinbaum.

The interest of longstanding friends—Eli Lederhendler, Menachem Bar Shalom, and Netty Levine—has helped sustain me during more taxing moments. My dear friend since graduate school, historian David Biale, died just as I was putting the finishing touches on this book. Our conversations about it, much like nearly all we enjoyed during our half-century friendship, were bracing, tough, immensely satisfying. I miss him greatly, and wish we had been able to argue—as I'm certain we would have—about what I've done with Roth, who intrigued David nearly as much as he did me.

Permission to cite Roth's unpublished and published work was granted to me by Roth's literary executors Julia Golier and Andrew Wiley. This book would have been vastly different without this happy decision. Daniel J. Linke, University Archivist and Deputy

Head of Special Collections at Princeton University, helped greatly in rendering that valuable collection accessible.

I've been the beneficiary of editorial help from Noa Silver and Jennifer Gordon, as well as my colleagues on the Jewish Lives series and at Yale University Press Ileene Smith, Anita Shapira, Rebecca Keys, Heather Gold, Elizabeth Sylvia, and Erica Hanson. And I was blessed with the most astute and proficient of all copyeditors, Dan Heaton. Director of Yale University Press John Donatich has become a dear friend and warm supporter; Charlotte Sheedy remains my agent—and friend—now for forty or more years. The talented Paul Bogaards agreed to tackle the book's publicity, together with Senior Publicist for Yale University Press Liz Pelton. Suzi Tibor dealt with a wide range of permissions with an uncanny calm and patience.

With the assistance of research funds from my Stanford University chair as well as the encouragement of my deans Debra Satz and Gabriella Safran, I worked with a remarkable team of researchers: Anna Pirkarska, Chana Lanter, Kira Webb, Phil Kreisman, Madeleine E. Joelson, Sofie Zorica Finn Storan, Riley Seow, Ben Streeter, Jacob Andrew Soliman, Zheran He, and Emma Alexandra Bates.

Staff at Stanford's History Department and the Taube Center for Jewish Studies have helped in ways indispensable: Thanks to Shaina Hammerman, Iva Klemm, Maria Von Buiten, Burçak Keskin Kozat, Maria Moreno-Lane, and Colin Hamil.

Finally, my wife, Susan Berrin, consented for the last several years to live in the closest proximity to Philip Roth. So preoccupied was I that near the end of the writing of this book, when making hotel reservations for a trip to Paris, I inadvertently reserved a room in what turned out to be a rather shoddy hotel—I couldn't recall where I'd heard of it—only realizing somewhat later that Roth had noted its amenities in his novel *Sabbath's Theater* published twenty-nine years earlier. Returning to the prospect of living—without these distractions—beside her is the greatest of life's gifts.

INDEX

Note: The abbreviation PR refers to Philip Roth. Italic page numbers refer to photographs.

Akhtar, Ayad, 289
Alcott, Louisa May, 157
Alfred Hitchcock Presents, 11, 58
Algren, Nelson, 159
Allen, Woody, 286
Alter, Robert, 102, 179–80, 181
Alterman, Eric, 270
American Imago, 108
American Jewish Committee, 76
Americanness, 10, 42, 66
American Pastoral (Roth): and American Trilogy, 218–19, 229, 241; critical reception of, 218, 225; on getting people wrong, 7–8, 185; on leather-working, 193, 223–24; and life's uncertainty, 221; and Newark, 25, 219; PR's writing of, 14, 146, 167, 185, 218, 221; publishing of, 218; Pulitzer Prize for, 218; and senselessness of everyday existence, 219; "the Swede" of, 219–24, 274; and Vietnam War, 220, 221–22; and Weequahic neighborhood, 32–33, 219–21
American Place Theatre, and PR's "Good Jewish Boy," 93, 99
American Trilogy (Roth), 218–19, 229, 241, 243, 286
Amis, Martin, 170
Amnesty International, 136, 146–47
The Anatomy Lesson (Roth): critical reception of, 132, 170; on Irving Howe, 135; PR's fictionalized experiences in, 169–70; PR's writing of, 163, 168, 169, 188–89, 294; publishing of, 167; on Weequahic neighborhood, 31–32; on work, 24; and Zuckerman saga, 150

Anderson, Sherwood, 110, 268
Andreas-Salomé, Lou, 122
Angoff, Charles, 83
Anti-Defamation League, 3, 80, 81
anti-Nazi groups, 27
antisemitism: Jewish intellectuals on, 65; and military duty, 76, 80; and PR's *The Plot Against America*, 11, 251, 253, 254; PR's responses to, 11, 72, 149–50, 173
Appelfeld, Aharon, 11, 175, 202, 204
Aristophanes, 203
Arno, Nat, 27–28
Asher, Aaron, 242
Atlantic, 123
Atlas, James, 246–48, 271
Atwood, Margaret, 191
Avishai, Bernard: on Irving Howe, 134; on *Portnoy's Complaint*, 5; and PR's death, 284; and PR's marriage to Claire Bloom, 199; PR's relationship with, 98, 134, 167, 175, 185–86, 277; *The Tragedy of Zionism*, 175, 186

Babel, Isaac, 139, 157–58, 162
Bailey, Blake: claims of sexual impropriety of, 275, 287, 288; *Philip Roth: The Biography*, 3–4, 5, 275, 281, 283, 287–88; PR conflated with, 4; and PR's description of mother, 39; and PR's education, 32; on PR's friendship with Alan Lelchuk, 13–14, 126; and PR's marriage to Claire Bloom, 209; on PR's marriage to Maggie Roth, 90; and PR's relationship with Minette Marrin, 191; and PR's relationship with Ross Miller, 188; and PR's relationship with Maletta Pfeiffer, 206, 207, 209; on PR's writing of *American Pastoral*, 221; on reception of *Letting Go*, 96
Bailey, Clinton, 174–75
Baldwin, James, 72, 293
Bamberger, Louis, 27
Barth, John, 129, 159
Barthelme, Donald, 159
Baruch, Bernard, 27, 44
Beckett, Samuel, 6, 38
Bellow, Janis, 246
Bellow, Saul: *The Adventures of Augie March*, 65–66, 247; biography of, 246–48, 271; *Humboldt's Gift*, 247; influence of, 288; and Israel, 135; and Library of America, 243; and memories, 203; as model for character in *The Ghost Writer*, 246–47; PR compared to, 62, 72, 76, 141; PR on sons of, 265–66; PR's criticism of, 92–93; PR's kinship with, 42, 110; PR's relationship with, 246–48; PR's study and imitation of, 57
Ben-Gurion, David, 81, 174
Ben-Horin, Eliyahu, 80
Benjamin, Richard, 120
Benny, Jack, 79
Berkowitz, Robert Leonard, 43
Berman, Paul, 249
"Beyond the Last Rope" essay (Roth), 16–17
Bloch, J. W., 80–81
Block, Abraham, 28
Bloom, Claire: acting career of, 168; *Leaving a Doll's House*, 3, 136, 185, 207, 208, 209, 225, 241, 243, 244, 269, 287; PR's correspondence with, 172; and PR's *Deception*, 190, 207; PR's divorce from, 208, 209, 213; PR's manuscript on, 257, 275; PR's marriage to, 198–99, 207, 209; and PR's mental breakdown, 207, 208; PR's *My Life as a Man* dedicated to, 140; PR's *The Professor of Desire* dedicated to, 151; PR's relationship with, 151–53, 154, 164, 167, 168, 169, 171–72, 174, 181, 182, 185, 186, 190, 193, 198, 205, 206, 209
Bloom, Harold, 168, 203
Boroff, David, 65
Borowitz, Eugene, 81

Boudin, Kathy, 221
Bradley Beach, New Jersey, 16–18, *17*, 30, 36, 264–65
Braudy, Susan, 90, 99
The Breast (Roth): critical reception of, 122, 131–32, 133, 218; Irving Howe on, 134; PR's interview on, 123, 130; PR's writing of, 122, 130, 136, 167, 218; release of, 51, 130–31, 142; Barbara Sproul as model for character in, 141–42
Breuer, Josef, 122
Brod, Max, 148
Brodesser-Akner, Taffy, 289
Brown, Norman O., 109–10
Bruce, Lenny, 110, 115, 117
Brustein, Barbara, 99
Brustein, Robert, 99
Buber, Martin, 68, 72, 81, 138
Buck, Pearl, 40
Buckley, William, 44
Bucknellian, 50
Bucknell University, PR studying at, 49–52, 57, 98, 187
Bush, George W., 10, 250, 251, 271

Callil, Carmen, 287
Camus, Albert, 6, 292–93
Capote, Truman, 50, 52
Carruth, Hayden, 111
Carver, Raymond, 144
Céline, Louis-Ferdinand, 6, 155
Chabon, Michael, 289
Cheever, John, 72, 288
Chekhov, Anton, 149, 157, 265, 273
Chicago Review, 57–58, 62
Christian Science Monitor, 228
Clinton, Bill, 231–32
Coetzee, J. M., 5, 251, 254–55
Cohen, David, 46
Cohen, Florence, 39, 48, 226
Cohen, Irving, 46, 48, 226
Cohen, Joshua, 289
Cohen, Leah Hager, 280
Cohen, Oscar, 81
Cohn, Robert, 222
Cohn, Roy, 93
Commentary: Irving Howe's "Philip Roth Reconsidered" essay, 133–37, 167, 170, 196; PR's fiction and essays in, 63, 67, 75–76; on PR's *When She Was Good*, 102; Isaac Rosenfeld's essay on Jewish life, 106
Conarroe, Joel, 129, 143, 153, 169, 185, 262, 277
Conrad, Joseph, 6, 64, 157, 273
"The Contest for Aaron Gold" (Roth), 58, 62
"The Conversion of the Jews" (Roth), 64
Coover, Robert, 159
Cosmopolitan, 93
The Counterlife (Roth): and Clinton Bailey, 175; critical reception of, 218, 267; and cusp of adolescence, 8–9; incompatible narratives of, 171, 294–95; interplay between counterintuitive and concrete, 177; and Israel, 10, 170–71, 172, 174–78; and Minette Marin's voice, 182; and Ross Miller, 169, 170, 171, 172, 241; *My Life as a Man* compared to, 140; and National Book Critics Circle Award, 181; and National Jewish Book prize, 181; and need to lose oneself, 176–77; as nonfiction, 171; and persistent talk, 180; and David Plante's trip with PR to Israel, 170–72, 174, 176; and politics, 227; PR's writing of, 170–71, 187; release of, 150, 183; and responses to life's provocations, 179–80, 295; and theatricality, 179; and Weequahic neighborhood, 33–34; West Bank description in, 176–79; Zuckerman's funeral depicted in, 173–74
Covid epidemic, 286
Crystal Lake, 32
cummings, e. e., 50, 58–59
Czech writers, 98, 115, 136, 138, 147, 149–50

Dana, John Cotton, 25
Dateline NBC, 208
Davis, Philip, 259
Dayan, Yael, 175
"The Day It Snowed" (Roth), 58
Deception (Roth), 189–91, 193, 194, 202, 207
Deconstructing Harry (film), 286
"Defender of the Faith" (Roth), 60, 72, 76–77, 80–81, 92
Definitely, Maybe (film), 286
DeLillo, Don, 196, 198, 286
Demjanjuk, John, 201–2
Denham, Alice, 13–14, 92
Diamant, Dora, 147
Dickens, Charles, 30
Dickstein, Morris, 141
di Donato, Pietro, 79, 82
Dissent magazine, 134
Doctorow, E. L., 4
Donoghue, Denis, 282
Dos Passos, John, 221
Dostoevsky, Fyodor, 155
Drabble, Margaret, 131
Dreiser, Theodore, 221
Dunham, Lena, 290–91
Durante, Jimmy, 155
The Dying Animal (Roth): critical reception of, 238, 239–40; and friendship between men, 238–41; and jealousy, 237–38; and old age, 236–37, 238; and sexual revolution of sixties, 238, 240

Eckstine, Billy, 45
Einstein, Albert, 43
Eisen, Arnold, 267
Eisenhower, Dwight David, 93
"Eli, the Fanatic" (Roth), 53, 74, 75–76
Eliot, T. S., 51
Ellenstein, Meyer, 28
Ellison, Ralph, 79, 82, 138, 230, 234
Ellmann, Richard, 7, 77
Elman, Richard, 201
Elon, Amos, 174–76
Emerson, Ralph Waldo, 66
Englander, Nathan, 289
Epstein, Barbara, 199
Epstein, Jason, 52
"Epstein" (Roth): and fissures in lives of characters, 8; and Jewish life, 75; and PR's story of letter writer, 82, 83; and Weequahic neighborhood, 64
Esquire, 64, 92, 93, 100, 104
Everyman (Roth): and diamond trade, 193, 223; and old age, 264–65, 267; PEN/Faulkner Award for, 266; PR's writing of, 245–46, 261, 264–66
Exit Ghost (Roth): and biography, 3, 270–71; characters of, 163, 270–73; and Joseph Conrad, 157, 273; PR's writing of, 257, 260, 264, 273–74; and youth, 92, 272
"Expect the Vandals" (Roth), 64
Ezrahi, Sidra DeKoven, 186, 193, 223

The Facts (Roth): and childhood recollections, 30; critical reception of, 187; epilogue of, 187–89; and family, 22, 187–88; Ross Miller on, 242; *My Life as a Man* compared to, 140; as nonfiction, 186, 189; PR on father in, 36, 187; PR on Jewish self-definition, 81; PR on mother in, 36–38, 188; PR on Maggie Roth in, 85–86, 90, 188; PR on Yeshiva University forum, 78, 79, 81–82; PR's description of family in, 187; PR's writing of, 186–89; as virtual autobiography, 36, 78, 186, 189, 202; and Weequahic neighborhood, 33; and Andrew Wylie's negotiation of price, 192
Farrar, Straus and Giroux, 110, 175
Farrow, Mia, 277, 286
Fast, Howard, *Citizen Tom Paine*, 47, 48, 157
Faulkner, William, 66
Feiffer, Jules, 99, 127
feminism, 103, 141, 190–91, 232, 238, 244, 260, 269–70
Fiedler, Leslie, 24, 87

"The Final Delivery of Mr. Thorn" (Roth), 53–54
Finkel, Mickey (uncle), 48
Finkielkraut, Alain, 42
Fitzgerald, F. Scott, 3, 66, 69, 72
Fitzgerald, Penelope, 241
Flaschner, Lemmel, 22
Flaschner Family: Victory Edition, 21–22
Flaschner Family Association, 20–21, 34
Flaubert, Gustave, 6, 227
Fleischer, David, 82
Foley, Martha, 58
Ford Foundation, 93
Forest Lodge YMHA camp, 54
Forster, E. M., 77, 87
Foucault, Michel, 153, 157–60
Frank, Anne: *The Diary of a Young Girl*, 65, 157; in *Exit Ghost*, 272–73; in *The Ghost Writer*, 7, 125, 157, 158–63; PR's wanting to write about, 11, 163
Franklin, Ruth, 157
Freud, Sigmund, 6, 107, 109–10, 115, 122, 138–40, 180
Friedman, Bruce Jay, 106
Frosch, William, 87

Garbus, Martin (Marty), 60, 284
Gardner, Ava, 1
Gardner, John, 129, 131
Gass, William H., 159, 181
Gates, David, 285
Gauguin, Paul, 71
Geffen, Arthur, 63–64, 88
Genet, Jean, 6, 8
Gens, Jacob, 11
Gessen, Keith, 239–40
The Ghost Writer (Roth): and anti-semitism, 149–50; characters of, 153–55, 246–47; critical reception of, 14, 153, 162, 165, 218, 294; dedication to Milan Kundera, 138; discussion of books in, 157, 162; Anne Frank in, 7, 125, 157, 158–63; and interplay between self and text, 159; PR's fictionalized experiences in, 7, 158, 160; PR's writing of, 138, 151, 153, 155–56, 159, 161, 165, 166, 167
Girls (television series), 290–91
Gogol, Nikolai, 132, 139
Gold, Herbert, 86, 93
Golden, Harry, 85
Golding, William, 292
Goldman, Albert: *Life* portrait of PR, 104–5, 114–18; on *Portnoy's Complaint*, 104–5, 110, 114–15, 116; PR's friendship with, 46, 90, 95, 99, 116, 185–86; PR's ideas for collaboration with, 38–39; and PR's *The Professor of Desire*, 125; on Barbara Sproul, 116, 127–28
Golier, Julia, 212, 267, 273–74, 277, 283–84
Goodbye, Columbus (film), 1, 56, 120
"Goodbye, Columbus" (Roth): bitterness of, 72; and ethnography of Jewish suburbia, 71–72, 75; fear of being overwhelmed in, 73; film version of, 1; and fissures in the lives of characters, 8; *The Ghost Writer* compared to, 153; models for characters in, 3, 55–56, 67, 68–70; and Newark, 24, 279; parents in, 15, 70, 71; PR's resemblance to main character of, 48, 49, 68–69; PR's writing of, 63, 68, 69–71, 158; reliance on books, 6; Ted Solotaroff on, 62; and work, 24
Goodbye, Columbus and Five Short Stories (Roth): and Americanness, 10; and attacks on PR by Jewish critics of, 72, 76, 78–81, 83–84; cover design of, 91; critical reception of, 77–81, 133, 174, 288; and demands of realism, 53; Irving Howe on, 134; *I Married a Communist* compared to, 228; and Jewish life, 74–75; *Letting Go* compared to, 96; and Mark Daroff Award, 77; Modern Library edition of, 138; and National Book Award for fiction, 77–78, 127; PR on criticism of, 73;

Goodbye, Columbus and Five Short Stories (Roth) (*continued*)
and PR's distance from characters, 230; PR's dry spell after, 146; and PR's role as Jewish writer, 84; PR's writing of, 63–64, 68, 167; publicity for, 92; publishing of, 66–67, 76, 78, 87, 91–92, 96, 247; stories selected for, 74, 76; success of, 16; thirtieth-anniversary edition preface of, 106–7; twentieth anniversary of, 138
Goodman, Paul, 6, 72, 127
Gopnik, Adam, 107, 109
Gornick, Vivian, 141
Gorra, Michael, 6, 72
Grady, Constance, 288
The Great American Novel (Roth), 2, 121, 123, 147, 167
Green, Martin, 156–57
Greenberg, Clement, 136
Greer, Germaine, 171
Groffsky, Maxine: on "Goodbye, Columbus," 69; as *Paris Review* editor, 68; PR's relationship with, 3, 55–56, 59–60, 67–68, 72, 73, 89, 242, 281
Gruenbaum, Henry, 81
Guston, Philip, 143

Haetzni, Elyakim, 177
Halkin, Hillel, 101, 122, 140
Halliday, Lisa, 2, 255, 259, 262–63, 282, 284, 288
Harel, Israel, 176
Harper's: PR's essay "Beyond the Last Rope" in, 16; PR's writing in, 93
Hawthorne, Nathaniel, 270, 272–73
Hayes, Patrick, 109, 160
Hefner, Hugh, 91
Hellman, Lillian, 94
Hemingway, Ernest, 58, 62, 66
Hersey, John, 65
Hertzberg, Hendrik, 231, 232
Heyman, Bob, 48, 59, 86
Heymann, Eileen, 81
"His Mistress's Voice" (Roth), 39
Hiss, Alger, 1
Hitchens, Christopher, 263
Hitler, Adolph, 201
Hobhouse, Janet, 12–13, 144–45, 182, 213
Hochman, Sandra, 103
Hoffman, Dustin, 93
Holocaust: Aharon Appelfeld on, 202; in *The Counterlife*, 175; and PR's experience of Yeshiva University forum, 82; PR's friendships with survivors of, 11–12; PR's play about, 58–59; PR's short stories on, 74; role in contemporary culture, 161
The Holocaust (television series), 161
Hooks, Sean, 191
Houghton Mifflin, 62–63, 66–67, 75, 87, 92
Houston Chronicle, 104
Howe, Irving: "The Age of Conformity," 135; and Bernard Avishai, 185; and Czech writers, 147; on Ralph Ellison, 234; on kinship of Jewish writers, 66; "Philip Roth Reconsidered" essay, 133–37, 167, 170, 196; on *Portnoy's Complaint*, 133, 134, 135; PR distinguished from, 43, 138; PR's response to, 135
Hudson, Judith, 256, 257, 260
The Human Stain (Roth): and American Trilogy, 219, 229, 241; on betrayal of mother and African American family, 22–23, 230, 233–34; and biography, 5, 229–30, 232; chaos in, 232; critical reception of, 228–29, 244; feminists on, 244; and fissures in the lives of characters, 8; freedom in, 22–23, 230, 234, 235; model for Coleman Silk in, 143, 230; and old age, 237; openings for story of, 231–32; passing in, 5, 232–34; PR's fictionalized experiences in, 230; and unkindness of fate, 230
The Humbling (Roth), 255, 264

Huvelle, C. H., 169, 205, 240
Huxley, Aldous, 54
Hyman, Stanley Edgar, 87, 96

"'I Always Wanted You to Admire My Fasting'; or Looking at Kafka" (Roth), 21–22, 136, 147–48
I Married a Communist (Roth): and American Trilogy, 219, 229, 241; Saul Bellow on, 247; critical reception of, 228; *Goodbye, Columbus* compared to, 228; and McCarthyism, 225–26; and Arthur Miller, 157; model for Ira Ringold in, 46, 225–27, 228; model for Murray Ringold in, 32, 225, 226, 227, 228; and Thomas Paine, 47; publishing of, 225; and Weequahic neighborhood, 34–35
Indignation (Roth), 264, 266, 267–70
Israel: and Saul Bellow, 135; and PR, 10–11, 65, 81, 135, 170–76, 200; and PR's *The Counterlife*, 10, 170–71, 172, 174–78; and PR's *Operation Shylock*, 11, 174, 198, 201, 202–3; Herman Roth on, 174
Itzkowitz, Harold, 54–55

Jakobson, Barbara, 99, 108, 142, 182, 284
Jakobson, John, 99
James, Henry: "The Figure in the Carpet," 164–65; Janet Hobhouse compared to, 144; and PR's *Exit Ghost*, 273; and PR's *The Ghost Writer*, 160, 162; and PR's *I Married a Communist*, 227; and PR's *Letting Go*, 6, 88, 110, 157; and PR's *My Life as a Man*, 139; PR's reading of, 153, 157; PR's study and imitation of, 57, 64, 100
Jewish family associations, 21
Jewish fiction, 75, 84, 85
Jewish Theological Seminary, 267
Johnson, John, 32, 33
Johnson, Lyndon, 10, 174
Joyce, James, 6, 7, 31, 57, 77, 157, 230
Jung, Carl, 200

Kafka, Franz: "The Burrow," 148; "The Hunger Artist," 125; "The Judgement," 148; "The Metamorphosis," 130; and PR's *The Anatomy Lesson*, 170; and PR's *The Breast*, 131, 132; and PR's *The Dying Animal*, 236, 237; and PR's *The Ghost Writer*, 157, 167; and PR's "'I Always Wanted You to Admire My Fasting'; or, Looking at Kafka," 21–22, 136, 147–48; PR's interest in, 136, 137, 146, 147–49; and PR's *My Life as a Man*, 139; and PR's *Portnoy's Complaint*, 6, 110, 114; and PR's *Zuckerman Unbound*, 167; *The Trial*, 148
Kahane, Meir, 200
Kakutani, Michiko, 215–16, 229
Karr, Mary, 260, 284
Kauffmann, Stanley, 66
Kazin, Alfred, 19–20, 43, 77, 135, 136, 137
Kazin, Judith, 19–20
Kelly, Robert, 63
Kennedy, Jackie, 1, 94
Kennedy family, 2, 43
Kermode, Frank, 216
Kerouac, Jack, 78, 127
Kierkegaard, Søren, 6
Kirsch, Adam, 119
Kissinger, Henry, 201
Kitaj, R. B., 98, 172–73, 202
Kleinschmidt, Hans J., 107–9, 142–43
Klima, Ivan, 11, 136, 137, 150, 151
Kline, Kevin, 286
Klinghoffer, Leon, 200
Korean War, 21, 267–69, 278
Kozodoy, Neal, 195–96
Krauss, Nicole, 277, 289
Kuemmerle, Lucy Warner, 222, 281–83
Kundera, Milan, 136, 138
Kurosawa, Akira, 276

Lahr, John, 168
Laing, R. D., 127
Landes, Daniel, 81
Lansky, Meyer, 28
Leader, Zachary, 247–48
Lee, Hermione, 63, 122, 171, 188, 241
Lehman, Betty, 55
Lehman, Stuart, 58–59, 267
Lelchuk, Alan: *American Mischief*, 123–24; disintegration of PR's friendship with, 125–26; and Irving Howe, 135; on *Letting Go*, 97; photograph of, *124*; and PR on *The Breast*, 130; and PR on *Portnoy's Complaint*, 114; and PR on *When She Was Good*, 102–3; and PR on writing "Goodbye, Columbus," 68, 69; and PR's *American Pastoral*, 221; PR's championing of, 98, 123–24; PR's correspondence with, 13–14, 128–29, 142; PR's *The Great American Novel*, 123; and PR's literary aspirations, 49; and PR's *My Life as a Man*, 125; and PR's *The Professor of Desire*, 125; PR's taped conversation with, 45, 157–58; and Yaddo, 123; *Ziff: A Life?*, 125–26
Lennon, John, 115
Lerner, Ben, 289
Lethem, Jonathan, 289
Letting Go (Roth): critical reception of, 81, 96–97, 101; film treatment of, 93; Irving Howe on, 133–34; and Henry James, 6, 88, 110, 157; letter to son in, 36; and PR's dedication, 87; PR's writing of, 110, 167; release of, 91; Maggie Roth as model of character in, 87–88; Ted Solotaroff as model for character in, 61–62; George Starbuck on, 90–91
Levi, Primo, 11, 150, 183–85, *184*
Levinger, Miriam, 177–78
Levinger, Moshe, 177–78
Lewinsky, Monica, 231
Lewis, Sinclair, 96
Library of America, 243, 245
Lichtenstein, Gene, 88, 91
Life, 104–5, 114–18
Limelight (film), 152
Lincoln, Abraham, 226
Lindbergh, Charles, 11, 249–54
Listen Up Philip (film), 289–90
Llewellyn, Caro, 255–57, 259–60
London Review of Books, 187
"Looking at Kafka" (Roth), 21–22, 136, 147–48
Lowell, Robert, 58, 77
Luciano, Lucky, 28
Lucretius, 175
Lurie, Alison, 4, 94–95, 100–101

McCarthy, Cormac, 286
McCarthy, Joseph, 51, 225–26
McCarthyism, 49, 225–26
McEwan, Ian, 4
McGrath, Charles, 222, 285
MacGraw, Ali, 56, 120
Mademoiselle, 93
Mad magazine, 120
Mailer, Norman, 58, 92–93, 154, 159, 262, 288
Malamud, Bernard: biography of, 259; *Dubin's Lives*, 154; and Alan Lelchuk, 126; as model for character in *The Ghost Writer*, 154; PR compared to, 62, 72, 76; PR's criticism of, 92–93; PR's kinship with, 42, 65; on Maggie Roth, 87
Malcolm, Janet, 121–22, 179
Mandela, Nelson, 199
Manea, Cella, 150–51, 257
Manea, Norman, 11, 98, 150–51, 207, 257
Mann, Thomas, 6, 139, 157, 218
Marcus, Greil, 115
Markfield, Wallace, 106
Marrin, Minette, 181–82, 190–91
Martin, Dean, 29
Martin, Mildred, 50–51, 57, 171
Martin, Tony, 45
Marx, Karl, 146, 293
Marx Brothers, 115

Mather, Cotton, 210
Maurer, Bob, 50–52, 57
Maurer, Charlotte, 50–52, 57
Maurer, Harry, 51, 98
Melville, Herman, 6, 139
Menand, Louis, 65
Mercer, Johnny, 221
Merkin, Daphne, 144
Milbauer, Asher, 11–12
Miles, Jack, 144, 257
Miller, Arthur, 157, 168–69
Miller, Kermit, 168–69
Miller, Ross: and biography of PR, 108, 167, 169, 229, 241–42, 244, 245–46; and *The Counterlife*, 169, 170, 171, 172, 241; and Jack Miles, 144; on Arthur Miller, 168–69; and Maletta Pfeiffer, 205, 211; on *Portnoy's Complaint*, 40–41; PR's manuscript on, 257, 275; PR's relationship with, 168–69, 186, 188–89, 240, 241–46, 274
Minutemen, 27–29
Moe, Henry Allen, 14
Moore, Deborah Dash, 44
Morrison, Toni, 290
Motion Picture Association of America, 120
Mudge, Ann, 98–99, 142, 188, 265, 284
Musil, Robert, 216
My Life as a Man (Roth): critical reception of, 141, 156; and Alan Lelchuk, 125; narrators of, 138, 139; PR's fictionalized experiences in, 51, 59, 88, 139–41, 142, 153, 182, 242, 282; PR's writing of, 122, 138–39, 155, 161, 162–63

Nabokov, Vladimir, 96, 218
Nadel, Ira, 136, 173
National Jewish Book Council, 77
Nazis: and Minutemen, 27–28; and PR's *The Plot Against America*, 251
Nazism, 200
Nehring, Cristina, 198
Nemesis (Roth): and community, 278–79; critical reception of, 279–80; and family, 277, 278, 280–81; fatherly love in, 36; on Newark, 30, 277–79; and polio epidemic, 277–79, 286; PR's writing of, 256, 264, 275
New American Review, 61, 104
Newark, New Jersey: and African American music, 45; African Americans of, 29; airport of, 26; Chancellor Elementary School, 44; civic culture of, 25, 29; Clinton Hill neighborhood of, 43; economy of, 29–30; factories of, 25, 26, 31; family associations of, 21; gangsters of, 27–29; geography of, 25; immigrants of, 25, 33; Ironbound neighborhood of, 26; Irvington neighborhood of, 72; Jewish community of, 26–28, 30–31, 33, 43–44, 51; Jewish elite of, 26–27, 28; library system of, 25, 49; Mosque Theater, 45; Museum of Art, 26; PR on social history of, 2, 29, 30, 34–35, 51, 70, 72, 101; and PR's *American Pastoral*, 25, 219; PR's family living in, 16, 24–25, 26, 28, 29, 30, 69; and PR's "Goodbye, Columbus," 24, 279; and PR's *Nemesis*, 30, 277–79; PR's relationship with, 24, 25, 69, 73, 106–7, 114, 122, 165, 170, 182, 229, 249–50, 277, 279; Temple B'nai Abraham, 26; Third Ward of, 26, 28, 31; Weequahic High School, 32; Weequahic neighborhood of, 26, 28, 29, 30–34, 43, 64, 250, 278–79, 283; Weequahic Park, 31, 32, 250; and work, 24–25
Newark Museum, 216–17
Newark Public Library, 25, 49, 70, 72
New England writers, 66
New Republic: on *Letting Go*, 96; PR's fiction and essays in, 63; PR's movie reviews for, 66
New Yorker: PR's *The Ghost Writer* previewed in, 153; PR's stories published in, 76, 80; review of

New Yorker (*continued*)
Alan Lelchuk's *American Mischief*, 124; vignettes of, 50
New York magazine, 208
New York Review of Books: and PR's interview about *The Breast*, 123, 130; PR's theatrical reviews in, 93; and Edward Rothstein's review of *Zuckerman Unbound*, 166–67
New York Times: Michiko Kakutani's review of *Sabbath's Theater*, 215–16; PR's essay on Primo Levi, 183–84; on PR's *The Human Stain*, 229; PR's obituary in, 285–86; Fay Weldon's review of *Deception*, 191
New York Times Book Review: on Blake Bailey's *Philip Roth: The Biography*, 3, 287; on *When She Was Good*, 102
New York Times Magazine, 94
Nietzsche, Friedrich, 6, 109–10
Nixon, Richard, 2–3, 10
Nobel Prize, 3, 126, 209, 211, 244, 276, 285, 291
Norton, 3, 275, 287
"Novotny's Pain" (Roth), 60

Oates, Joyce Carol, 129, 139
Obama, Barack, 281
O'Brien, Edna, 6, 153
Olmsted, Frederick Law, 32
Olmsted Brothers, 32
O'Neill, Eugene, 293
O'Neill, Joseph, 2
"On the Air" (Roth), 122
Operation Shylock (Roth): Janis Bellow on, 246; critical reception of, 199–200, 241; and Israel, 11, 174, 198, 201, 202–3; King Lear in, 201; as nonfiction, 189, 203; PR's fictionalized experiences in, 6, 18, 198, 202, 203–4; and PR's sense of validation, 121; PR's writing of, 200, 201; release of, 207
Oppenheimer, Mark, 287
Oren, Dan, 21
Orwell, George, 30
Orwell, Sonia, 171
Our Gang (Roth), 2, 134, 167
Out of Africa (film), 164
Ozick, Cynthia, 287

Paine, Thomas, 47
Paramount, 120
Paris Review: Maxine Groffsky as managing editor of, 68; and George Plimpton, 22, 273; PR interview in, 5, 63; PR's fiction and essays in, 63, 64, 76
Parrish, Timothy, 78
Partisan Review, 104, 292–93
Passin, Ruth, 86
Patrimony (Roth): critical reception of, 193, 196–97; Neal Kozodoy's review of, 195–96; and National Book Critics Circle Award, 193; as nonfiction, 189; PR's depiction of father in, 16, 35, 97, 187, 189, 192, 193–97; PR's depiction of paternal grandfather in, 34, 194; PR's tour promoting, 197–98; PR's writing of, 196; as virtual autobiography, 189, 202
PEN American Center, 258
Perry, Alex Ross, 289
Pfeiffer, Maletta: and Claire Bloom, 152, 207, 209, 211, 225; diary of, 209–10, 212; friendships of, 241; *Overcoming*, 209; PR's relationship with, 145, 152–53, 172, 182, 199, 205–12, 213, 225, 241
Pfeiffer, Werner, 205, 207
Pierpont, Claudia Roth: and PR in Prague, 137–38, 149; and PR on J. D. Salinger, 50; and PR's death, 284; on PR's *Exit Ghost*, 273; on PR's father, mother, family as subject, 15; on PR's *Operation Shylock*, 200–201; on PR's *Sabbath's Theater*, 213, 214, 217
Plante, David: and PR on Claire Bloom, 152, 168; on PR's candid nature, 4; PR's relationship with, 98, 170–72, 174, 176, 260
Plath, Sylvia, 77

Playhouse 90, PR's play for, 11
Pléiade series of Gallimard, 266
Plimpton, George, 22, 64, 263, 270, 273
The Plot Against America (Roth): on antisemitism, 11, 251, 253, 254; Aunt Evelyn in, 253, 254; characters of, 252–53; critical reception of, 249, 251, 288; family in, 249–50, 251, 253–54; on fascism, 249, 250; father in, 35, 249, 254; HBO adaptation of, 254, 286; and Jewish life, 251–55; Charles Lindbergh in, 11, 249–54; Ross Miller on, 245; mother in, 249, 250, 253, 254; neighbor Seldon in, 253, 254; and Newark, 249, 250; older brother in, 49, 249, 253, 254; PR's writing of, 242, 243, 255; rabbis in, 252–53, 254; realism of, 254; Franklin Roosevelt in, 249–51, 254; *Sabbath's Theater* compared to, 254–55
Podhoretz, Norman, 42–43, 133, 136
Poland, rumors of fate of Jews in, 43
Pollard, Jonathan, 200
Portnoy's Complaint (Roth): adolescence captured in, 45; Bernard Avishai on, 5; as bestseller, 7, 104, *105*, 119, 122, 126–27, 128, 129, 156, 167, 289; on Christianity, 113; critical reception of, 103, 106, 119, 121, 122, 127, 132, 165, 187, 199; description of sexual impotence in, 174; double consciousness in, 106; and family, 114, 115; freedom in, 19, 33, 235; Sigmund Freud and Friedrich Nietzsche's unresolved combat in, 6; *The Ghost Writer* compared to, 138; Albert Goldman on, 104–5, 110, 114–15, 116; Irving Howe on, 133, 134, 135; humor in, 111; inspiration for characters in, 9–10; Jewish characters in, 76; and Jewish life, 110, 111, 113, 114, 119; masturbation in, 4, 119, 187; model of Sophie Portnoy in, 38, 39, 40–41, 111, 113, 250; mother in, 39–40, 111, 113, 250; parental devotion in, 33; parents in, 41; popularity of, 1, 104; PR's writing of, 95, 99–101, 106, 141; redemption in, 113; release of, 43, 44, 45, 48, 50, 104, 114, 139; as response to Yeshiva University forum, 78; J. D. Salinger compared to, 52; samples published in magazines, 104; sexuality in, 33, 293–94; Zadie Smith on, 110–11; Ted Solotaroff's praise of, 61; theatrical version of, 93; and Weequahic neighborhood, 33
Posnock, Ross, 24, 71, 218
Pozorski, Aimee L., 6
The Prague Orgy (Roth), 150, 168
Presley, Elvis, 115
Pretenkin, Blanda, 120
Prevatt, Nicole, 234
Price, Richard, 129
Priesand, Sally, 41
Princeton University: Institute for Advanced Study at, 27; PR's teaching at, 81, 93, 230
Prinz, Joachim, 26–28, 81
The Professor of Desire (Roth), 116, 125, 149, 151, 155, 156
Prose, Francine, 157
Proust, Marcel, 78
Puzo, Mario, 7
Pynchon, Thomas, 286

Rackman, Emanuel, 80
Rahv, Philip, 136
Random House, 92
Reagan, Ronald, 174
Remnick, David, 277
"Revenge" (Roth), 158
Rhys, Jean, 171
Ribalow, Harold, 84
Richman, Peter Mark, 93
Rieff, David, 110, 175, 179, 185, 277, 281
Riesman, David, 6, 69, 71, 158
Robeson, Paul, 227
Rogers, Jacqueline, 88, 242

Rogers, Susan, 242, 255, 260, 284
Rogers, Thomas, 88, 242
Roosevelt, Eleanor, 10, 227
Roosevelt, Franklin, 10, 22, 27, 42, 44, 249–51, 254
Rosenbloom, "Slapsie Maxie," 43
Rosenfeld, Isaac, 106, 198
Roth, Bertha (grandmother), 19–20, 34
Roth, Bess (mother): at Bradley Beach, *17*; death of, 189, 194; family background of, 39; and Flaschner Family Association, 20; marriage of, 41, 189; as model for mother in *Portnoy's Complaint*, 111, 250; with PR at fortieth-birthday party, *112*; PR's descriptions of, 9, 16, 36–38, 39, 40; PR's relationship with, 38–39, 41–42, 108, 189, 195; Sandy Roth's description of, 40; Judith Thurman's description of, 41; and Weequahic neighborhood, 35; whistling of, 41
Roth, Doreen, 40
Roth, Henry, 154, 271
Roth, Herman (father): anti-German rants of, 64; and boxing, 43; death of, 16, 19, 192, 193–95; and "Epstein," 64; family background of, 35, 194–95; financial mishaps of, 35, 44, 46, 194, 233; heirloom from Sender Roth, 34; on Israel, 174; Jewishness of, 194, 196; marriage of, 41, 189; meddling of, 97–98; photograph of, *37*; protection of sons from sexual mishaps, 35; in PR's *Patrimony*, 16, 35, 97, 187, 189, 192, 193–97; PR's reciting sayings of, 36; PR's relationship with, 15–16, 18, 35–36, 41, 45–46, 49, 89, 97, 149, 166, 174, 182–83, 187, 189, 193, 195; Sandy Roth's relationship with, 48, 97–98; temperament of, 35–36, 40; whistling of, 41
Roth, Jonathan, 40, 97, 195
Roth, Margaret Martinson Williams "Maggie": death of, 90, 95, 108; diary of, 90; *Esquire* work of, 88; as model for *Letting Go* character, 87–88; as model for *When She Was Good* character, 101–2; PR's argument with, 90; PR's divorce from, 94, 95; in PR's *The Facts*, 85–86, 90, 188; PR's marriage to, 88–91, 99, 108–9, 222, 282; and PR's *My Life as a Man*, 88, 140–41; PR's relationship with, 67–68, 85–88
Roth, Milton, 194
Roth, Philip Milton: on adolescence, 44–45; ambition of, 9; American Academy of Arts and Sciences award, 62–63, 243; on Americanness, 10, 42; anti-nostalgic stance of, 18; Army enlistment of, 59–61, 63, 67, 86; astringency of, 8; Bernard Avishai's relationship with, 98, 134, 167, 175, 185–86, 277; back pain of, 61, 169, 199, 207; back surgery of, 256; and baseball, 42; Saul Bellow's relationship with, 246–48; biographers of, 3–4, 5; biographical portraits of, 12; on biography, 229–30, 248; birth of, 24, 35; Claire Bloom's divorce from, 208, 209, 213; Claire Bloom's marriage to, 198–99, 207, 209; Claire Bloom's relationship with, 151–53, 154, 164, 167, 168, 169, 171–72, 174, 181, 182, 185, 186, 190, 193, 198, 205, 206, 209; and boxing, 43–44; on Bradley Beach, 16–18, *17*, 30, 36, 264; as camp counselor, 54–55; and capture of colloquial prose, 76; as celebrity, 120–21, 126–27; childhood recollections of, 30–31, 38, 41–42; collegiate look in clothing of, 57, 144; comedy developed by, 46, 57, 60, 99, 110, 115, 148–49, 185–86, 260, 285; Commander of the Legion of Honour, 266; commitment to writing, 6–7, 9, 10, 12, 13, 14, 61, 63, 129, 263; confessional voice of, 289, 293; and counterculture,

127; death of, 258, 260, 284, 285; on diasporism, 9, 178, 202; on disguise, 5; early girlfriends of, 55–56; early jobs of, 48–49; early life of, 28–29, 30, 44–46, 60; early reading habits of, 47–48; in East Village, 63; education of, 32, 44, 46, 49–52, 57–59, 63, 64–65, 66, 187, 234; and *Et Cetera* literary magazine, 49, 50, 52, 53, 57; and falling in love quickly, 55; and fame, 91; on family, 19–23, 24, 41, 102, 195, 249, 277; on father as second-generation American Jew, 16; father in fiction of, 15, 16, 22; father's relationship with, 15–16, 18, 35–36, 41, 45–46, 49, 89, 97, 149, 166, 174, 182–83, 187, 189, 193, 195; female characters of, 103; on fiction, 5, 6, 189–90, 202, 228; fictionalized experiences in novels of, 6, 7, 18, 51, 59, 88, 139–41, 142, 153, 158, 160, 169–70, 182, 198, 202, 203–4, 230, 242, 282, 289; Frankfurt manuscript, 67, 97; on freedom in literature, 48, 235, 293; on freedom in relationships, 59–60, 103; funeral of, 4, 217, 283–84; on generational differences, 129; Maxine Groffsky's relationship with, 3, 55–56, 59–60, 67–68, 72, 73, 89, 242, 281; Guggenheim Award of, 62; and Halcion withdrawal, 169, 185–86, 189, 202; health of, 169, 172, 185, 192, 198, 256, 275, 276, 281, 282, 283–84; on homosexuality, 95, 100; honorary doctorates of, 243, 267; and Houghton Mifflin, 62–63, 66–67; hunger for validation, 121; and Israel, 10–11, 65, 81, 135, 170–76, 200; on Jewish life, 2, 9–12, 16, 21–22, 42–44, 64–65, 74–76, 83, 84, 106–7, 110, 137, 172–73, 193, 194; Jewishness of, 10, 42, 43, 69, 110, 123, 172, 184, 196, 200, 203; Hans J. Kleinschmidt's psychoanalysis of, 107–8; knee surgery of, 185; lack of scholarly cultivation, 58; legacy of, 290; legal career considered by, 3; with Primo Levi, *184*; life refashioned into art, 79; life with women, 2, 12–13; and literary life, 57–58, 63, 66, 120–21; literary standing of, 289; male friendships of, 241–42; Man Booker International Prize, 287; meddling of, 98–99; and memories, 203; mental breakdown of, 207–8, 211, 213, 241; Ross Miller's relationship with, 168–69, 186, 188–89, 240, 241–46, 274; misogyny of, 141, 244, 286, 288; on monogamy, 183; with mother at fortieth-birthday party, *112*; mother's relationship with, 38–39, 41–42, 108, 189, 195; Ann Mudge's relationship with, 98–99, 188, 265, 284; and Nobel Prize, 3, 126, 209, 211, 244, 276, 285, 291; patriotism of, 10; PEN/Saul Bellow Award for Achievement in American Fiction, 266, 290; Maletta Pfeiffer's relationship with, 145, 152–53, 172, 182, 199, 205–12, 213, 225, 241; physical appearance of, 54–55; David Plante's relationship with, 98, 170–72, 174, 176, 260; and portrayals of women, 288–89; promise in writing of, 66; protagonists resembling himself, 4; quadruple bypass of, 192; rage as theme of, 73, 79, 109, 113, 178, 220, 228, 229, 231–32; reactions to, 1–2; reading audience of, 167; reading interests of, 48–49, 54, 101, 110, 136, 137, 153, 175, 281; rebelliousness of, 50; reliance on books, 6; reputation of, 2, 164, 243, 269–70, 286–87; responses to antisemitism, 11, 72, 149–50, 173; on restrictions of recent past, 18; retirement of, 7, 85, 163, 245–46, 256–57, 275; on rigors of academic

Roth, Philip Milton (*continued*) study, 58–59; Margaret Martinson Williams Roth's divorce from, 94, 95; Margaret Martinson Williams Roth's marriage to, 88–91, 99, 108–9, 222, 282; Sandy Roth's relationship with, 42, 48, 87, 90, 195, 244; as self-referential writer, 4, 5–6; on sentimentality, 30, 77; sexual energy exuded by, 54–55; short stories of, 1, 3, 8, 50, 52–53, 57–58, 60, 61; Barbara Sproul's breakup with, 142–43, 153, 205; Barbara Sproul's friendship with, 126, 130, 136, 277, 284; Barbara Sproul's romantic relationship with, 12, 40, 116, 121, 127–29; teaching positions of, 61, 81, 86, 93, 100, 102, 136, 137, 143, 230, 282; on unruliness of *shmutz*, 7, 83; John Updike's relationship with, 136; on work, 24; Writers from the Other Europe imprint of, 98, 136; as "writer's writer," 289; on "written and unwritten world," 6; on Abner "Longy" Zwillman, 28. *See also specific works*

Roth, Sandy (brother): advertising career of, 48; artistic talent of, 42, 45, 48; birth of, 35; at Bradley Beach, *17*; father's relationship with, 48, 97–98; mother's relationship with, 38, 40; physical appearance of, 54; and PR's *Everyman*, 265; and PR's "Expect the Vandals," 64; PR's relationship with, 42, 48, 87, 90, 195, 244; reading habits of, 48

Roth, Sender (grandfather), 20, 31, 34, 35, 194

Roth, Seth, 195

Roth, Sonny, 34

Rothstein, Edward, 166–67

Russell, Bertrand, 268, 293

Rutgers University, Newark branch, 49

Sabbath's Theater (Roth): critical reception of, 215–16; and fissures in the life of characters, 8; and inevitable oblivion, 214; King Lear in, 157, 201, 216; model for Drenka in, 145, 182, 206, 207; and National Book Award, 216; Claudia Roth Pierpont on, 213, 214, 217; *The Plot Against America* compared to, 254–55; portrayal of Mickey Sabbath in, 154, 213–15, 216, 217, 219; PR as model for Mickey Sabbath in, 206, 210; PR's fantasies, nightmares, and appetites in, 4–5; PR's writing of, 213; publishing of, 209–10, 218; Benjamin Taylor on, 215, 216–17; treatment of Drenka in, 141, 213, 214, 237

Said, Edward, 6, 200

Salinger, J. D., 50, 52, 75, 77, 292

Sartre, Jean-Paul, 65, 292

Saturday Review, 93

Saul, Scott, 106

Schlesinger, Arthur M., 6, 250–51

Schloss, Roslyn, 189

Schulz, Bruno, 11, 98

Schwartz, Delmore, 246

Schwartzman, Jason, 289–90

Second World War: and Flaschner Family Association, 21; Jewish intellectuals on Jewish horrors of, 65; and Newark, 29; PR's interest in Jewish catastrophe in, 11, 137

Seventeen, 93–94

Shakespeare, William, 6, 200–201, 216

Sharon, Arik, 200

Shawn, William, 50

Shechner, Mark, 25, 28

Shurlock, Geoffrey, 120

Siegel, Bugsy, 28

Sinatra, Frank, 256

Singer, Isaac Bashevis, 154

Sissman, L. E., 124

Skyhorse, 288

Smith, Zadie, 110–11, 289

Solotaroff, Ted: as editor of *New American Review*, 61, 104, 115, 123; first impression of PR, 57, 60; on Jewish fiction, 75, 84; on Jewish life, 65; as model for *Letting Go* character, 61–62; and PR on marriage to Maggie Roth, 88–89; and PR on writing, 159, 161, 165–66; and PR on Yeshiva University event, 82; and PR's description of mother, 41; and PR's feeling misunderstood as a novelist, 151; PR's friendship with, 61–62, 166, 174; on Maggie Roth, 86; as writer, 61, 62
Sontag, Susan, 292–93
Southern writers, 66
Spinoza, Baruch, 293
Sport, 104
Sproul, Barbara: and Amnesty International, 136, 146–47; breakup with PR, 142–43, 153, 205; family background of, 127–28; on Albert Goldman, 116, 127–28; on Alan Lelchuk, 126; as model for character in *The Breast*, 141–42; photograph of, *131*; PR's friendship with, 126, 130, 136, 277, 284; on PR's mother, 40; PR's romantic relationship with, 12, 40, 116, 121, 127–29
Stanford University, PR's forum at, 92–93
Starbuck, George, 66–67, 74, 87, 90–91
Stavitsky, Michael, 33
Steiger, Anna, 168, 181, 193, 208–9
Steiger, Rod, 168
Stein, Gertrude, 12, 144
Steinbeck, John, 292
Steindler, Catherine, 260–62
Stern, Richard, 67, 145, 196–97, 200, 242
Stolz, Allie, 43–44
Streep, Meryl, 164
Streisand, Barbra, 2
Stroup, Rachel, 238
Styron, Rose, 143
Styron, William, 110, 121, 135, 143, 159, 169, 288
Susann, Jacqueline, 120
Swift, Jonathan, 50

Tanner, Tony, 203
Taranto, Julius, 291–92
Tartici, Ayten, 2
Taylor, Benjamin: *Here We Are*, 275–77; and PR's death, 284; on PR's failed marriages, 276; on PR's inner anarchy, 38, 210; on PR's marriage to Maggie Roth, 89–90; and PR's mental breakdown, 208; and PR's moral reputation, 243; on PR's reaction to Anti-Defamation League, 81; on PR's rejection for Nobel Prize, 276; on PR's *Sabbath's Theater*, 215, 216–17; on Catherine von Klitzing, 258
Tel Aviv writer's conference, 99–100
Teplitz, Saul I., 83–84
Thoreau, Henry David, 66
Thurman, Judith, 41, 164–65, 241, 243, 262, 277, 284
Times Literary Supplement, 84
Tisch, Jesse, 48
Tolstoy, Leo, 100, 239–40
Trilling, Lionel, 6, 109–10, 115, 158, 292
Truman, Harry, 42, 226, 227
Trump, Donald, 10, 250, 281, 286, 288
Tumin, Melvin, 143, 230
Turgenev, Ivan, 138
Turner, Kathleen, 292
Twitter, 191

University of Chicago: PR's lecturer's position at, 86, 136; PR's offer of instructorship at, 61; PR studying at, 57–59, 63, 64–65, 66, 187, 234
University of Iowa Writers' Workshop, PR's teaching at, 93, 100, 102, 282
University of Pennsylvania, PR's teaching at, 137, 143

Updike, John: and generational differences, 129; influence of, 288; and PR's *The Facts*, 188; and PR's *Operation Shylock*, 200, 203; PR's relationship with, 136; review of PR's *The Anatomy Lesson*, 170; scholarly approach of, 58; and Bruno Schulz, 98
Uris, Leon, 41, 65, 77, 85

Valentino, Rudolph, 154
Van Doren, Charles, 93
Vanity Fair, 208
Velazquez, Diego, 237
Village Voice, on PR's *When She Was Good*, 103
von Klitzing, Catherine, 257–60, *259*, 284

Wagman, Fredrica, 98
Wallace, George, 29
Wallace, Henry, 227
Wallace, Mike, 77–78, 127
Washington Post, 104
Weil, Robert, 271
Weitzmann, Marc, 242, 261, 265
Weldon, Fay, 190–91
Welty, Eudora, 243
Wheatcroft, John, 50–51
When She Was Good (Roth): complex treatment of Lucy in, 141; critical reception of, 102–3, 234, 290–91; and Gustave Flaubert, 6; Irving Howe on, 133–34; PR's writing of, 78–79, 95, 100–102, 106, 136, 234; release of, 104
Whitman, Walt, 66
Wilentz, Sean, 277
Wiley, Andrew, 277, 284
Williams, David (Maggie's son), 86, 222
Williams, Holly (Maggie's daughter), 86, 222
Wilson, Edmund, 94
Winchell, Walter, 252
Wolcott, James, 115
Wolfe, Thomas, 48, 139, 288
Wood, James, 7, 72, 138, 228–29, 266
Woodson, Kirby, 255, 257
Woolf, Virginia, 77, 157
Wouk, Herman, 65, 85
Writers from the Other Europe imprint, 98, 136, 147
Wylie, Andrew, 192, 199, 244

Yaddo, 29, 94–95, 100, 123, 128, 129
Yardley, Jonathan, 131–32
Yeats, William Butler, 109–10
Yeshiva University: PR's experience of forum of March 1962, 78–83, 146, 230, 234; recording of forum, 79, 82
Youngman, Henny, 110

Zionism, 175, 176, 177, 200
Zuckerman Unbound (Roth), 150, 165–67, 294
Zwillman, Abner "Longy," 27–29

Jewish Lives is a prizewinning series of interpretative biography designed to explore the many facets of Jewish identity. Individual volumes illuminate the imprint of Jewish figures upon literature, religion, philosophy, politics, cultural and economic life, and the arts and sciences. Subjects are paired with authors to elicit lively, deeply informed books that explore the range and depth of the Jewish experience from antiquity to the present.

Jewish Lives is a partnership of Yale University Press and the Leon D. Black Foundation. Ileene Smith is editorial director. Anita Shapira and Steven J. Zipperstein are series editors.

PUBLISHED TITLES INCLUDE:

Abraham: The First Jew, by Anthony Julius
Rabbi Akiva: Sage of the Talmud, by Barry W. Holtz
Ben-Gurion: Father of Modern Israel, by Anita Shapira
Judah Benjamin: Counselor to the Confederacy, by James Traub
Bernard Berenson: A Life in the Picture Trade, by Rachel Cohen
Irving Berlin: New York Genius, by James Kaplan
Sarah: The Life of Sarah Bernhardt, by Robert Gottlieb
Leonard Bernstein: An American Musician, by Allen Shawn
Hayim Nahman Bialik: Poet of Hebrew, by Avner Holtzman
Léon Blum: Prime Minister, Socialist, Zionist, by Pierre Birnbaum
Franz Boas: In Praise of Open Minds, by Noga Arikha
Louis D. Brandeis: American Prophet, by Jeffrey Rosen
Mel Brooks: Disobedient Jew, by Jeremy Dauber
Martin Buber: A Life of Faith and Dissent, by Paul Mendes-Flohr
David: The Divided Heart, by David Wolpe
Moshe Dayan: Israel's Controversial Hero, by Mordechai Bar-On
Disraeli: The Novel Politician, by David Cesarani
Alfred Dreyfus: The Man at the Center of the Affair, by Maurice Samuels
Einstein: His Space and Times, by Steven Gimbel
Becoming Elijah: Prophet of Transformation, by Daniel Matt
The Many Lives of Anne Frank, by Ruth Franklin
Becoming Freud: The Making of a Psychoanalyst, by Adam Phillips
Betty Friedan: Magnificent Disrupter, by Rachel Shteir

Emma Goldman: Revolution as a Way of Life, by Vivian Gornick
Hank Greenberg: The Hero Who Didn't Want to Be One, by Mark Kurlansky
Peggy Guggenheim: The Shock of the Modern, by Francine Prose
Ben Hecht: Fighting Words, Moving Pictures, by Adina Hoffman
Heinrich Heine: Writing the Revolution, by George Prochnik
Lillian Hellman: An Imperious Life, by Dorothy Gallagher
Herod the Great: Jewish King in a Roman World, by Martin Goodman
Theodor Herzl: The Charismatic Leader, by Derek Penslar
Abraham Joshua Heschel: A Life of Radical Amazement, by Julian Zelizer
Houdini: The Elusive American, by Adam Begley
Jabotinsky: A Life, by Hillel Halkin
Jacob: Unexpected Patriarch, by Yair Zakovitch
Franz Kafka: The Poet of Shame and Guilt, by Saul Friedländer
Carole King: She Made the Earth Move, by Jane Eisner
Rav Kook: Mystic in a Time of Revolution, by Yehudah Mirsky
Stanley Kubrick: American Filmmaker, by David Mikics
Stan Lee: A Life in Comics, by Liel Leibovitz
Primo Levi: The Matter of a Life, by Berel Lang
Maimonides: Faith in Reason, by Alberto Manguel
Groucho Marx: The Comedy of Existence, by Lee Siegel
Karl Marx: Philosophy and Revolution, by Shlomo Avineri
Louis B. Mayer and Irving Thalberg: The Whole Equation, by Kenneth Turan
Golda Meir: Israel's Matriarch, by Deborah E. Lipstadt
Menasseh ben Israel: Rabbi of Amsterdam, by Steven Nadler
Moses Mendelssohn: Sage of Modernity, by Shmuel Feiner
Harvey Milk: His Lives and Death, by Lillian Faderman
Arthur Miller: American Witness, by John Lahr

Moses: A Human Life, by Avivah Gottlieb Zornberg
Amos Oz: Writer, Activist, Icon, by Robert Alter
Proust: The Search, by Benjamin Taylor
Yitzhak Rabin: Soldier, Leader, Statesman, by Itamar Rabinovich
Ayn Rand: Writing a Gospel of Success, by Alexandra Popoff
Walther Rathenau: Weimar's Fallen Statesman, by Shulamit Volkov
Man Ray: The Artist and His Shadows, by Arthur Lubow
Sidney Reilly: Master Spy, by Benny Morris
Admiral Hyman Rickover: Engineer of Power, by Marc Wortman
Jerome Robbins: A Life in Dance, by Wendy Lesser
Julius Rosenwald: Repairing the World, by Hasia R. Diner
Philip Roth: Stung by Life, by Steven J. Zipperstein
Mark Rothko: Toward the Light in the Chapel,
by Annie Cohen-Solal
Ruth: A Migrant's Tale, by Ilana Pardes
Menachem Mendel Schneerson: Becoming the Messiah,
by Ezra Glinter
Gershom Scholem: Master of the Kabbalah, by David Biale
Bugsy Siegel: The Dark Side of the American Dream,
by Michael Shnayerson
Solomon: The Lure of Wisdom, by Steven Weitzman
Steven Spielberg: A Life in Films, by Molly Haskell
Spinoza: Freedom's Messiah, by Ian Buruma
Alfred Stieglitz: Taking Pictures, Making Painters, by Phyllis Rose
Barbra Streisand: Redefining Beauty, Femininity, and Power,
by Neal Gabler
Henrietta Szold: Hadassah and the Zionist Dream,
by Francine Klagsbrun
Leon Trotsky: A Revolutionary's Life, by Joshua Rubenstein
Warner Bros: The Making of an American Movie Studio,
by David Thomson

Elie Wiesel: Confronting the Silence, by Joseph Berger
Ludwig Wittgenstein: Philosophy in the Age of Airplanes, by Anthony Gottlieb

FORTHCOMING TITLES INCLUDE:

Hannah Arendt, by Masha Gessen
The Ba'al Shem Tov, by Ariel Mayse
Walter Benjamin, by Peter E. Gordon
Bob Dylan, by Sasha Frere-Jones
George Gershwin, by Gary Giddins
Ruth Bader Ginsburg, by Jeffrey Rosen
Jesus, by Jack Miles
Josephus, by Daniel Boyarin
Louis Kahn, by Gini Alhadeff
Mordecai Kaplan, by Jenna Weissman Joselit
Henry Kissinger, by Dennis Ross
Fiorello La Guardia, by Brenda Wineapple
Mahler, by Leon Botstein
Norman Mailer, by David Bromwich
Robert Oppenheimer, by David Rieff
Rebecca, by Judith Shulevitz
Edmond de Rothschild, by James McAuley
Jonas Salk, by David Margolick
Stephen Sondheim, by Daniel Okrent
Susan Sontag, by Benjamin Taylor
Gertrude Stein, by Lauren Elkin
Sabbatai Tsevi, by Pawel Maciejko
Billy Wilder, by Noah Isenberg